HOUGHTON MIFFLIN

Explore

INVITATIONS
TO LITERACY

Houghton Mifflin Company • Boston

Atlanta • Dallas • Geneva, Illinois • Palo Alto • Princeton

Reading Is An Adventure That Makes Every Day Special

Book Adventure™

www.bookadventure.org

read.

Use the on-line "Book Finder" to find a book you want to read.

click.

After reading, return on-line to take a fun interactive quiz.

win.

For every correct answer, you can earn points. Redeem the points for prizes.

When you read, use these Reading Strategies to become a better reader.

- Predict/Infer
- Think About Words
- Self-Question

- Monitor
- Evaluate
- Summarize

HOUGHTON MIFFLIN

Explore

Senior Authors

J. David Cooper
John J. Pikulski

Authors

Kathryn H. Au
Margarita Calderón
Jacqueline C. Comas
Marjorie Y. Lipson
J. Sabrina Mims
Susan E. Page
Sheila W. Valencia
MaryEllen Vogt

Consultants

Dolores Malcolm
Tina Saldivar
Shane Templeton

INVITATIONS
TO LITERACY

Houghton Mifflin Company • Boston
Atlanta • Dallas • Geneva, Illinois • Palo Alto • Princeton

Cover and title page photography by Tim Turner.

Cover photo by Tom and Pat Leeson.

Acknowledgments begin on page 647.

Printed in the U.S.A.

ISBN: 0-618-05789-7

23456789-VH-05 04 03 02 01 00

Introductory Selection

Themes

CONTENTS

PAPERBACK **PLUS**

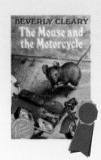

The Mouse and the Motorcycle
narrative fiction by Beverly Cleary

In the same book . . .
More about real mice and cool and daring fictional mice on motorcycles

From the Mixed-up Files of Mrs. Basil E. Frankweiler
narrative fiction by E. L. Konigsburg

In the same book . . .
Lots more about Michelangelo and the world of art

In the
WILD

A Closer Look

It's Up to You!

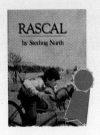

PAPERBACK **PLUS**

Come Back, Salmon
narrative nonfiction by
Molly Cone

In the same book . . .
More about Pigeon Creek,
Pacific salmon, and a
Tlingit tale about salmon

Rascal
personal narrative by
Sterling North

In the same book . . .
Information about raccoons,
unusual pets, and pet ownership

CONTENTS

Try to See It My Way

PAPERBACK **PLUS**

The Hundred Penny Box
realistic fiction by
Sharon Bell Mathis

In the same book . . .
More about Aunt Dew's
family tree, pennies through
history, and another seasoned
storyteller

Dear Mr. Henshaw
realistic fiction by
Beverly Cleary

In the same book . . .
Much more, including Beverly
Cleary and her readers, trucks,
and monarch butterflies

CATASTROPHE!

In an Instant

PAPERBACK **PLUS**

Head for the Hills!
narrative nonfiction by
Paul Robert Walker

In the same book . . .
More about modern-day
dams and how to build
an embankment dam of
your own

Volcano: The Eruption
and Healing of Mount
St. Helens
expository nonfiction by
Patricia Lauber

In the same book . . .
Human stories from Mount
St. Helens, and fact and folklore
about volcanoes

FROM THE PRAIRIE TO THE SEA

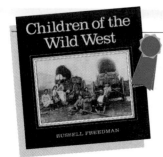

PAPERBACK **PLUS**

Skylark
fiction by
Patricia MacLachlan

In the same book . . .
More about life on the
prairie and love of the sea

Old Yeller
fiction by Fred Gipson

In the same book . . .
More about the people
and animals of the Texas hill
country, and a look at life
on the cattle trail

CONTENTS

Do You Believe This??

What a Character!

You Won't Believe Your Eyes

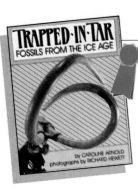
PAPERBACK PLUS

The Kid in the
Red Jacket
narrative fiction by
Barbara Park

In the same book . . .
More about moving and
being the new kid on the
block

The Whipping Boy
narrative fiction by Sid
Fleischman

In the same book . . .
More about Sid Fleischman and
castles of the world

A Package for Mrs. Jewls

by Louis Sachar

Louis, the yard teacher, frowned.

The school yard was a mess. There were pencils and pieces of paper everywhere. How'd all this junk get here? he wondered. Well, I'm not going to pick it up!

It wasn't his job to pick up garbage. He was just supposed to pass out the balls during lunch and recess, and also make sure the kids didn't kill each other.

He sighed, then began cleaning it up. He loved all the children at Wayside School. He didn't want them playing on a dirty playground.

As he was picking up the pencils and pieces of paper, a large truck drove into the parking lot. It honked its horn twice, then twice more.

Louis ran to the truck. "Quiet!" he whispered. "Children are trying to learn in there!" He pointed at the school.

19

A short man with big, bushy hair stepped out of the truck. "I have a package for somebody named Mrs. Jewls," he said.

"I'll take it," said Louis.

"Are you Mrs. Jewls?" asked the man.

"No," said Louis.

"I have to give it to Mrs. Jewls," said the man.

Louis thought a moment. He didn't want the man disturbing the children. He knew how much they hated to be interrupted when they were working.

"I'm Mrs. Jewls," he said.

"But you just said you weren't Mrs. Jewls," said the man.

"I changed my mind," said Louis.

The man got the package out of the back of the truck and gave it to Louis. "Here you go, Mrs. Jewls," he said.

"Uhh!" Louis grunted. It was a very heavy package. The word FRAGILE was printed on every side. He had to be careful not to drop it.

The package was so big, Louis couldn't see where he was going. Fortunately, he knew the way to Mrs. Jewls's class by heart. It was straight up.

Wayside School was thirty stories high, with only one room on each story. Mrs. Jewls's class was at the very top. It was Louis's favorite class.

He pushed through the door to the school, then started up the stairs. There was no elevator.

There were stairs that led down to the basement, too, but nobody ever went down there. There were dead rats living in the basement.

The box was pressed against Louis's face, squashing his nose. Even so, when he reached the fifteenth floor, he could smell Miss Mush cooking in the cafeteria. It smelled like she was making mushrooms. Maybe on my way back I'll stop by Miss Mush's room and get some mushrooms, he thought. He didn't want to miss Miss Mush's mushrooms. They were her specialty.

He huffed and groaned and continued up the stairs. His arms and legs were very sore, but he didn't want to rest. This package might be important, he thought. I have to get it to Mrs. Jewls right away.

He stepped easily from the eighteenth story to the twentieth. There was no nineteenth story.

Miss Zarves taught the class on the nineteenth story. There was no Miss Zarves.

At last he struggled up the final step to the thirtieth story. He knocked on Mrs. Jewls's door with his head.

Mrs. Jewls was in the middle of teaching her class about gravity when she heard the knock. "Come in," she called.

"I can't open the door," Louis gasped. "My hands are full. I have a package for you."

Mrs. Jewls faced the class. "Who wants to open the door for Louis?" she asked.

All the children raised their hands. They loved to be interrupted when they were working.

"Oh dear, how shall I choose?" asked Mrs. Jewls. "I have to be fair about this. I know! We'll have a spelling bee. And the winner will get to open the door."

Louis knocked his head against the door again. "It's heavy," he complained. "And I'm very tired."

"Just a second," Mrs. Jewls called back. "Allison, the first word's for you. Heavy."

"Heavy," said Allison. "H-E-A-V-Y. Heavy."

"Very good. Jason, you're next. Tired."

"Tired," said Jason. "S-L-E-E-P-Y. Tired."

Louis felt the package slipping from his sweaty fingers. He shifted his weight to get a better grip. The corners of the box dug into the sides of his arms. He felt his hands go numb.

Actually, he *didn't* feel them go numb.

"Jenny, package."

"Package," said Jenny. "B-O-X. Package."

"Excellent!" said Mrs. Jewls.

Louis felt like he was going to faint.

At last John opened the door. "I won the spelling bee, Louis!" he said.

"Very good, John," muttered Louis.

"Aren't you going to shake my hand?" asked John.

Louis shifted the box to one arm, quickly shook John's hand, then grabbed the box again and staggered into the room.

"Where do you want it, Mrs. Jewls?" he asked.

"I don't know," said Mrs. Jewls. "What is it?"

"I don't know," said Louis. "I'll have to put it down someplace so you can open it."

"But how can I tell you where to put it until I know what it is?" asked Mrs. Jewls. "You might put it in the wrong place."

So Louis held the box as Mrs. Jewls stood on a chair next to him and tore open the top. His legs wobbled beneath him.

"It's a computer!" exclaimed Mrs. Jewls.

Everybody booed.

"What's the matter?" asked Louis. "I thought everyone loved computers."

"We don't want it, Louis," said Eric Bacon.

"Take it back, Jack," said Terrence.

"Get that piece of junk out of here," said Maurecia.

"Now, don't be that way," said Mrs. Jewls. "The computer will help us learn. It's a lot quicker than a pencil and paper."

"But the quicker we learn, the more work we have to do," complained Todd.

"You may set it over there on the counter, Louis," said Mrs. Jewls.

Louis set the computer on the counter next to Sharie's desk. Then he collapsed on the floor.

"Now watch closely," said Mrs. Jewls.

Everyone gathered around the new computer. It had a full-color monitor and two disk drives.

Mrs. Jewls pushed it out the window.

They all watched it fall and smash against the sidewalk.

"See?" said Mrs. Jewls. "That's gravity."

"Oh, now I get it!" said Joe.

"Thank you, Louis," said Mrs. Jewls. "I've been trying to teach them about gravity all morning. We had been using pencils and pieces of paper, but the computer was a lot quicker."

Meet the Author

It's not just a coincidence that Louis Sachar (it rhymes with *cracker*) has the same first name as Louis, the yard teacher of Wayside School. Sachar was once a lunchtime supervisor of elementary school children. The kids called him "Louis the Yard Teacher," and his experiences with them led to many of the stories in his Wayside School books.

Sachar was simply practicing his hobby when he wrote the first book, *Sideways Stories from Wayside School.* "I never truly expected to be published," he says.

Sachar tried to remember his childhood in that book and its sequel, *Wayside School Is Falling Down,* in which "A Package for Mrs. Jewls" is the opening story. He observes, "I think that kids in grade school are basically the same as they were when I was young."

Sachar's latest Wayside School book is *Wayside School Gets a Little Stranger.*

Meet the Illustrator

Michele Noiset (*Nwah-ZAY*) grew up in a family of seven brothers and sisters in Connecticut. When she was seven years old and first became interested in art, Noiset didn't have to look far to find an instructor. Her grandfather was a painter. "He used to bring home art books for me and give me little assignments," she remembers. Noiset lives in Massachusetts with her husband and son and a very old dog named Poochy.

Michele Noiset

Big Ideas Come in Small Packages!

Draw a Cartoon

Aaaaargh!

With its zany characters and events, "A Package for Mrs. Jewls" might make a great comic strip. You be the cartoonist. Retell the story in a series of cartoon drawings with speech balloons.

Make a Model or a Diagram

Building Going Up!

Think about the description of Wayside School in the selection. Then use the description to help you make a model or a diagram of the school.

Act Out a Scene

S·P·E·L·L·I·N·G B·E·E

Step into the story for a spell. Act out the scene in which Mrs. Jewls's class has a spelling bee. Spell words from the selection, plus any other words you choose.

Compare and Contrast

Schools of Thought

How weird is weird? Maybe Wayside School isn't so weird after all. Write a paragraph telling how Wayside School and your school are different and how they are alike.

JOURNEY TO

ADVENTURE!

JOURNEY TO ADVENTURE!

Contents

Read On Your Own

PAPERBACK PLUS

The Mouse and the Motorcycle
by Beverly Cleary

Join Ralph the mouse as he zooms along on a motorcycle.

In the same book . . .
More about real mice and cool and daring fictional mice on motorcycles

PAPERBACK PLUS

From the Mixed-up Files of Mrs. Basil E. Frankweiler

by E. L. Konigsburg

Share Claudia and her brother Jamie's adventures at the Metropolitan Museum of Art in New York City.

In the same book . . .

Lots more about Michelangelo and the world of art

Black Stars in Orbit: NASA's African American Astronauts

by Khephra Burns and William Miles
Share the experiences of the first African Americans in space and their fellow scientists who worked behind the scenes.

Coast to Coast

by Betsy Byars
Birch's grandfather wants to sell his antique Piper Cub airplane. But first Birch wants him to fly across the country and take her along.

To the Top of the World: Adventures with Arctic Wolves

by Jim Brandenburg
The author is "adopted" by a pack of Arctic wolves on remote Ellesmere Island.

The Black Pearl

by Scott O'Dell
Learning the family art of pearl diving provides Ramon with an unexpected — and dangerous — adventure.

The Grand Escape

by Phyllis Reynolds Naylor
Marco and Polo, two pampered house cats, think life out West will be exciting.

The Haymeadow

by Gary Paulsen
Unexpected events occur when John spends the summer alone, tending the family's herd of 6000 sheep.

JAMES and the GIANT PEACH

by Roald Dahl

James receives a sack of strange crystals and accidentally spills them by a peach tree, causing a peach on the tree to grow until it's gigantic! Crawling into the giant fruit, James discovers a group of talking bugs and worms as big as he is. When the peach breaks free and rolls down to the ocean, James and his friends are bound for adventure!

"Look!" cried the Centipede just as they were finishing their meal. "Look at that funny thin black thing gliding through the water over there!"

They all swung around to look.

"There are two of them," said Miss Spider.

"There are *lots* of them!" said the Ladybug.

"What are they?" asked the Earthworm, getting worried.

"They must be some kind of fish," said the Old-Green-Grasshopper. "Perhaps they have come along to say hello."

"They are sharks!" cried the Earthworm. "I'll bet you anything you like that they are sharks and they have come along to eat us up!"

"What absolute rot!" the Centipede said, but his voice seemed suddenly to have become a little shaky, and he wasn't laughing.

"I am *positive* they are sharks!" said the Earthworm. "I just *know* they are sharks!"

And so, in actual fact, did everybody else, but they were too frightened to admit it.

There was a short silence. They all peered down anxiously at the sharks who were cruising slowly round and round the peach.

"Just assuming that they *are* sharks," the Centipede said, "there still can't possibly be any danger if we stay up here."

But even as he spoke, one of those thin black fins suddenly changed direction and came cutting swiftly through the water right up to the side of the peach itself. The shark paused and stared up at the company with small evil eyes.

"Go away!" they shouted. "Go away, you filthy beast!"

Slowly, almost lazily, the shark opened his mouth (which was big enough to have swallowed a perambulator) and made a lunge at the peach.

They all watched, aghast.

And now, as though at a signal from the leader, all the other sharks came swimming in toward the peach, and they clustered around it and began to attack it furiously. There must have been twenty or thirty of them at least, all pushing and fighting and lashing their tails and churning the water into a froth.

Panic and pandemonium broke out immediately on top of the peach.

"Oh, we are finished now!" cried Miss Spider, wringing her feet. "They will eat up the whole peach and then there'll be nothing left for us to stand on and they'll start on us!"

"She is right!" shouted the Ladybug. "We are lost forever!"

"Oh, I don't want to be eaten!" wailed the Earthworm. "But they will take me first of all because I am so fat and juicy and I have no bones!"

"Is there *nothing* we can do?" asked the Ladybug, appealing to James. "Surely *you* can think of a way out of this."

Suddenly they were all looking at James.

"Think!" begged Miss Spider. "*Think*, James, *think*!"

"Come on," said the Centipede. "Come on, James. There *must* be *something* we can do."

Their eyes waited upon him, tense, anxious, pathetically hopeful.

"There is *something* that I believe we might try," James Henry Trotter said slowly. "I'm not saying it'll work . . ."

"Tell us!" cried the Earthworm. "Tell us quick!"

"We'll try anything you say!" said the Centipede. "But hurry, hurry, hurry!"

"Be quiet and let the boy speak!" said the Ladybug. "Go on, James."

They all moved a little closer to him. There was a longish pause.

"Go *on*!" they cried frantically. "*Go on!*"

And all the time while they were waiting they could hear the sharks threshing around in the water below them. It was enough to make anyone frantic.

"Come on, James," the Ladybug said, coaxing him.

"I . . . I . . . I'm afraid it's no good after all," James murmured, shaking his head. "I'm terribly sorry. I forgot. We don't have any string. We'd need hundreds of yards of string to make this work."

"What sort of string?" asked the Old-Green-Grasshopper sharply.

"Any sort, just so long as it's strong."

"But my dear boy, that's exactly what we do have! We've got all you want!"

"How? Where?"

"The Silkworm!" cried the Old-Green-Grasshopper. "Didn't you ever notice the Silkworm? He's still downstairs! He never moves! He just lies there sleeping all day long, but we can easily wake him up and make him spin!"

"And what about me, may I ask?" said Miss Spider. "I can spin *just* as well as any Silkworm. What's more, *I* can spin patterns."

"Can you make enough between you?" asked James.

"As much as you want."

"And quickly?"

"Of course! Of course!"

"And would it be strong?"

"The strongest there is! It's as thick as your finger! But why? What are you going to do?"

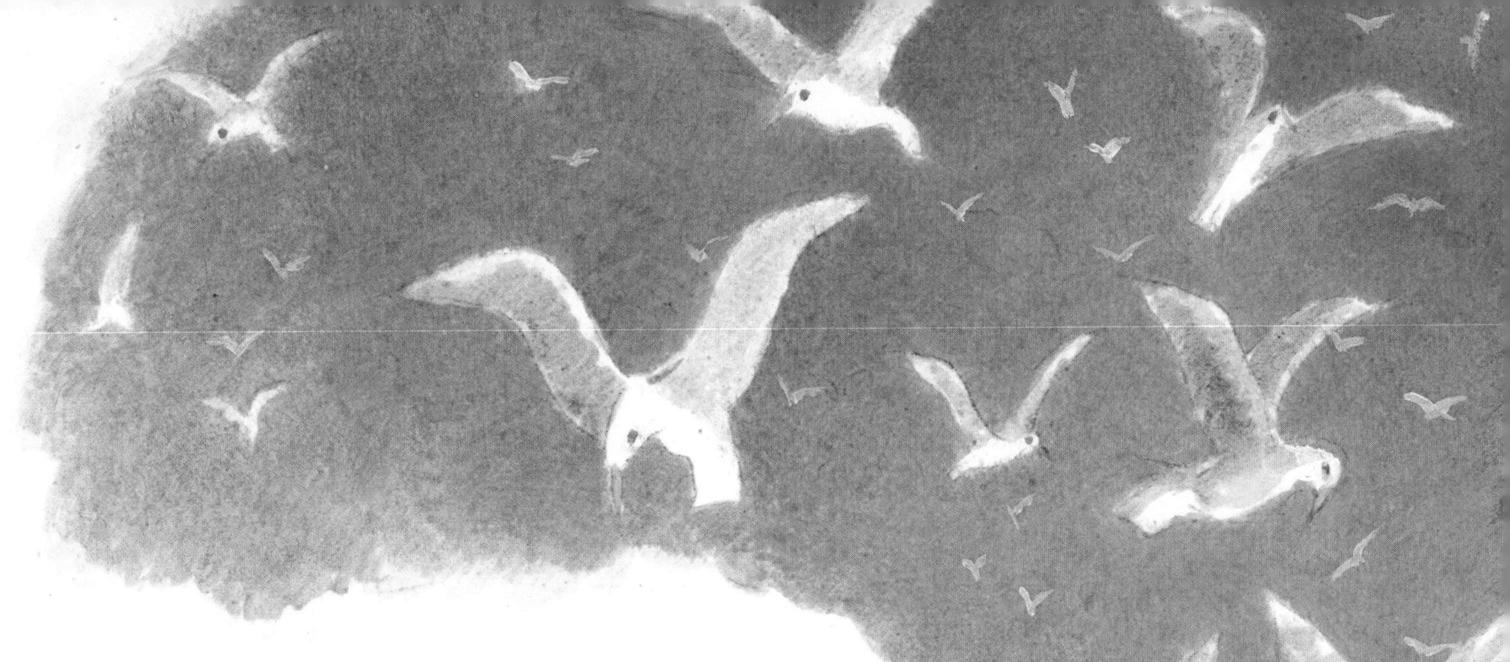

"I'm going to lift this peach clear out of the water!" James announced firmly.

"You're mad!" cried the Earthworm.

"It's our only chance."

"The boy's crazy!" "He's joking!"

"Go on, James," the Ladybug said gently. "How are you going to do it?"

"Skyhooks, I suppose," jeered the Centipede.

"Seagulls," James answered calmly. "The place is full of them. Look up there!"

They all looked up and saw a great mass of seagulls wheeling round and round in the sky.

"I'm going to take a long silk string," James went on, "and I'm going to loop one end of it around a seagull's neck. And then I'm going to tie the other end to the stem of the peach." He pointed to the peach stem, which was standing up like a short thick mast in the middle of the deck.

"Then I'm going to get another seagull and do the same thing again, then another and another—"

"Ridiculous!" they shouted.

"Absurd!"

"Poppycock!"

"Balderdash!"

"Madness!"

And the Old-Green-Grasshopper said, "How can a few seagulls lift an enormous thing like this up into the air, and all of us as well? It would take hundreds . . . thousands . . ."

"There is no shortage of seagulls," James answered. "Look for yourself. We'll probably need four hundred, five hundred, six hundred . . . maybe even a thousand . . . I don't know . . . I shall simply go on hooking them up to the stem until we have enough to lift us. They'll be bound to lift us in the end. It's like balloons. You give someone enough balloons to hold, I mean *really* enough, then up he goes. And a seagull has far more lifting power than a balloon. If only we have the *time* to do it. If only we are not sunk first by those awful sharks. . . ."

"You're absolutely off your head!" said the Earthworm. "How on earth do you propose to get a loop of string around a seagull's neck? I suppose you're going to fly up there yourself and catch it!"

"The boy's dotty!" said the Centipede.

"Let him finish," said the Ladybug. "Go on, James. How *would* you do it?"

"With bait."

"Bait! What sort of bait?"

"With a worm, of course. Seagulls love worms, didn't you know that? And luckily for us, we have here the biggest, fattest, pinkest, juiciest Earthworm in the world."

"You can stop right there!" the Earthworm said sharply. "That's quite enough!"

"Go on," the others said, beginning to grow interested. "Go on!"

"The seagulls have already spotted him," James continued. "That's why there are so many of them circling around. But they daren't come down to get him while all the rest of us are standing here. So this is what—"

"Stop!" cried the Earthworm. "Stop, stop, stop! I won't have it! I refuse! I—I—I—I—"

"Be quiet!" said the Centipede. "Mind your own business!"

"I *like* that!"

"My dear Earthworm, you're going to be eaten anyway, so what difference does it make whether it's sharks or seagulls?"

"I won't do it!"

"Why don't we hear what the plan is first?" said the Old-Green-Grasshopper.

"I don't give a hoot what the plan is!" cried the Earthworm. "I am not going to be pecked to death by a bunch of seagulls!"

"You will be a martyr," said the Centipede. "I shall respect you for the rest of my life."

"So will I," said Miss Spider. "And your name will be in all the newspapers. Earthworm gives life to save friends . . ."

"But he won't *have* to give his life," James told them. "Now listen to me. This is what we'll do . . ."

"Why, it's absolutely brilliant!" cried the Old-Green-Grasshopper when James had explained his plan.

"The boy's a genius!" the Centipede announced. "Now I can keep my boots on after all."

"Oh, I shall be pecked to death!" wailed the poor Earthworm.

"Of course you won't."

"I will, I know I will! And I won't even be able to see them coming at me because I have no eyes!"

James went over and put an arm gently around the Earthworm's shoulders. "I won't let them *touch* you," he said. "I promise I won't. But we've *got* to hurry! Look down there!"

There were more sharks than ever now around the peach. The water was boiling with them. There must have been ninety or a hundred at least. And to the travelers up on top, it certainly seemed as though the peach were sinking lower and lower into the water.

"Action stations!" James shouted. "Jump to it! There's not a moment to lose!" He was the captain now, and everyone knew it. They would do whatever he told them.

"All hands below deck except Earthworm!" he ordered.

"Yes, yes!" they said eagerly as they scuttled into the tunnel entrance. "Come on! Let's hurry!"

"And you—Centipede!" James shouted. "Hop downstairs and get that Silkworm to work at once! Tell him to spin as he's never spun before! Our lives depend upon it! And the same applies to you, Miss Spider! Hurry on down! Start spinning!"

In a few minutes everything was ready.

It was very quiet now on the top of the peach. There was nobody in sight—nobody except the Earthworm.

One half of the Earthworm, looking like a great, thick, juicy, pink sausage, lay innocently in the sun for all the seagulls to see.

The other half of him was dangling down the tunnel.

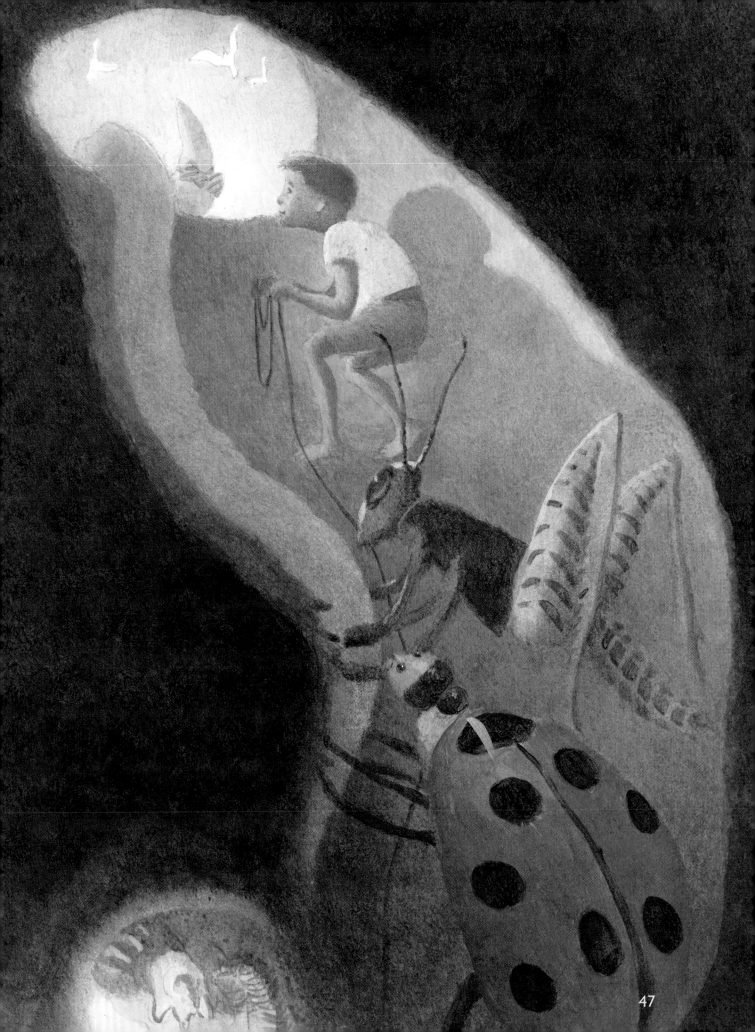

James was crouching close beside the Earthworm in the tunnel entrance, just below the surface, waiting for the first seagull. He had a loop of silk string in his hands.

The Old-Green-Grasshopper and the Ladybug were further down the tunnel, holding onto the Earthworm's tail, ready to pull him quickly in out of danger as soon as James gave the word.

And far below, in the great hollow stone of the peach, the Glow-worm was lighting up the room so that the two spinners, the Silkworm and Miss Spider, could see what they were doing. The Centipede was down there, too, exhorting them both frantically to greater efforts, and every now and again James could hear his voice coming up faintly from the depths, shouting, "Spin, Silkworm, spin, you great fat lazy brute! Faster, faster, or we'll throw you to the sharks!"

"Here comes the first seagull!" whispered James. "Keep still now, Earthworm. Keep still. The rest of you get ready to pull."

"Please don't let it spike me," begged the Earthworm.

"I won't, I won't. Ssshhh . . ."

Out of the corner of one eye, James watched the seagull as it came swooping down toward the Earthworm. And then suddenly it was so close that he could see its small black eyes and its curved beak, and the beak was open, ready to grab a nice piece of flesh out of the Earthworm's back.

"Pull!" shouted James.

The Old-Green-Grasshopper and the Ladybug gave the Earthworm's tail an enormous tug, and like magic the Earthworm disappeared into the tunnel. At the same time, up went James's hand and the seagull flew right into the loop of silk that he was holding out. The loop, which had been cleverly made, tightened just the right amount (but not too much) around its neck, and the seagull was captured.

"Hooray!" shouted the Old-Green-Grasshopper, peering out of the tunnel. "Well done, James!"

Up flew the seagull with James paying out the silk string as it went. He gave it about fifty yards and then tied the string to the stem of the peach.

"Next one!" he shouted, jumping back into the tunnel. "Up you get again, Earthworm! Bring up some more silk, Centipede!"

"Oh, I don't like this at all," wailed the Earthworm. "It only just missed me! I even felt the wind on my back as it went swishing past!"

"Ssshh!" whispered James. "Keep still! Here comes another one!"

So they did it again.

And again, and again, and again.

And the seagulls kept coming, and James caught them one after the other and tethered them to the peach stem.

"One hundred seagulls!" he shouted, wiping the sweat from his face.

"Keep going!" they cried. "Keep going, James!"

"Two hundred seagulls!"

"Three hundred seagulls!"

"Four hundred seagulls!"

The sharks, as though sensing that they were in danger of losing their prey, were hurling themselves at the peach more furiously than ever, and the peach was sinking lower and lower still in the water.

"Five hundred seagulls!" James shouted.

"Silkworm says he's running out of silk!" yelled the Centipede from below. "He says he can't keep it up much longer. Nor can Miss Spider!"

"Tell them they've *got* to!" James answered. "They can't stop now!"

"We're lifting!" somebody shouted.

"No, we're not!"

"I felt it!"

"Put on another seagull, quick!"

"Quiet, everybody! Quiet! Here's one coming now!"

This was the five hundred and first seagull, and the moment that James caught it and tethered it to the stem with all the others, the whole enormous peach suddenly started rising up slowly out of the water.

"Look out! Here we go! Hold on, boys!"

But then it stopped.

And there it hung.

It hovered and swayed, but it went no higher.

The bottom of it was just touching the water. It was like a delicately balanced scale that needed only the tiniest push to tip it one way or the other.

"One more will do it!" shouted the Old-Green-Grasshopper, looking out of the tunnel. "We're almost there!"

And now came the big moment. Quickly, the five hundred and second seagull was caught and harnessed to the peach stem . . .

And then suddenly . . .

But slowly . . .

Majestically . . .

Like some fabulous golden balloon . . .

With all the seagulls straining at the strings above . . .

The giant peach rose up dripping out of the water and began climbing toward the heavens.

About the Author

Roald Dahl lived in England until his death in 1990, but he considered Norway his home. As a child he developed a love for adventure on family trips to a small island off the Norwegian coast. There Dahl spent the long summer days swimming, boating, and exploring.

Dahl began *James and the Giant Peach,* his second children's book, as a bedtime story for his two young daughters. "It was very rare to hit upon something that really made them sit up and sparkle," Dahl recalled. But he went on to attract a large reading audience with nearly twenty children's books, some of which have been made into movies. One of Dahl's books that you may enjoy is *Matilda,* about a young girl who uses her genius to combat a bullying headmistress.

About the Illustrator

"There seems to be a theme of huge things in my work," Kevin Hawkes says. In addition to a giant peach, he has illustrated *The Nose* and *The Turnip,* both children's books about oversized objects. Hawkes lives on an island off the coast of Maine with his wife and two children.

Grab On to Some Peachy Ideas!

Stage a Puppet Show

Give Those Bugs a Hand!

Use socks, paper bags, or cardboard cutouts on sticks to make puppets of the characters from *James and the Giant Peach*. Then put on a puppet show of a scene from the story. Read from the selection or write your own dramatization.

Write a Dialogue

Shark Talk

Up on the peach, James and the crew are busily making and carrying out their escape plan. What are the sharks saying as they look forward to a bite to eat and then see their meal fly away? Write a dialogue between two of the sharks.

Problem Solve

Scram, Sharks!

Now it's your turn to be the captain. What are some other ways James and his friends could have solved the problem of the sharks? Get together with a group and brainstorm different solutions — the wilder the better!

Make a Mobile

Air Craft

Show how James and his crew saved the day! Make a *James and the Giant Peach* mobile. Use cardboard, paper, or foil to create a giant peach and characters from the story. Decorate your creations with markers or crayons, thread string through your creations, and tie them to a hanger. Then hang up your mobile and wait for a breeze!

The Glass Canoe
by John Ciardi

There was a man in a glass canoe.
    (So he could see the fish.)
He paddled out to watch a trout.
    It gave its tail a swish.

It swished downriver. Trout can do
    A remarkable lot of swishing
When they see you in a glass canoe
    And guess you may be fishing.

It swished downriver — toward the falls,
    A rather daft thing to do.
It was even dafter to follow after,
    I'd say, in a glass canoe.

But that's what they did, and what came next
    The trout just will not say.
(I know a pool where it goes to school
    And I spoke to it there today.)

I haven't seen the glass canoe.
    I hear it tried to split
A rock in two (which it couldn't do)
    And that the rock split it.

I did see a very wet sort of man
    Come shivering out of the mist,
And I heard him sigh as he passed by,
    "I knew, but I couldn't resist!"

Then he shivered into the mist again.
    And I couldn't be sure, but I guessed
I had seen him before. If you want to know more,
    You'll have to make up the rest.

The Poor Boy Was Wrong
by John Ciardi

There was a young fellow named Sid
Who thought he knew more than he did.
    He thought that a shark
    Would turn tail if you bark.
So he swam out to try it — poor kid!

57

DAUNTLESS DIMBLE

by Jack Prelutsky

Dauntless Dimble was the bravest
of the bravest of the brave,
Dimble climbed the highest mountain,
he explored the deepest cave,
Dimble fought the fiercest creatures,
but he never met his match,
Dimble often wrestled tigers
and escaped without a scratch.

Not a challenge went unanswered,
he accepted every dare,
Dimble walked on blazing embers
and was none the worse for wear,
Dimble exited an airplane
high above a rocky butte,
he escaped with minor bruises
though he wore no parachute.

$39.50

Dimble diving in the ocean
was beset by hungry sharks,
yet the only wounds he suffered
were some superficial marks,
once a polar bear attacked him
on the icy arctic floes,
the result of that adventure
was a slightly bloody nose.

Dimble danced with deadly cobras,
Dimble toyed with killer bees,
Dimble dangled by one finger
from a tiny greased trapeze,
but he rose from sleep one morning,
and while getting out of bed,
Dimble tripped upon the carpet,
where he cracked his dauntless head.

59

Arctic Explorer:
The Story of Matthew Henson

by Jeri Ferris

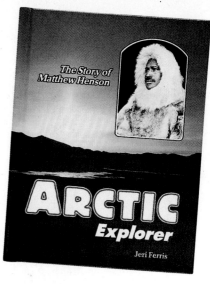

It's early summer, 1908. Since 1891, explorers
Robert Peary and Matthew Henson have been trying
to be the first to reach the North Pole. This is their sixth and final attempt.
They are experienced and determined, but the Arctic is fierce and unpre-
dictable. Peary's wife, Josephine, and Henson's wife, Lucy, may well wonder
whether they will see their husbands again.

Matt moved to the newly repaired *Roosevelt* to help or-
ganize the supplies for the 1908 expedition. The small ship
settled lower and lower in the water as the crew carried on
dynamite for blasting ice; pickaxes; shovels; guns; kerosene;
and thousands of pounds of tea, coffee, dried fish, bacon,
sugar, biscuits, flour, and pemmican. There were cameras,
maps and charts, navigational equipment, thermometers,
compasses, books, and materials for building sledges. Coal
was stuffed into any space left over.

On July 6, 1908, the *Roosevelt* steamed out of New York
to the sound of whistles and bells and shouts. Matt thought
of Lucy. "I hoped when she next heard of me it would be
with feelings of joy and happiness,"

he said, "and that she would be glad she had permitted me to leave her." The next day, at Oyster Bay, New York, President Theodore Roosevelt came on board. He poked into all the corners, shook hands with all the men, cried "Bully!" and said he knew they would bring home the Pole this time. (Some folks did expect Peary to return with a pole, probably striped.) Then they were off.

President Theodore Roosevelt wishes Peary luck on his sixth attempt to reach the Pole.

Peary had selected the bravest, strongest, most intelligent men he could find for his last try. There was Matt, of course, there had to be Matt. There were Captain Bartlett and Ross Marvin again. And there were three new men: George Borup, a young Yale graduate; Donald MacMillan, a teacher; and J.W. Goodsell, a doctor.

When MacMillan boarded the *Roosevelt,* he looked for Matt. "I had read so much about [Henson]," he said, "that naturally I studied him with interest." Matt greeted MacMillan with a handshake and a smile, and right away MacMillan saw the easy way Matt had of making friends. Later he saw Matt's courage in a terrible storm when he did the work of three men without thinking of his own safety. Donald MacMillan wrote it all down in his diary (and Matt wrote in *his* diary that he hoped he and MacMillan would become friends). In fact, all the men kept diaries of this expedition. They expected it to be successful and wanted to have the details right.

At Etah Peary learned that Dr. Cook, the same Dr. Cook who had gone north with him in 1891, was again in the Arctic, but no one knew just where. Also at Etah 49 Eskimos came aboard, and 550 tons of coal, 70 tons of whale meat, 50 dead walruses, and 246 screaming dogs were added to the overloaded ship. "The ship," Matt said, "is now in a most perfect state of dirtiness."

Some of the 246 dogs aboard the *Roosevelt* in 1908. In addition to the dogs and whale meat and dead walruses, the 10,000 pounds of sugar took up a space 10-by-10-by-6 feet all by itself. Then there was bacon, pemmican, biscuits, coffee . . .

Henson (right) poses on one of the sledges he built for travel in the Arctic.

The *Roosevelt*'s egg-shaped sides, designed by Peary, help it to avoid being crushed by the ice.

The *Roosevelt* arrived at Cape Sheridan on September 5, and Matt began training the new men in the art of dog driving, igloo building, and survival. He was also the interpreter. Besides all his other work, Matt made the sledges and alcohol stoves for the spring trip and sledged supplies north to Cape Columbia. On one of the trips, the cold was so awful that an Eskimo's foot began to freeze. Matt said he "thawed it out in the usual way, . . . his freezing foot under my bearskin shirt."

Between sledge trips the men lived on the ship. They ate musk ox steaks, stuffed walrus heart, and fresh bread (the cook baked 18,000 pounds of bread on this expedition). As usual, Matt ate with the crew, not with the other expedition members.

When the sun disappeared, Matt wrote, "The night is coming quickly, the long months of darkness, of quiet and cold, that . . . I can never get used to." The sailors played dominoes and checkers to pass the time. Some of the sailors had banjos and accordions, and the explorers often heard the song "Home Sweet Home" during that long winter.

In February 1909 they were ready to go to the Pole. Each man took one special possession — for Matt it was his Bible. Each sledge carried 450 pounds of supplies — enough pemmican, biscuits, tea, and stove alcohol to last the driver and team 50 days.

On February 28 Bartlett and Borup left Cape Columbia to pioneer the trail. At 6:30 the next morning, Henson, the leader of the main group, waited for Peary's command. At last he heard "Forward, march!" Matt's whip snapped out, and a double crack, like gunshots, cut through the silence. The eager dogs were off, yelping in their happiness.

The line of sledges heading toward the North Pole in March 1909

Dogs in their traces fan out in front of a sledge. If they are starving, the dogs will eat their traces, which are made of sealskin.

The trail was so choppy that Matt's sledge broke. The dogs sat and rested while Matt drilled new holes and threaded sealskin lines through them, with his bare hands, to put the pieces together. Every few seconds he would have to stop and put his freezing hands under his reindeer fur jacket to warm them.

Henson and Peary caught up with Bartlett on March 4 at the Big Lead. It was as wide and fearful-looking as it had been in 1906. On March 5, still waiting beside the Big Lead, Matt saw the sun reappear, a "crimson sphere, just balanced on the brink of the world." The weather was perfect — clear with a light wind — but they could not cross the lead. Bartlett and

Dogs curl up outside Peary's igloo.

Peary corrected their compasses, Peary paced up and down, and Matt worked on the sledges.

On March 11 it was clear and calm and -45°F, and the Big Lead was frozen over. The men hurried across.

On March 26, at 86°38', it was Ross Marvin's turn to go back (three men had already returned, as planned). Henson and Marvin shook hands warmly. Marvin congratulated Matt for continuing on and wished him success in getting to the Pole.

This left Henson, Peary, Bartlett, and their teams of Eskimos. Bartlett set out again as pioneer, and on March 29 Peary and Henson caught up with him beside a wide lead. Bartlett and his team of Eskimos were asleep in their igloos, so Henson and Peary quietly built their igloos one hundred yards east of them and went to sleep. A few hours later Matt heard a great crashing and grinding. He kicked out the snow door of his igloo and saw the Arctic Ocean rolling and pitching wildly, the ice separating and huge ice blocks piling up right beside the terrified dogs. Then the ice split with the sound of a shot and zigzagged

Explorers of the Arctic face more obstacles than just cold and darkness. Expedition members need to lift and push their sledges over the ice blocks.

Captain Bob Bartlett (far right) with his sledge team. The Inuit Ooqueah is sitting next to Bartlett.

apart between Henson and Peary's igloos and Bartlett's igloos. Bartlett, his team of Eskimos, and his dogs were on a loose floating island, which began to revolve and drift into the lead, toward Matt. Bartlett had his dogs harnessed in a flash, and as the ice floe passed Matt, Bartlett, the Eskimos, and the dogs leaped across the swirling water to safety. The men were too stunned to speak. The empty igloos floated away and were gone.

On April 1, at 87°46', it was Bartlett's turn to go back. Bartlett was disappointed at not being the one to go to the Pole with Peary, but he knew Matt Henson should go. Peary had told MacMillan earlier that it had to be Matt. "I can't get along without him," Peary had said.

Now it was Henson and Peary against the Arctic, as it had been for 18 years. They had only 135 miles to go; 40 strong, fresh dogs; the 4 bravest Eskimos (Ootah, Ooqueah, Egingwah, and Seegloo); and a brilliant sparkling snow highway lit by a sun that never set. Peary wrote, "My party, my equipment, and my supplies, they were perfect."

Peary searches the horizon with his telescope.

All day April 1 they repaired sledges and rested. The Eskimos had a special treat — boiled dog. At midnight April 2 Peary started out on foot in front, then rode on a sledge, as was his custom. They marched for 10 hours, and in the sunlight that night, Matt saw a marvelous sight. The full moon and the sun circled the sky opposite each other — a disk of silver and a disk of gold.

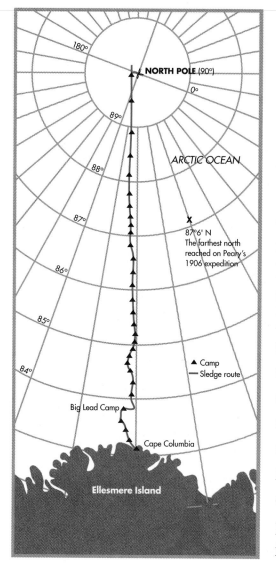

Peary and Henson's route to the North Pole, 1909. In 1902 the Big Lead halted the men; in 1906 a blizzard forced them to turn back.

On April 3 they came to a lead covered with thin ice. As Matt drove his sledge across, the runners broke through. Matt shouted to the dogs to pull the sledge to safety, and the ice opened under his feet. He went straight down into the Arctic Ocean. It was, he said, a moment of "hideous horror." Suddenly he felt something lift him up. Ootah had raced over, grabbed Matt by the hood, and dragged him out. Matt lay in a wet, frozen heap on the ice for a few seconds, trying to get his breath back. Ootah had saved his life. "But I did not tell him so, for such occurrences are taken as part of the day's work," Matt said. Matt stripped off his wet boots, put on dry ones from the sledge, and pounded the icy water out of his furs before they could freeze solid around him. Then they hurried on.

The bitter east wind was like frozen steel, so cold that even the Eskimos complained. But the closer the group got to the top of the world, the more the shattered ice smoothed out. Peary was so anxious to reach the Pole that he would hardly stop to rest the dogs. Hour after hour, around the 24-hour day, they hurried toward the Pole. Matt could estimate mileage accurately, and on April 5 he calculated that they had marched 100 miles since Bartlett had turned back. Peary stopped and took an observation of the sun. It showed they were at 89°25'. Only 35 miles to go, he told Matt.

Before midnight on April 6 they raced off again, and at 10:00 in the morning they stopped. Matt later said, "I was driving ahead and was swinging around to the right. . . . The Commander, who was about 50' behind, called to me and said we would go into camp. . . ." The ice was smooth and blindingly white in all directions, with patches of sapphire blue. At exactly noon Peary took his observations with the artificial horizon of warm mercury that Matt had prepared. The latitude reading showed them to be about three miles from the exact top of the world.

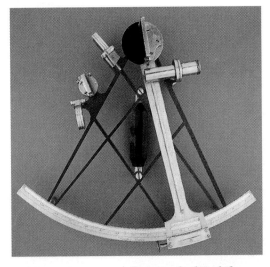

Peary calculated the explorers' position by using a sextant to measure the angular distance between the sun and the horizon. He used warm mercury to create an artificial horizon when the actual horizon was obscured.

Matt felt tremendously proud. "I was confident that the journey had ended," he said. They had done it! He and Peary and their team of Eskimos were the *first* to reach the North Pole. He pulled off his mitten and hurried over to shake Peary's hand, but to Matt's surprise Peary turned aside. Matt decided that Peary had not seen his outstretched hand. He wrote, "I ungloved my right hand and went forward to congratulate him, . . . but a gust of wind blew something in his eye, or else [the pain of looking at the sun] forced him to turn aside. . . ."

At 6:00 that evening, clouds covered the sun where they were, so Peary sledged 10 miles north to take more observations. When he did so he learned that he was traveling south. To get back to camp he would travel north and then south, all in one straight line. This could only happen at the Pole.

Peary had to be absolutely sure he was in the right place, so beginning at 6:00 the next morning, he took more observations. Then he crisscrossed an area of 8-by-10 miles and took a fourth set of observations at noon.

At last Peary said, "We will plant the stars and stripes — *at the North Pole!*" Peary took a picture of Matt holding the American flag, with the Eskimos on either side also holding flags.

They gave three cheers while the dogs looked on, puzzled. While Matt arranged the sledges for the journey home, Peary cut a diagonal strip from the flag and placed it in a bottle along with the record of his discovery, to leave at the top of the world. Peary had written in his diary for April 6, "The Pole at last!!! The prize of three centuries, my dream and ambition for twenty-three years. *Mine* at last."

Matt (center) and the four Eskimos at the North Pole. Matt holds the American flag Josephine Peary made years before. It is covered with patches to replace pieces cut out and left at various "farthest north" camps.

Now they only had to get home. Peary was worn out, so Matt helped him onto a sledge. Then Matt took the group south. Although the trail was broken in places by the drifting of the ice, Matt found it far easier to travel south with light sledges than it had been to make a new trail north. Even so, he wrote, it was "17 days of haste, toil, and misery. . . . We crossed lead after lead, sometimes like a bareback rider in the circus, balancing on cake after cake of ice."

On April 23 they were back at Cape Columbia. When they were a day's march away from the ship, Peary hurried on ahead. Soon Matt could see the *Roosevelt* and smell hot coffee in the clear air. When Matt reached the ship, his friends rushed to greet him and pull him up the side. He was "overjoyed to find [himself] once more safe among friends." They helped Matt to his cabin, and he took off his furs and relaxed for the first time in 68 days.

Meet Jeri Ferris

Growing up on the Nebraska prairie gave Jeri Ferris a lifelong interest in American history and the people who helped shape it. As Matthew Henson did, Ferris enjoys traveling and exploring. She has crisscrossed the globe. She often collects folk art from the countries she visits. Ferris now lives in Los Angeles, California, where she teaches elementary school and writes biographies for children. She writes biographies, she says, because she wants to "make these determined men and women inescapably real," and to inspire similar determination and self-confidence in her readers.

Some of Ferris's other biographies include *What I Had Was Singing: The Story of Marian Anderson* and *Native American Doctor: The Story of Susan LaFlesche Picotte.*

Jeri Ferris has loved horses since she was a child.

Go Exploring!

Write a Newspaper Article

Dateline: North Pole

The year is 1909. You are a newspaper reporter assigned to cover Matthew Henson and Robert Peary's polar expedition. Use the selection to gather the facts — who, what, where, when, why, and how — and write a newspaper article about Henson and Peary's arrival at the North Pole.

Have a Discussion

Co-Explorers

What are your thoughts and feelings about the relationship between Robert Peary and Matthew Henson? Discuss how the two men got along on the way to the North Pole and at the moment of their success. How do you think their relationship might be different if they were co-explorers today?

Expedition at a Glance

July 1908 to April 1909: New York to the
North Pole! Use the selection to make a time
line of Peary and Henson's final expedition,
from the day they steamed out of New York
Harbor to the day they arrived back at
Ellesmere Island in triumph. Include all
the important events along the way.

Compare and Contrast

Two Heroes

In *James and the Giant Peach,* a boy on a
giant peach harnesses a flock of seagulls. In
Arctic Explorer: The Story of Matthew Henson,
an Arctic explorer on a sledge drives a pack of
dogs. How are James and Matthew Henson
both heroes in their adventures? How are they
different from each other?

EVERYDAY ADVENTURERS:
People Who Work in High Places

Hang ten!

A construction worker clings to a girder on the John Hancock Center in Chicago, Illinois.

Treetop rafters

Using a giant raft that has been placed on the treetops, scientists collect specimens from the canopy of a tropical rain forest.

Nose job

Despite a fear of heights, Robert Crisman patches cracks in the faces of Mount Rushmore National Memorial, South Dakota.

Pinnacle painting

More than two hundred feet up, painter Don Harry adds a fresh coat to Cinderella Castle in the Magic Kingdom at the Walt Disney World Resort.

At home on the dome

Judy O'Neil, a member of a family of steeple-jacks, applies a coat of primer before painting gold leaf on the dome of the State Capitol in Atlanta, Georgia.

Call to Adventure

by Hillary Hauser

> *The day shall not be up so soon as I,*
> *To try the fair adventure of tomorrow.*
> — Shakespeare
> *King John*

Adventure — what a magic word!

By it you enter into worlds previously unseen and unknown. It is the key to individuality, the courage to chart your own life and the strength to think for yourself. When you decide to be an adventurer, you have committed yourself to trying something new and different, something that has never been done by anyone else, at least not in the same way as it has been done before.

To be adventurous does not necessarily mean that one must perform a physical feat. Some of the greatest adventurers of all time have changed the world while staying in the solitude of their rooms, allowing only their minds to travel. Innovative scientists, writers, or philosophers, for example, constantly try to think about things in new ways. They also have the courage to express their ideas publicly.

The type of adventurer we can become depends upon the degree of our curiosity — how much we want to learn about something we don't know, how much we want to test ourselves against the forces of nature or the obstacles that stand in the way of the discovery that we are sure exists even though we can't see it. The unknown world we choose to discover may be the North Pole or the bottom of the sea, or it may be at the bottom of pages and pages of calculations or words. Even if someone else has been there before, discovered the thing before, perhaps we'll try to get there by some other way, or perhaps we'll simply do the thing alone, to prove that we can do difficult things by ourselves.

In fact, the adventurer may find that in actuality, he or she IS the adventure. That's because each one has a unique approach to every possibility on the planet, and how an individual sees a thing or a challenge is what makes the challenge unique.

FEAR

A Personal Essay by Tristan Overcashier

Being an adventurer often involves overcoming fear. Tristan explores his thoughts about conquering fear in this essay.

FEAR

Fear — everybody has one, if it's a fear of spiders or a fear of heights. Throughout your lifetime you should try to conquer your dread. You will need to take risks, but if you overcome your fear there is usually something good in it for you.

When you're going through the process of defeating your trepidation, you have many thoughts. You may think, "Is this O.K.? Would my parents approve of it? Could I seriously injure myself? What will my peers say?" When you answer these questions and others for yourself, you then decide to either walk away or go for it.

When I was seven years old, I had one procedure left to get my swimming card — jumping off a diving board, my greatest fear. Thoughts ran through my mind. "Why me? Maybe I should walk away."

I came back to the sound of my swimming teacher. "Come on, let's go!" I realized I was safe. I gathered up all my strength.

Wait! Oh, no. Buzz, buzz. Wasps.

"I'm dead," I thought. See, wasps are another one of my fears, and there I was face to face with one on a diving board!

I thought about that dreaded word C-H-I-C-K-E-N. So I went, praying that the wasp would leave.

CRUNCH. SPLASH! That was what it sounded like to step on a wasp and then land in the water. I got out of the water to find out that diving boards aren't that scary, wasp stings hurt, and it felt good to receive my swim card.

If you walk away, your friends may call you a baby, but remember, only listen to your own criticism. If you decide to go on and overcome your fear, you will feel contentment or even pride.

Fear — you'll always have one, but you can always attempt to prevail.

Tristan Overcashier
Plumb Elementary School
Clearwater, Florida

Tristan was in the fifth grade when he wrote this essay. He enjoys playing soccer and collecting sports cards. He is thinking about becoming a marine biologist because he loves sea animals, such as dolphins. He is also considering becoming a pharmacist because he likes to mix chemicals.

ADVENTURES IN FLIGHT:
From Balloon to the Moon

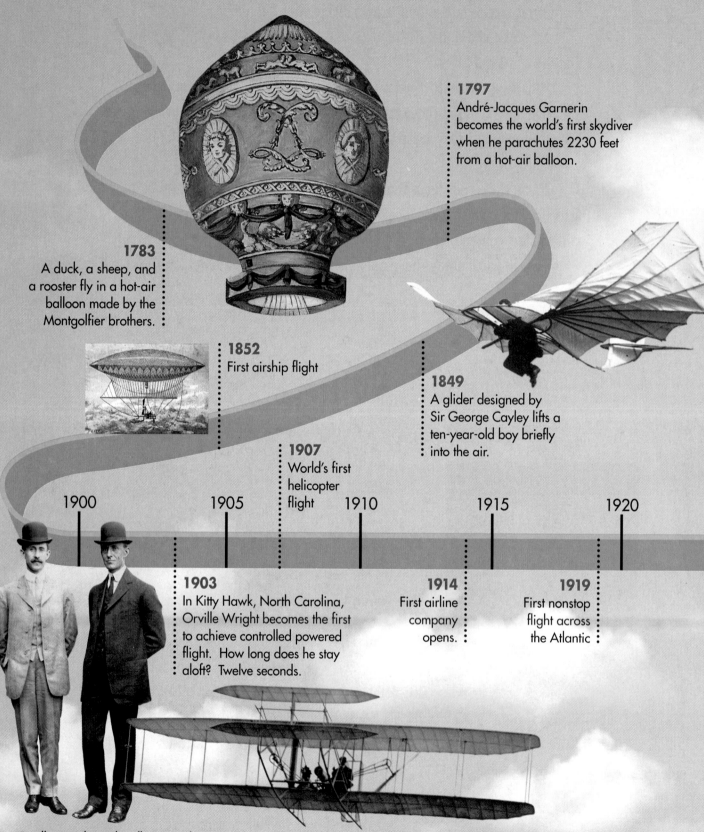

1797
André-Jacques Garnerin becomes the world's first skydiver when he parachutes 2230 feet from a hot-air balloon.

1783
A duck, a sheep, and a rooster fly in a hot-air balloon made by the Montgolfier brothers.

1852
First airship flight

1849
A glider designed by Sir George Cayley lifts a ten-year-old boy briefly into the air.

1907
World's first helicopter flight

1900 1905 1910 1915 1920

1903
In Kitty Hawk, North Carolina, Orville Wright becomes the first to achieve controlled powered flight. How long does he stay aloft? Twelve seconds.

1914
First airline company opens.

1919
First nonstop flight across the Atlantic

Orville Wright and Wilbur Wright

1921
Excluded from
United States
aviation schools, Bessie
Coleman studies flying
in Europe. She becomes
the world's first licensed
African American pilot.

1931
Ruth Nichols flies
her plane to an
altitude of 28,743
feet — higher than
any woman has
flown before.

1933
The first modern airliner, the
Boeing 247, makes its initial
flight. It can carry ten passengers
and four hundred pounds of
baggage. People love its luxuries:
armchair seats, a flight attendant,
and a bathroom.

1925   1930   1935   1940   1945

1927
Charles Lindbergh
flies solo across
the Atlantic.

1935
Having soloed
across the
Atlantic in 1932,
Amelia Earhart
soloes across the
Pacific from
Hawaii to
California.

85

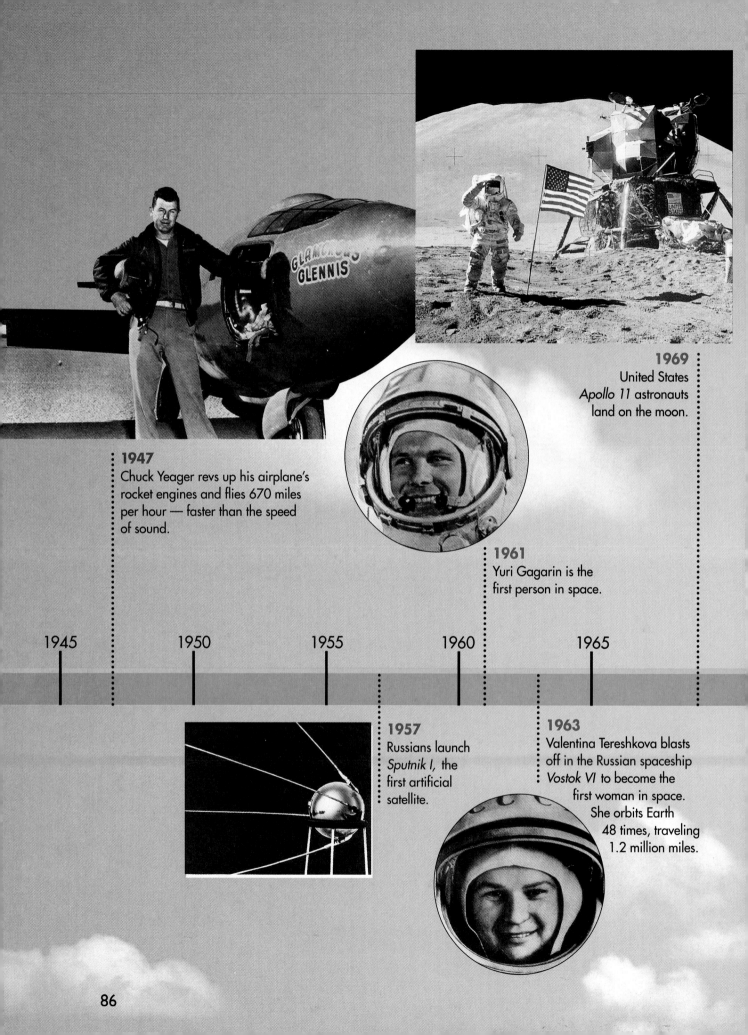

1947
Chuck Yeager revs up his airplane's rocket engines and flies 670 miles per hour — faster than the speed of sound.

1969
United States *Apollo 11* astronauts land on the moon.

1961
Yuri Gagarin is the first person in space.

1945

1950

1955

1960

1965

1957
Russians launch *Sputnik I*, the first artificial satellite.

1963
Valentina Tereshkova blasts off in the Russian spaceship *Vostok VI* to become the first woman in space. She orbits Earth 48 times, traveling 1.2 million miles.

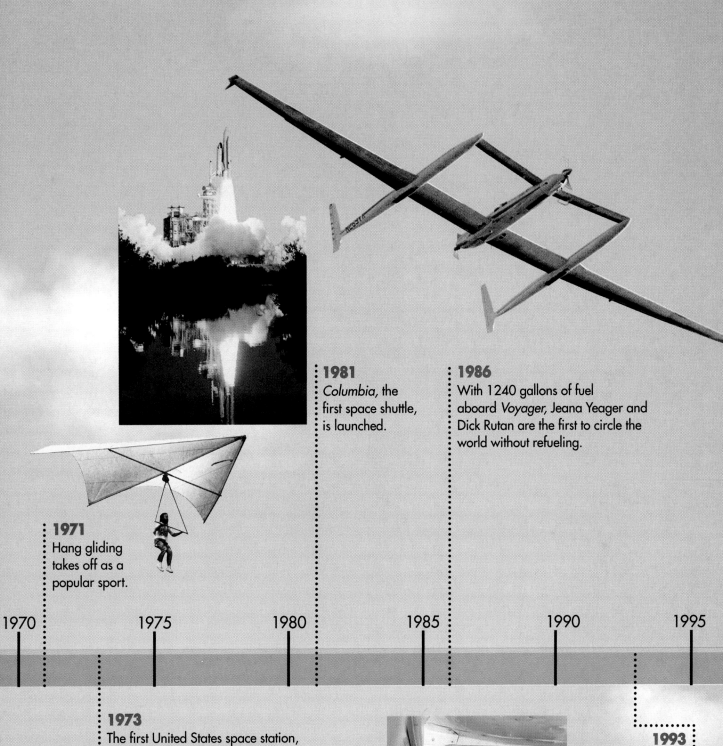

1981
Columbia, the first space shuttle, is launched.

1986
With 1240 gallons of fuel aboard *Voyager*, Jeana Yeager and Dick Rutan are the first to circle the world without refueling.

1971
Hang gliding takes off as a popular sport.

1970   1975   1980   1985   1990   1995

1973
The first United States space station, *Skylab* — built out of old spaceship parts — proves that people can live for long periods in space.

1993
Victoria Van Meter, 11, becomes the youngest girl to fly across the United States. Her flight instructor sits alongside her the whole way but never once takes the controls.

87

Moon

by Myra Cohn Livingston

Moon remembers.

Marooned in shadowed night,

white powder plastered
on her pockmarked face,
scarred with craters,
filled with waterless seas,

she thinks back
to the Eagle,
to the flight
of men from Earth,
of rocks sent back in space,
and one
faint
footprint
in the Sea of Tranquility.

Again and again

by Kazue Mizumura

Again and again,

The wind wipes away the clouds

And shines up the moon.

Winter Moon

by Langston Hughes

How thin and sharp is the moon tonight!

How thin and sharp and ghostly white

Is the slim curved crook of the moon tonight!

Alice Neel, *Harlem Nocturne,* oil on canvas, 1952

VOYAGER

An Adventure to the Edge of the Solar System

SALLY RIDE
TAM O'SHAUGHNESSY

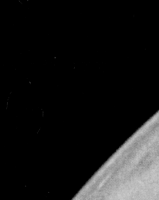

This is the story of two spacecraft: *Voyager* 1 and *Voyager* 2. They were launched from Earth to explore four distant planets: Jupiter, Saturn, Uranus, and Neptune.

Earth is the third of nine planets that circle the star we call the Sun. Jupiter, Saturn, Uranus, and Neptune are the fifth, sixth, seventh, and eighth. They are very, very far away. Jupiter, even when it is closest to Earth, is 400 million miles away. Neptune is 3 billion miles away.

All four of these planets are very different from Earth.

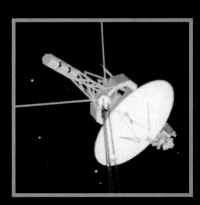

The first two, Jupiter and Saturn, are like each other in many ways. Both of them are huge. Jupiter is the biggest planet in the solar system — more than one thousand Earths would fit inside it. Both are made up mostly of hydrogen and helium gas, the two lightest gases in the universe. Toward the center of each planet the gas gets thicker and thicker, until it is so thick that it becomes liquid. Jupiter and Saturn have no solid ground to stand on. Because they are so big, and are made up mostly of gas, they are called "gas giants."

Uranus and Neptune are also giant planets. Although they are not as big as Jupiter and Saturn, both are much, much bigger than Earth. Their atmospheres are also made up mostly of hydrogen and helium gas. Because they are so far away from the Sun, they are cold, dark planets.

Scientists had studied the four giant planets through telescopes and learned a lot about them, but even the most powerful telescopes could not answer all their questions. A spacecraft designed to explore the giant planets would give them a closer view. But it would have been impossible to send astronauts so far. Astronauts have never traveled beyond our own moon. A trip to the giant planets would be thousands of times farther and would take several years. Only a robot spacecraft could make the long journey.

The mission was so important that two spacecraft were built, *Voyager* 1 and *Voyager* 2. If one broke down on the long trip, there would still be one left.

The *Voyager*s were not very big — each one was about the size of a small car — but they were the most advanced spacecraft ever designed. The scientific instruments they carried included special cameras with telescopic lenses. These cameras would take close-up pictures of the giant planets and the surfaces of their moons. Other instruments would measure ultraviolet and infrared light. This light, invisible to normal cameras, would tell scientists more about the temperatures of the planets and what they are made of.

MISSION CONTROL

During their long trip through space, the *Voyager*s would be controlled from Earth. Scientists would radio commands to the spacecraft telling them what path to follow, what to photograph, and when to send back information. The *Voyager*s' antennas would always be pointed toward Earth, ready to receive instructions.

Radio signals from the *Voyager*s were picked up by large antennas in California, Australia, and Spain. The signals were then relayed by satellite to Mission Control in Pasadena, California. ▶

The pictures and information collected by the spacecraft would be radioed back to Earth. But the *Voyagers'* radio transmitters were not very powerful, and by the time their signals reached Earth, they would be very, very weak. Many large antennas all over the world would be needed to pick them up. It would be like listening for a whisper from thousands of miles away.

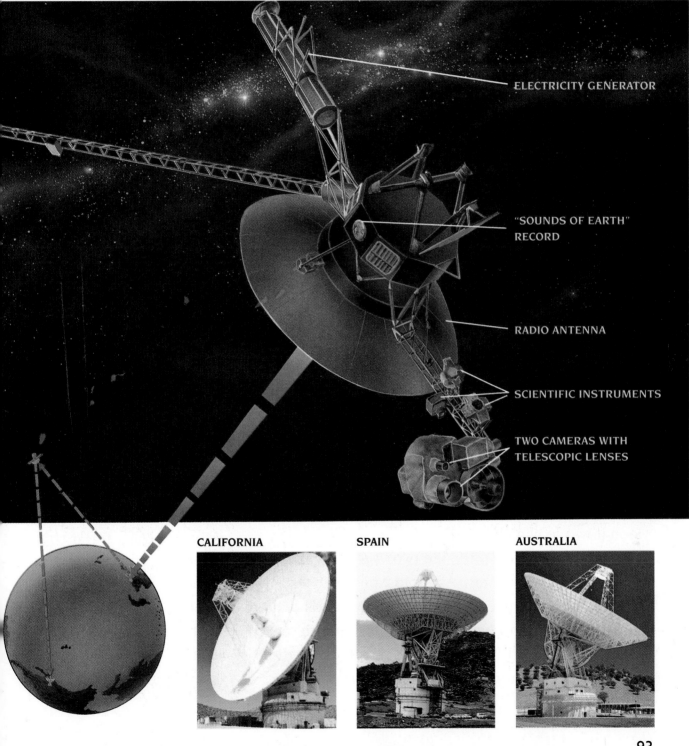

ELECTRICITY GENERATOR

"SOUNDS OF EARTH" RECORD

RADIO ANTENNA

SCIENTIFIC INSTRUMENTS

TWO CAMERAS WITH TELESCOPIC LENSES

CALIFORNIA

SPAIN

AUSTRALIA

Exploring all four giant planets is possible only when the planets are lined up correctly in their orbits. Then each planet's gravity can be used — like a slingshot — to speed up the spacecraft and bend its path toward the next planet. The *Voyagers* would fly to Jupiter, then use Jupiter's gravity to accelerate them toward Saturn. If both *Voyagers* were still working when they got to Saturn, one spacecraft would be sent to study Saturn's largest moon, Titan, and the other would continue on to explore Uranus and Neptune.

The planets do not line up this way often — only once every 176 years! The *Voyager* mission was a rare opportunity.

In the summer of 1977, the *Voyagers* were launched into space by two powerful rockets. Leaving Earth, they were flying so fast that it took them only ten hours to pass the Moon. As it was racing away, *Voyager* 1 looked back to take this picture of the Earth and Moon it was leaving behind.

On their way to Jupiter, the two *Voyagers* would have to pass through the asteroid belt. Asteroids are huge, fast-moving rocks that orbit around the Sun. There are thousands of them between the planets Mars and Jupiter, and a collision with one could destroy the spacecraft. Both *Voyagers* made it safely past them. *Voyager* 1 led the way to Jupiter, the first gas giant.

▲ The four giant planets, Jupiter, Saturn, Uranus, and Neptune, shown to scale. Earth is also shown to scale.

◀ The Earth and the Moon, photographed by the rapidly departing *Voyager* 1.

JUPITER

The *Voyager*s sped closer and closer to Jupiter. As the spacecraft approached the planet, hundreds of scientists crowded into Mission Control to see the close-up pictures of this faraway world.

The radio signals that carry *Voyager*s' pictures travel at the speed of light. So although it had taken the *Voyager*s one and a half years to travel to Jupiter, their pictures traveled back to Earth in about 45 minutes. As soon as the pictures were received by the huge antennas on Earth, they were relayed to Mission Control, then displayed on TV screens. The scientists were stunned by what they saw.

The giant planet has bright colors and complex patterns that scientists had never seen through their telescopes. It is covered with wide bands of yellow, orange, red, and white clouds. Violent storms move through the clouds.

The Great Red Spot is a huge storm in Jupiter's atmosphere that never disappears. Scientists had looked at it through telescopes for over three hundred years, but they had never been able to study its motion. Hundreds of the *Voyager*s' pictures were put together into a movie so that the motions of the Great Red Spot and the other storms could be seen. The movie showed the Great Red Spot swirling violently around its center, with hurricane-force winds around its edges.

Each of the smaller white circles is also a violent, swirling storm. Scientists do not understand why some storms are bright red and others are white. Although the white storms look small next to the Great Red Spot, some of them are as big as the Earth.

A picture of Jupiter's Great Red Spot. ▶

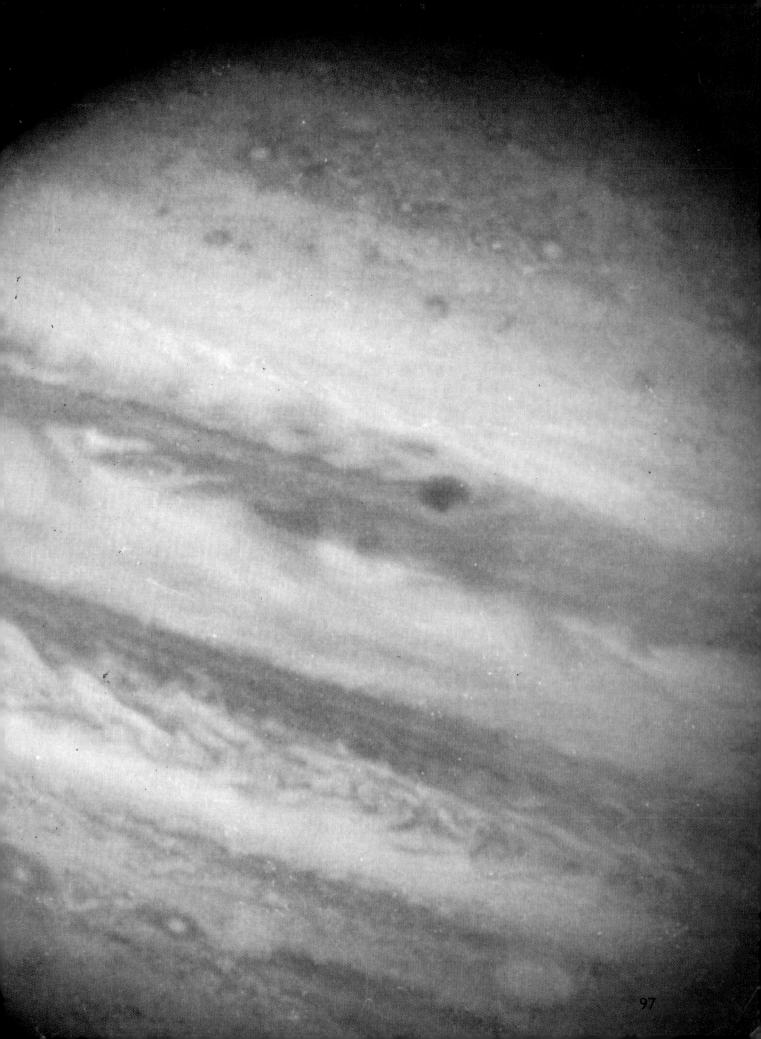

Jupiter has 16 moons that circle around it like a miniature solar system. Three of these moons were discovered by the *Voyager*s. Some of the other moons were seen close up for the first time.

Jupiter's moon Callisto has been hit by rocks and meteorites for over 4 billion years. Each of these collisions left a crater in Callisto's icy surface. Some of the craters look very bright. These are the newer ones. Each collision sprays fresh ice over the surface, and the freshest ice is the brightest.

Long ago, a very big object — maybe an asteroid — crashed into Callisto. Callisto's icy surface wasn't strong enough to hold the shape of the huge crater left by the collision. Its surface sagged back to its original shape, and now all that's left is a bright patch of ice and a series of faint rings that formed at the time of the collision.

Scientists expected most of the moons in the solar system to look like Callisto — dark, frozen, and covered with craters. They were shocked when they saw the *Voyager*s' pictures of Io, another of Jupiter's moons. There were no craters, and its surface looked orange and splotchy. At first Io was a mystery. But then one of the *Voyager*s' pictures showed something completely unexpected: a volcano erupting! There are active volcanoes on Earth, but scientists did not expect to find them anywhere else in the solar system. Nine volcanoes were erupting on Io while the

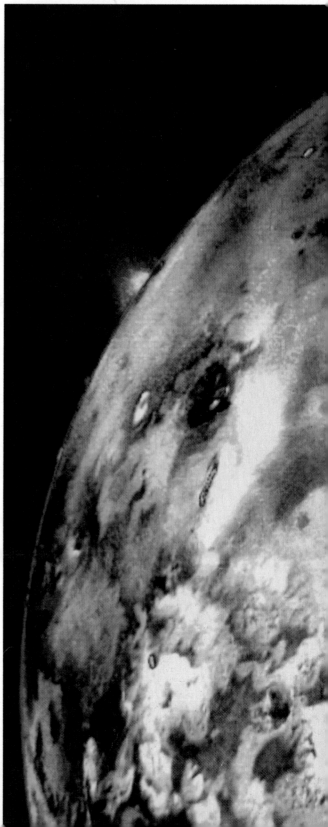

Voyager 1 took this photo of a volcano erupting on Io. The plume of gas is more than 100 miles high.

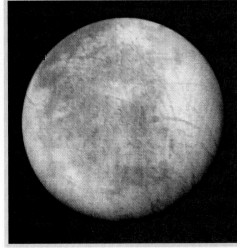

Voyagers flew past, some throwing hot gas hundreds of miles high. There are no craters on Io because lava from the volcanoes flows over its surface and fills in the craters. The cooled lava contains the chemical sulfur, which gives Io's surface its orange, yellow, red, and black colors.

Europa is Jupiter's brightest moon. Like Io, Europa did not look the way scientists expected a moon to look. It is bright because it is covered with a very smooth layer of ice that reflects the sunlight. Scientists believe that the lines on Europa's surface are cracks in the ice. Fresh ice from below the surface oozes up through the cracks and forms long, flat ridges.

Like Callisto, Europa has been hit by thousands of rocks and meteorites. But there are very few craters left on its surface. Europa's layer of ice must have once been soft, or even liquid, and erased the craters.

For hundreds of years, scientists thought that Saturn was the only planet with rings, but the *Voyagers* discovered a thin ring around Jupiter. The ring could not be seen from Earth. Even the *Voyagers'* sensitive cameras could barely make it out.

The ring is made up of very small dust particles that are circling the planet. Where does the dust come from? The *Voyagers* discovered two tiny moons at the edge of the ring. Scientists think that meteorites hit those moons and knock dust off their surfaces. The dust goes into orbit around the planet and becomes part of the ring.

The *Voyagers* relayed more than 30,000 pictures of Jupiter and its moons back to Earth. As scientists settled down to study the pictures and other scientific information, the spacecraft began their two-year trip to the next planet, Saturn.

SATURN

Saturn is the second largest planet in the solar system — only Jupiter is bigger. But although Saturn is big, it is very light. It is not like a big rock. A rock would sink in a bucket of water. If you could find a bucket big enough, Saturn would float in it.

When astronomers look at Saturn through telescopes on Earth, they see a yellow, hazy planet with three beautiful rings. But as the *Voyagers* got closer and closer, they showed Saturn as it had never been seen before. The planet turned out to have broad belts of brown, yellow, and orange clouds. Its striped atmosphere reminded scientists of Jupiter, but the colors weren't as bright, and the bands weren't as sharp.

High winds howl through Saturn's atmosphere, blowing much faster than any winds on Earth. Jet streams near Saturn's equator can reach 1,000 miles per hour. The *Voyagers* also discovered wild, swirling storms, like those in Jupiter's atmosphere.

Saturn's famous rings are made up of countless pieces of rock and ice in high-speed orbits around the planet. If you could scoop up all the particles in the rings, you would have enough rock and ice to make a medium-sized moon. Scientists think that the rings may be what's left of a moon that was shattered by collisions.

As part of an experiment, the *Voyagers* sent radio signals through the rings back to Earth. The radio signals were changed a little bit as they went through the rings. By studying these changes, scientists learned that the pieces of rock and ice that make up the rings come in many different sizes. Some are as small as grains of sand. Some are as big as trucks.

From Earth, Saturn appears to have three broad rings. In the *Voyagers'* pictures it looked as if there were thousands and thousands of rings. *Voyagers'* other instruments showed that the rings are all part of a huge sheet of particles. There are no completely empty gaps. The thin sheet starts close to Saturn's cloud tops and extends out 40,000 miles. Three very faint rings orbit outside the main sheet.

The *Voyagers* discovered a very small moon, invisible from Earth, at the outer edge of the main sheet of rings. This moon, like the rings themselves, is probably a piece of a larger moon that was shattered when it was hit by a comet or an asteroid. There are other small moons like this one that help shape the rings and sweep the edges clean.

Saturn has at least 18 moons, more than any other planet. Four of them, including the one at the edge of the main sheet of rings, were discovered by the *Voyagers*.

The *Voyagers'* pictures of Saturn's moons show that the solar system can be a dangerous place. One of the moons, Mimas, barely survived a collision that left an enormous crater on its surface. The crater is 80 miles wide, and the mountain at its center is higher than Mount Everest. If the collision had been much harder, Mimas would have split apart.

Saturn's rings. Colors have been added to the photograph by a computer to show different parts of the rings.

This picture shows Saturn, its rings, and two of its 18 moons, Tethys and Dione.

MIMAS

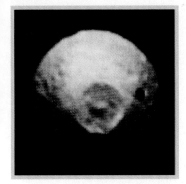

HYPERION

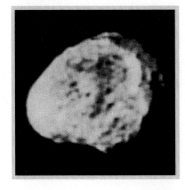

PHOEBE

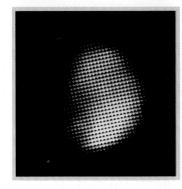

TITAN

Another moon, Hyperion, is probably a piece of what was once a larger moon that did break apart.

Most of Saturn's moons are icy balls that were formed at the same time as the planet. But Phoebe is different. It is probably an asteroid that came too close to the planet and was captured by the pull of Saturn's gravity. The picture is blurry because Phoebe is small and *Voyager* was far away.

Titan, Saturn's largest moon, fascinated scientists. Before the *Voyager* mission, it was the only moon in the solar system known to have an atmosphere. From Earth, scientists had detected methane gas around Titan, but they could not tell whether there were other gases in its atmosphere. To find out more, scientists sent *Voyager* 1 on a path that would take it very close to this unusual moon.

When the spacecraft arrived at Titan, it found a thick orange haze covering the moon. Titan's atmosphere is very thick — more than one and a half times thicker than the air on Earth. It is made up mostly of nitrogen gas, just like Earth's atmosphere. But unlike the air we breathe, Titan's atmosphere contains no oxygen.

What is below the orange haze? *Voyager* 1's cameras could not see to Titan's surface, but its other instruments sent back clues. The chemical ethane is as abundant on Titan as water is on Earth. Scientists think that Titan might have ethane rainstorms, and maybe even ethane rivers and lakes on its frozen surface.

Because *Voyager* 1's path took it so close to Titan, it would not be able to go on to Uranus and Neptune. Instead, the spacecraft headed up and out of the main plane of the solar system.

Voyager 2 was on a path that would enable it to visit the last two giant planets. Using Saturn's gravity like a giant sling-shot, *Voyager* 2 said good-bye to its twin and headed for Uranus alone.

URANUS

Uranus is so far away that it took *Voyager* 2 more than four years to travel there from Saturn. The planet was still 150 million miles away when *Voyager* took this picture.

Because Uranus is so far from the Sun, it does not get much heat or light. It is a cold, dark planet. Taking pictures at Uranus is like taking pictures at twilight on Earth. So as *Voyager* approached Uranus, scientists adjusted its cameras to take pictures in this dim light.

Voyager got closer and closer to the planet, but all the pictures relayed back to Earth looked the same. Uranus does not have streaming bands of color or swirling storms like Jupiter and Saturn. Its pale blue atmosphere is almost featureless. *Voyager* did measure strong winds, but they are not as strong as the winds on the other two planets.

Uranus' atmosphere is made up mostly of hydrogen and helium gas, like Jupiter and Saturn. But it also has small amounts of methane. It is the methane that gives Uranus its blue color.

Although this pale blue planet looks calm and peaceful, scientists think it had a violent past. Early in its history, Uranus probably collided with a huge object, maybe a comet the size of Earth. This collision was so violent that Uranus was knocked over. Now the planet lies on its side. As it orbits around the Sun, first its south pole then its north pole point toward the Sun.

The same year that the *Voyager*s were launched from Earth, scientists looking through telescopes discovered nine narrow rings around Uranus. When *Voyager* 2 got there, it found two more.

Uranus' rings are very different from both the faint ring around Jupiter and the broad sheet of rings around Saturn. The rings of Jupiter and Saturn have many tiny particles in them, but Uranus' rings seem to be made up mostly of big chunks of rock and ice the size of boulders. Scientists were puzzled. Shouldn't the boulders crash into each other and break into smaller pieces? Scientists are still studying the information *Voyager* sent back, looking for the small particles they think should be there.

The rings are also much darker than those of Jupiter and Saturn. The boulders in Uranus' rings are as black as charcoal.

The picture to the right, and a picture like it from Saturn, gave scientists a clue to the mystery of what holds a ring together. Because of *Voyager*'s photographs, scientists now think that particles can be held in the shape of a ring by two small moons, one on each side of the ring. Each moon's gravity pulls on the particles in a kind of tug-of-war, which keeps the particles in a ring between them.

The *Voyager*s showed that moons and rings are closely related. Not only can rings be held in place by small moons, but the rings themselves may be what's left of moons that were shattered by collisions with comets or asteroids.

▲ Uranus' rings. The two rings *Voyager* discovered are so faint that they don't show up in this picture.

▼ Two tiny moons (*circled*), close to one of Uranus' rings.

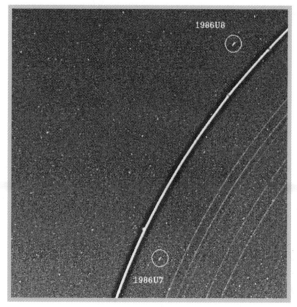

Before *Voyager* 2 visited Uranus, scientists had found five moons around the planet, but they did not know how big they were, or what they were made of. In just a few hours, *Voyager* discovered ten new moons. It found that Uranus' moons are made up mostly of ice and rock, and that even its largest moons, Titania and Oberon, are only half the size of Earth's moon.

Miranda is the closest moon to the planet. It looks like a jigsaw puzzle whose pieces have been scrambled. Part of its surface looks old and cratered, and part of it looks young and very rough. There are ice cliffs ten miles high and canyons ten miles deep. Scientists are puzzled by Miranda. Some think it is possible that Miranda was once torn apart by a collision. The pieces stayed in orbit around Uranus and were slowly drawn back together to form a moon again. This theory could explain the mixed-up appearance of the moon we see today.

Voyager 2's encounter with Uranus was very short. Most pictures of the planet, its rings, and its moons were taken in only six hours. But those six hours gave scientists their first real look at this pale blue planet.

After traveling nearly 3 billion miles, *Voyager* still had $1\frac{1}{2}$ billion miles to go before reaching Neptune, the last giant planet in our solar system.

NEPTUNE

Voyager 2 had been traveling for 12 years. The aging spacecraft had survived its long trip through space and was finally nearing Neptune. There was great excitement in Mission Control. Scientists had waited a long time for a close look at this mysterious planet.

Voyager did not disappoint them. In the very first close-up pictures, scientists discovered a new moon orbiting close to Neptune. The moon is small, dark, and bumpy. It looks as if it has lived through many collisions. *Voyager* would discover five more small moons before it left Neptune.

Voyager's next pictures brought another discovery: there are rings around this planet, too. Two are narrow, and two are broad. The particles that make up Neptune's rings are small, like those in Jupiter's rings. But they are also very black, like the big boulders circling Uranus.

Neptune's rings are unusual because some parts of them are thicker than others. The particles in the rings are not spread out evenly. Scientists do not understand why. There might be very small moons shaping the rings, but none have yet been found.

Scientists expected Neptune to be a lot like Uranus because the two planets are about the same size and are very, very far away from the Sun. But *Voyager*'s pictures surprised them. This cold, blue planet has violent weather. Its atmosphere has wild storms, like those on Jupiter and Saturn.

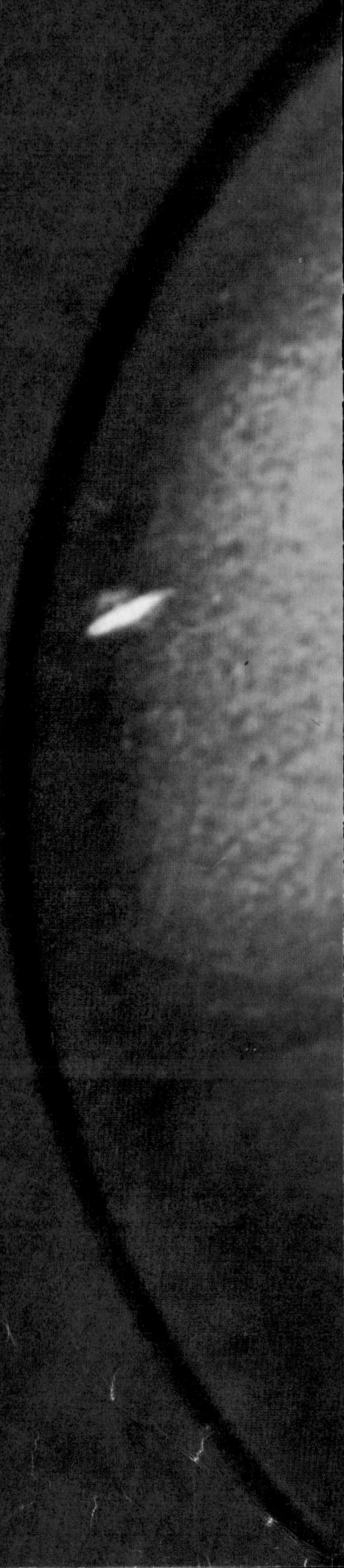

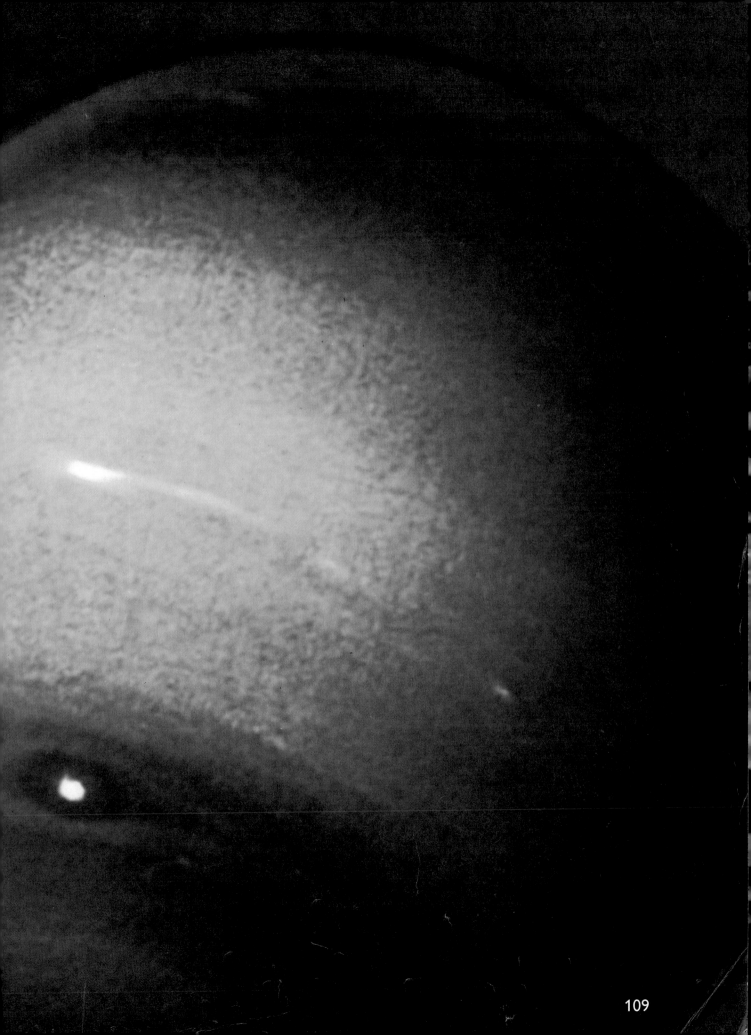

One huge storm was named the Great Dark Spot because it reminded scientists of Jupiter's Great Red Spot. Winds near its edges are the strongest measured on any planet — over 1,400 miles per hour!

Voyager flew closer to Neptune than to any other planet, skimming only three thousand miles above the tops of its clouds. The white clouds in Neptune's atmosphere look like high, thin clouds on Earth. You can see their dark shadows on the cloud layer below. From the shadows, scientists figured out that the white clouds are floating many miles above the others.

Voyager's flight path also took it very close to Neptune's rings. As it passed the rings, it was hit again and again by tiny dust particles. Even though the particles were very small, they were moving so fast that *Voyager* could have been damaged. But the bombardment lasted only a few moments, and *Voyager* made it safely past. *Voyager* raced toward its last target, Neptune's largest moon, Triton.

Very little was known about Triton, but observations from Earth led scientists to believe that it might have an atmosphere. *Voyager* found that it does. Triton's atmosphere is made up of the same gases — nitrogen and methane — as the atmosphere of Saturn's moon, Titan. But Triton's atmosphere is very, very thin. *Voyager's* cameras could easily see through it to the moon's surface.

▲ Two photographs were combined to make this picture of Neptune's rings.

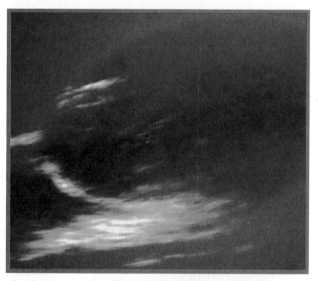

▲ A close-up picture of the Great Dark Spot.

▲ White clouds high in Neptune's atmosphere cast dark shadows on the blue cloud layer below.

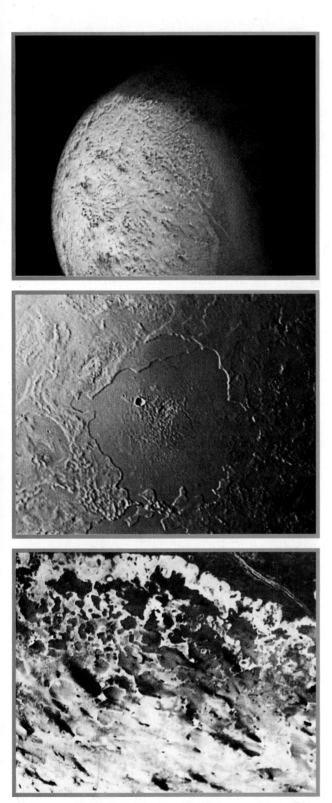

Most moons are formed with their planet, so they orbit in the same direction as the planet spins. Triton orbits Neptune in the "wrong" direction. This makes scientists think that Triton was formed somewhere else in the solar system but came too close to Neptune and was captured by the planet's gravity.

After Triton was captured, the forces pulling it toward Neptune may have heated Triton and melted it. It is possible that for a billion years Triton was a liquid moon. Today, Triton is the coldest place in the solar system — its temperature is 390 degrees (Fahrenheit) below zero. Its surface is frozen hard.

Parts of Triton are covered by pale ice caps. At first, scientists couldn't explain the dark streaks they saw on the ice. But as they looked at more pictures, they saw that dark jets of ice and gas were shooting up from the surface and then were being carried sideways by the wind. These jets, called geysers, occur when liquid below the surface explodes up through weak spots in the ice — like a warm soft drink when you pop open the can. Some geysers may erupt for months, spraying ice and gas miles into Triton's thin atmosphere and leaving dark streaks on its icy surface.

Top: Triton. *Center*: Part of Triton's surface. The distance across the photograph is about 300 miles. *Bottom*: Part of the ice cap at Triton's south pole. The dark smudges may be ice geysers.

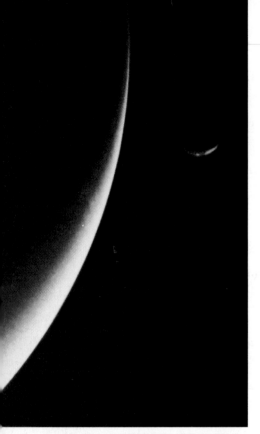

Ice geysers had never been seen before. This discovery, on the coldest moon in the solar system, was an exciting end to a 12-year adventure. Three days after leaving Triton, *Voyager* was already 3 million miles away. As it sped away, it gave scientists this last look at Neptune and Triton. It was not long before the last giant planet was just a dot in the distance.

The *Voyager*s are still traveling.

Since leaving Saturn, *Voyager* 1 has been heading north out of the solar system. *Voyager* 2 is now heading south. Although the *Voyager*s are no longer taking pictures, they are still collecting data. They will continue to radio information back to Earth until about the year 2020. Both spacecraft are studying the solar wind, high energy particles that stream out of the Sun. And they are searching for the edge of the solar system — the place where our Sun's influence ends.

The *Voyager*s won't stop there. They will continue on into interstellar space, the empty space between the stars. Although they are traveling at more than 35,000 miles per hour, neither spacecraft will come near another star for thousands and thousands of years.

It is very unlikely that either *Voyager* will be found by space travelers from another world. But just in case, they carry a message from their home planet, Earth. A copper record attached to the side of the spacecraft contains pictures and sounds from Earth. It begins:

> "This is a present from a small and distant world, a token of our sounds, our science, our images, our music, our thoughts, and our feelings."

The *Voyager*s are still traveling, heading toward the stars, carrying a message from all of us.

▲ *Voyager*'s last look at Neptune and Triton.

▲ The record attached to each *Voyager* contains greetings in more than 60 languages, music from many different cultures, and other sounds from Earth, such as the songs of humpback whales. The record's cover (*inset*) has symbols showing where Earth is located in the universe.

Meet the Authors

Sally Ride knows a lot about out-of-this-world travel. In 1983 she became the first American woman in space when she flew aboard the space shuttle *Challenger*. During the six-day flight, Ride did scientific experiments, helped launch satellites, and worked a fifty-foot robot arm. She even took part in a jellybean-catching contest — no hands allowed. "The thing that I'll remember most about the flight is that it was fun. In fact, I'm sure it was the most fun I will ever have in my life," she says.

Ride wrote her first children's book, *To Space and Back*, about living and working in space. In 1987 she hung up her flight suit for good, and now she is a professor of physics at the University of California at San Diego. Both of her careers helped her in writing *Voyager: An Adventure to the Edge of the Solar System*.

Tam O'Shaughnessy met Sally Ride when they were teenagers competing in national tennis tournaments. The two have been friends ever since. O'Shaughnessy played tennis professionally and then went on to become a biology professor in San Diego, California. *Voyager: An Adventure to the Edge of the Solar System* is her first book.

OUT-OF-THIS-WORLD IDEAS

Paint a Planet

What Color Is Your World?

Vibrant hues! Dazzling rings! Moons galore! How do you see the *Voyagers'* vistas? Use the information and photos in this selection to draw or paint pictures of the four planets visited by the *Voyagers*.

What I Want to Know Is . . .

What is Neptune's Great Dark Spot? How can a planet's moons look so different from each other? Your reading about *Voyager* may have raised many questions. Make a list of the questions you have about the planets, their moons, and other features of space.

Make a Model

Batteries Not Included

Although *Voyager* 1 and 2 look more like satellite dishes than sleek rocket ships, their design suits their mission. Use art materials to make a model of the *Voyager* spacecraft. Show what the parts do by labeling them, or draw a diagram of your model.

Compare Selections

Boast the Best!

From an ocean alive with sharks, to the frozen top of the world, to the outer reaches of our solar system — the major selections in this theme have taken you to some unusual places with some extraordinary characters. Write a paragraph or two explaining which adventure was most exciting to you and why.

SPACE CADETS

CONTACT VISITS A CAMP FOR KID ASTRONAUTS

by Russell Ginns

**"This is the flight director,"
says the voice over the radio.
"Prepare to separate solid
rocket boosters."**

You press two flashing yellow buttons. Then you hear the sound of two small explosions as the rockets separate from your ship. The whole cabin shakes.

The pilot taps you on the shoulder. She points out the window as the Earth seems to shrink and fall away.

"T plus eight minutes and 10 seconds," a voice crackles.

"The shuttle is now moving at a speed of 3,700 feet per second," says another voice.

Are you really flying in the space shuttle, 100 miles above the Earth? No — but you're doing the closest thing to it, as you complete your final mission at U.S. Space Camp in Huntsville, AL.

A space camper practices with the remote arm and "Five Degrees of Freedom" simulator.

Busy Schedule

From early morning until late at night, kids at Space Camp are very busy. "Sometimes they bring their skateboards or radios to camp," trainer Bridget Damberg told CONTACT. "But I've never seen anyone who had time to use them."

Starting at six in the morning, campers go to one training session after another, with just a little time in between to eat meals and phone home. They attend lectures about the history of space suits and learn all about the different parts of the space shuttle. They build and launch their own model rockets and tour the Space and Rocket Center, the largest space museum in the U.S. Each evening, campers watch movies about the history of space exploration.

Much of the equipment at Space Camp is similar to what real astronauts train on.

The "Five Degrees of Freedom" simulator was actually used by the early astronauts to practice moving about in zero gravity. Campers sit strapped into a chair that can swivel in any direction: up, down, left or right. The whole chair floats on a

Each year, thousands of kids from all over the U.S. travel there to learn about outer space and the U.S. space program. And the neatest part of all: Campers get hands-on astronaut training.

Space Camp is for kids in grades four through six. Space Academy is a similar program for kids in grades seven through twelve. Both are five and a half days of lessons, tours and practice missions that give kids a chance to experience what it's really like to be an astronaut.

So this is how weightlessness feels!

cushion of air. So the slightest push in any direction can start it sliding across the floor.

Holding a wrench in one hand, the trainee gets pushed towards a wall that has a bolt screwed into it. The object is to unscrew the bolt without touching the wall. "Until you get the hang of it, you start spinning while the bolt stays still," camper Danny Shaw, 11, told CONTACT.

Another simulator is called the "Microgravity Training Chair." It's a seat that hangs from the ceiling by a system of pulleys and springs. By adjusting it for each person, the wearers weigh one-sixth of their normal weight. "It's just like walking on the moon," says Danny.

But walking on the moon isn't easy. If you are strapped into the Microgravity Chair and try walking normally, you won't go forward. Instead, you'll bounce up and down in the same place. "The easiest way to walk on the moon is to pretend you're jogging in slow motion, swinging your arms and taking giant steps," trainer Paul Crawford tells the campers.

"That works," Danny agrees, "but it looks kind of silly."

Kids at Space Academy also go for a spin in the "Multi-Axis Training Simulator" — and they really go for a spin! The Multi-Axis is a system of large metal rings, one inside the other. The astronaut sits in the center. When the instructor starts up the motor, the astronaut spins randomly in three different directions — all at once.

"It looks like it could make you want to throw up!" Camper Robin Lundesh, 14, told CONTACT. "But it really isn't so bad." Because the astronaut's stomach is always in the very center of the spin, there is never enough force to make anyone feel sick. However, you do get a good idea what it's like to be spinning out of control in space. "You get very confused about which way is up," says Robin.

The "Multi-Axis Training Simulator" spins a camper three ways at once.

Mission control carefully tracks the shuttle.

The Final Mission

The main event of a week at Space Camp or Space Academy is the team mission. During a two-hour simulation, the team acts out an entire space shuttle flight. This includes takeoff, launching a satellite, docking with a space station, landing, and any emergency actions that have to be done along the way.

Each camper gets a different assignment. Some are sent to mission control, where they help direct the shuttle during takeoff and landing and keep track of life-support systems. Other campers are assigned to the cockpit where their main job is to fly the shuttle. Still others are payload specialists, who release satellites

into orbit and make repairs outside the ship while in outer space.

"At first, I was mad because I didn't get to be the pilot," says Sean Allen, 13. He was chosen to be the mission's Weather and Tracking Officer. "But my job turned out to be a big challenge. I had to keep track of everything that was happening during the launch. And at the end I decided where the shuttle had to land."

During the mission, each person follows a script that tells him or her what to do and say at certain times. Meanwhile, the trainers sit at a computer away from everyone and keep track of how the mission is running. They also create problems that the campers have to solve.

"There are 30 things that we can throw at the team," says trainer Tammy Motes. "We usually give them at least five or six."

For example, the trainers could decide to signal that the shuttle's cabin pressure is dropping. It's up to the pilot or the life supports systems officer to notice that the warning light is flashing. They must let the flight director know that something is wrong. Then, the flight director has to look through a book to find out what should be done, and radio back with instructions.

"While all this is going on, it's still up to the crew members to complete their other jobs," says Tammy Motes. "If they spend too much time fixing things and don't launch the satellite when they are supposed to, the whole mission is a flop."

Back Home

Once the campers have completed their final mission, they head to the graduation ceremony, where they receive a Space Camp Diploma and a pair of wings to pin on their shirts. After that, they head home.

Many of them will come back next year, moving up from Space Camp to Space Academy. Others may come back someday to take part in the more difficult Space Academy level II. And maybe some of them, just maybe, will go on to become the astronauts of tomorrow.

In the
WILD

In the
WILD

Contents

A CLOSER LOOK

IT'S UP TO YOU!

COME BACK, SALMON

HOW A GROUP OF DEDICATED KIDS ADOPTED
PIGEON CREEK AND BROUGHT IT BACK TO LIFE

by Molly Cone ❖ Photographs by Sidnee Wheelwright

PAPERBACK **PLUS**

Come Back, Salmon
by Molly Cone

A fifth-grade class from Everett,
Washington, restores the salmon to
Pigeon Creek.

In the same book . . .
More about Pigeon Creek, Pacific salmon,
and a Tlingit tale about salmon

RASCAL

by Sterling North

PAPERBACK **PLUS**

Rascal

by Sterling North

Keeping a pet raccoon turns out to be more than Sterling bargained for.

In the same book . . .

Information and poetry about raccoons and more about pet ownership

Track Down These Books!

Predator!
by Bruce Brooks
In the wild, many animals must *get* dinner without *becoming* dinner.

Dogs: The Wolf Within
by Dorothy Hinshaw Patent
How closely does your dog resemble its wolf ancestors?

The Moon of the Mountain Lions
by Jean Craighead George
Spend one month in the life of a young mountain lion in its natural habitat.

The Secret Moose
by Jean Rodgers
In a snow bank near his home in Alaska, Gerald discovers a wounded moose — and tries to return it to the wild.

Killer Bees
by Bianca Lavies
A photographer travels to Brazil to study the feared bees as they make their way north.

The American Alligator
by Dorothy Hinshaw Patent
Are they really dragons? Do they eat humans? Separate alligator fact from fiction.

WOLVES

SEYMOUR SIMON

Imagine snow falling silently in the great woodlands of North America. The only sounds are from the trees creaking and tossing in the wind. Suddenly the quiet is broken by the eerie howling of a wolf. And all the frightening stories and legends that you've heard about the treacherous and sly wolf and the evil werewolf begin to race through your mind.

But what is this animal of our imaginations truly like? Are wolves savage and destructive hunters of people and livestock? Or are they one of nature's most misunderstood creatures? It is possible that people don't like wolves because they don't know very much about them. For example, there is no record of a healthy wolf ever trying to kill a human in North America. Perhaps by learning about the wolf and how it lives in the natural world, we can begin to tell the difference between the real animal and the fables we've created.

In many ways, wolves are like dogs and lions; yet wolves have a bad reputation, unlike dogs and lions. Dogs are our "best friends," but all the dogs in the world are descended from wolves that were domesticated more than ten thousand years ago. And most of the things people like about dogs are also true about wolves.

Like dogs, wolves are very loyal to other wolves in their family. Wolves raised by people become loyal to those people as well. Dogs are friendly and intelligent, and these traits too come from wolves. Wolves in a pack are playful with each other. They are among the most intelligent animals in nature.

Like lions, wolves are marvelous hunters that work together in groups to catch their prey. Yet lions are called the "kings of the jungle," while wolves are described in many nursery tales as "sly and cowardly." It seems strange that people love dogs and admire lions but dislike wolves.

Wolves, like humans, are very adaptable to different climates and surroundings. At one time, wolves roamed across nearly all of North America, Europe, and Asia. Wolves can live in forests, grasslands, mountains, and swamps, even in the frozen, treeless tundras of the far north. Wolves can also eat almost anything they catch, from a moose to a mouse.

Wolves may look very different from each other. A wolf might be almost any color, from white to black, through shades and mixtures of cream, gray, brown, and red. Some wolves are heavily furred all over their bodies; others have more fur around their necks and backs. Some are large and powerful; others are smaller and quicker. Wolves even have different personalities; some are leaders, others are very social, and still others are "lone wolves."

Wolves may look and act differently from each other, but most wolves belong to the same species, called *Canis lupus* (*Canis* means dog and *lupus* means wolf). The wolf's closest relatives are the domestic dog, the coyote, the jackal, and a dog of Australia called the dingo.

There are many subspecies of North American wolves and also lots of common names for the same kind of wolf. These include tundra (or arctic) wolves, gray (or timber) wolves, and lots of location names for wolves, such as the Mexican wolf, the Rocky Mountain wolf, the eastern timber wolf (above right), the Texas gray wolf, and the Great Plains wolf (also called the lobo wolf or buffalo hunter). In colder locations, wolves usually have longer and thicker coats, smaller ears, and wider muzzles than do wolves that live in warmer regions.

Hybrids (mixtures) such as wolf-dogs or wolf-coyotes are not really wolves at all. Even though wolf-dogs may look much like dogs, they are very difficult to train and can be dangerous if kept as pets in homes with small children.

The red wolf, *Canis rufus* (*rufus* means red), once numbered in the thousands and roamed all over the southeastern United States. But by the 1970's, there were fewer than one hundred left. Biologists captured every one they could find in Texas and Louisiana and bred them carefully, so that the pups were as much like the original red wolf as possible.

In 1987, eight red wolves were released in North Carolina's Alligator River National Wildlife Refuge. There they have produced a number of litters. When wolves are set free, they wear collars with radio tracking devices in them, so any that stray onto private lands can be found and retrieved. Breeding pairs have also been released onto four islands off the southeastern coast of the United States.

Some scientists think that the red wolf is really a hybrid, a mixture of the wolf and the coyote. But there are no coyotes or gray wolves living in nature near the reds, so any interbreeding has stopped.

Wolves can run for miles without tiring when they are hunting moose, elk, or other large prey. Wolves have strong muscles, and their legs are long and almost spindly. Like dogs, and most other animals, wolves run on their toes. This makes their legs even longer and lets them take long steps, so that they can run fast. Wolves seem to glide effortlessly when they run, almost like the shadow of a cloud drifting along the ground.

Wolves are the largest members of the dog family, bigger than any wild dogs and most domestic dogs. The wolf looks much like a German shepherd with thick, shaggy fur and a bushy tail. The fur is extra thick in winter and is a good protection against rain or snow. Water runs off a wolf's fur the way it runs off a raincoat.

An adult wolf can weigh from 40 to 175 pounds (18 to 80 kilograms) and stretch more than 6 feet (2 meters) from the tip of its nose to the end of its tail. Male wolves are usually larger than female wolves.

Like lions' and tigers', wolves' teeth are well-suited for catching and eating other animals. Wolves have powerful jaws. The long, pointed teeth in the front sides of a wolf's jaws are called canines (KAY-nines). They are useful for grabbing and holding prey such as this moose. The small teeth in the front between the canines are incisors (in-SIGH-zors) useful for picking meat off bones. Two teeth along both sides of the jaws are carnassials (car-NASS-ee-uls). They work like scissors to slice food into pieces small enough to be swallowed.

Wolves have marvelous hearing. They can hear other wolves howling from three or four miles away. They can locate mice by the squeals they make even when the rodents are beneath a snowpack. Like bats and dolphins, wolves can also hear high-pitched sounds well above the range of human hearing. Wolves turn their ears from side to side. The direction the ears are pointing when the sound is loudest helps the wolf determine from where the sound is coming. Scientists believe that wolves hunt small prey more by sound than by smell or sight. Larger prey is often found by scent or by chance encounters.

Wolves live in packs, but that is just a name for a family of wolves. Packs are usually made up of a leader male and female wolf and their young along with some close relatives. An average wolf pack has five to eight wolves, but packs can have as few as two or three, or as many as twenty-five wolves.

The members of a pack are usually very friendly with each other. They hunt, travel, eat, and make noises together. Wolves bring bits of food to each other. They baby-sit each other's litters. They run around and play tag with each other and with the pups. They startle each other by hiding and then jumping out.

Wolves make all kinds of sounds besides howling; they bark, growl, whine, and squeak. Barking seems to be a warning when a wolf is surprised at its den. Growling is common among pups when they play, and adults growl when challenged by another wolf. Whines and squeaks are connected with playing, feeding, and general good feelings. Mothers squeak when the pups play too roughly; fathers squeak to call their pups.

Of all of the sounds a wolf makes, its howl is the most familiar. A wolf howls by pointing its nose to the sky and then giving voice to a single high-pitched sound that rises sharply and then slides down in rippling waves.

Wolves do not have to stand to howl; they can howl sitting or even lying on the ground. A wolf howls by itself or in groups of twos or threes. Often, other members of the pack join the chorus until the entire pack is howling.

Wolves howl at any time of day or night. Wolves howl to call the pack together before or after a hunt. They howl to locate each other when they are separated after a snowstorm or when in unfamiliar territory. They may howl to warn other wolf packs to stay away from their hunting grounds. And wolves even seem to howl just for the pleasure of it.

Howling increases seasonally during the winter months, and the sound may carry for six or more miles in cold, clear air. It's easy to see why people might have thought that the wolves were right at their doors when they heard the howling echoing across a shadowy moonlit snowscape.

Each wolf pack has a specific hierarchy. The leaders of a wolf pack are called the "alpha" male and the "alpha" female. They are usually the largest and strongest wolves in the pack, but packs may be as different from each other as individual wolves are different. A typical pack has an alpha male and an alpha female at the top, a lesser male and female in the middle called "beta" wolves, and less powerful wolves and pups at the bottom of the pack. (Alpha and beta are the letters A and B in the Greek alphabet.) Every member of a pack has a place or rank. Some wolves are higher and some are lower. This "dominance order" helps prevent fighting within the pack.

When two wolves in a pack have an argument, they may stick their ears and tails straight up, bare their teeth, and snarl at each other. Both wolves look fierce and ready to tear each other apart. But most times a wolf of a lower rank will give up before a fight starts with a wolf of a higher rank. To show that it has given up, the submissive wolf will lower its position or roll over on its back, flattening its ears and putting its tail between its legs. This behavior seems to prevent the dominant wolf from biting, so fights between pack members are usually settled without serious injuries.

Wolves hunt animals in different ways. A single wolf will hunt by itself for small prey including mice, rabbits, squirrels, beavers, ducks, geese, and even fish when available. But much of their prey are large animals such as deer, elk, moose, caribou, musk-oxen, and bighorn sheep. Most of these are hard to catch and can be dangerous when cornered, so wolves hunt them in packs.

One of the wolf's main prey is the moose. An adult moose may weigh over 1,000 pounds (450 kilograms) and stand over 6 feet (2 meters) tall at the shoulders. It has hoofs that can injure and even kill a wolf. It is also strong and a good runner. So it is not surprising that more than nine out of ten moose that wolves chase get away.

Wolves hunt moose by trying to encircle them and bring them to a standstill. One wolf may tear at the nose or the head of the moose while the others rip at the sides or the stomach. After wolves kill a large animal, they may rest for a brief time or eat right away. Each wolf eats 10 to 20 pounds (4 to 9 kilograms) of meat. If there is any left, the wolves may come back later.

Before babies are born, a mother and father wolf either dig a new den, enlarge an old fox den, or use a beaver lodge. Often, especially if food is scarce, only the male and female leaders of a pack mate and bear young. A wolf den may be 15 feet (4.5 meters) long and must be high enough for a wolf to stand in. Wolf babies are born in the spring, underground in dens like this one in Alaska.

A group of baby wolves born at the same time to one mother is called a litter. This litter has three pups, but some have ten or more. These pups are only about one week old. They have fine, dark, fuzzy hair, floppy ears, and blunt noses. They look much like dog puppies. Wolf pups cannot see at birth. Each of them weighs only about one pound (.5 kilograms). For the first few weeks of their lives, wolf pups nurse — their only food is the milk they get from their mothers. The mother stays close to the pups, making sure they are well fed, clean, and protected. She usually doesn't have to hunt for food herself because the father and other members of the pack bring food to her.

About two weeks after they are born, wolf pups open their eyes and begin to walk. At about three weeks they come out of their den and begin to play outside. Though they still nurse, they start to eat meat. All the members of the pack help care for the pups, bringing food to them. The pups rush up when a wolf returns from hunting. They wag their tails and whine and lick the adult's jaws. The wolf then brings up some of the food it has swallowed and gives it to the pups.

The pups grow very fast, and after about a month they start fighting and tumbling around with each other. After a while they begin to develop a dominance order among themselves. During a fight, one of the pups will roll over on its back to show that it gives up. The other raises its tail to show dominance. Pups also play at hunting by attacking each other, insects, and small animals. These games help pups practice hunting skills they will need when they grow up.

During the summer the pups begin to look like adult wolves, but they stay together in a safe place while the adults hunt. By fall the young wolves join the rest of the pack when it travels. They may join a hunt to help run down prey, but the older wolves make the kill. By winter the young are nearly grown. When they are about two years old, some will stay with the pack while others will leave to find mates and start new packs.

Two hundred years ago there were many thousands of wolves across much of the Northern Hemisphere. But wolves have been hunted, trapped, and poisoned, and only small numbers can still be found in eastern Europe, China, and parts of North America.

Henry David Thoreau, an American naturalist, once wrote, "In wildness is the preservation of the world." Conservationists want to reintroduce wolves into Yellowstone National Park in Wyoming. Some people see this as a threat to their livestock and even to themselves. Should we allow this symbol of wildness to hunt again in remote areas and the national parks where it once roamed free? The fate of the wolf is up to us and our willingness to share the earth with wild animals.

Meet Seymour Simon

Seymour Simon has loved science since he was a boy. As a teenager, his idea of a fun project was grinding his own telescope lenses! Simon taught in the public schools of New York City for over twenty years. He says, "It's questions... that occur to me and that have been asked of me by children (both my own and in my science classes) that make me want to write science books."

The subject of wolves came naturally to Simon because he studied animal behavior after college. He also encouraged his science students to study animals. Though he's never lived with a wolf pack, Simon says it helps to get a firsthand view of his subjects. "I like to try out the investigations and projects I write about. I've kept fishes, earthworms, gerbils, ants, crickets, and a host of other animals in my home."

Since Simon's first book, published in 1968, he has written over sixty books for children. Many of these books are about animals, including *Whales, Big Cats,* and *Snakes.* Simon also wrote *Earthquakes,* a fascinating look at the scientific causes and devastating consequences of earthquakes. Look for it in the "Catastrophe!" theme of this book.

Wondering About Wolves

Make a Chart

Spot vs. Lobo

One of the wolf's closest relatives is the domestic dog. Though they are similar in many ways, you wouldn't want to play fetch with a wolf. Keep them straight by making a chart that lists the similarities and the differences between the wolf and the dog.

A Wolf's Day

Now that you know a lot about wolves, write an account that tells about a day in the life of a wolf. If you prefer, you can act out what your wolf does during the day.

Create an Art Display

Wolf Gallery

With classmates, use the illustrations and information in *Wolves* to help create a gallery of wolf art. Draw, paint, or sculpt wolves! Experiment with different art materials. Then open your art gallery for a public viewing.

Put on a Quiz Show

"Wolves, for $500"

How much do you know about wolves? Find out. Gather with a few classmates and put on a quiz show. Write a list of questions that can be answered by reading *Wolves*. Then form teams and see which team answers the most questions correctly.

Lies (People Believe)

LIE: A pack rat never takes something without leaving another item in its place.

TRUTH: A pack rat may drop an item it's carrying in order to pick up something new. Just as often, however, it will scamper off with some nice shiny object — a button, coin, or nail — without leaving another item in its place.

LIE: You will die if you're bitten by a Gila monster or Mexican beaded lizard.

TRUTH: The Gila monster and the Mexican beaded lizard are the only poisonous lizards in the world. But even so, the bite of either is rarely fatal to humans.

LIE: The chameleon hides from enemies by changing color to blend in with its background.

TRUTH: The chameleon does not decide when to change its color. Its color changes, usually from shades of brown to green or green to brown, when it becomes excited or when there is a change in light or temperature.

About Animals

by Susan Sussman and Robert James

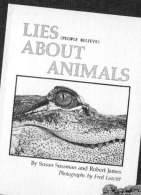

LIES (PEOPLE BELIEVE) ABOUT ANIMALS

By Susan Sussman and Robert James
Photographs by Fred Leavitt

LIE: If you touch a frog or toad, you'll get warts.

TRUTH: Neither animal can give you warts. The urine of a frog or toad can sting a cut, but this is harmless.

LIE: Birds hardly eat — thus, the expression "to eat like a bird."

TRUTH: Because of an enormously high metabolic rate (they burn up energy quickly), birds must eat most of the time they are awake. Some birds eat twice their body weight each day.

LIE: All fish die if kept out of water too long.

TRUTH: The African lungfish digs into the mud at the start of the dry season and builds a kind of cocoon around itself before the sun-baked ground hardens. It sleeps, living on its own fat, for a year or more until water returns to the river.

LIE: The hippopotamus sweats blood.

TRUTH: The hippopotamus protects its tender skin from the hot sun by secreting reddish oil that looks very much like blood.

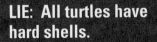

LIE: All turtles have hard shells.

TRUTH: There are soft-shelled turtles whose round, flat bodies are covered with flexible, tough skin. The leather-back sea turtle also has a soft covering.

LIE: Camels can travel for weeks on the desert without water.

TRUTH: To stay healthy, camels working in the hot desert should drink at least every three days and every day when possible. They can go longer, but their health would suffer. Camels are able to survive heat that would kill other animals. Their body temperature rises during the hottest part of the day so they absorb less heat. And a camel sweats very little, keeping fluids inside to nourish its body.

WOLF

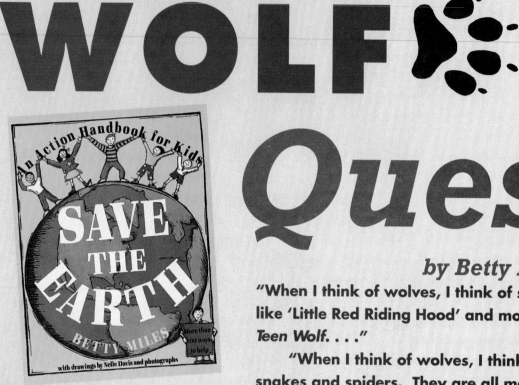

Quest

by Betty Miles

"When I think of wolves, I think of stories like 'Little Red Riding Hood' and movies like *Teen Wolf.* . . ."

"When I think of wolves, I think of bats, snakes and spiders. They are all mean!"

Most of the kids in the fifth grade of Mead School in Wisconsin Rapids, Wisconsin, felt that way about wolves — until they began to study them.

They learned how wolves raise their young, how they communicate and how they hunt for food. They found that wolves help to maintain the population and strengthen the herds of deer, elk and moose by preying on weak, old and sick animals. They came to see the timber wolf as a beautiful wild species and a valuable part of the Wisconsin ecosystem. They learned that there were once thousands of wolves in the state, but that people had killed so many that by

1960 wolves had almost disappeared. More recently, as a few wolves migrated to northern Wisconsin forests, people continued to fear — and even to kill — them.

As their own feelings about wolves were changing, the Mead School fifth-graders realized that most people's negative feelings came from misinformation and from childhood fears. They learned about Wisconsin groups like the Timber Wolf Alliance, which works to change people's attitudes through education.

Then they heard that the Wisconsin Bureau of Endangered Resources was considering a plan to expand the wolf population to eighty in northern Wisconsin. They wondered how people there would react. They decided to find out. They created a questionnaire which asked people to respond (strongly agree, agree, no opinion, disagree or strongly disagree) to ten statements, from "It is a good idea to try and save the timber wolf," to "The only good wolf is a dead wolf!"

They sent 350 questionnaires to people chosen randomly in seventeen northern Wisconsin counties and enclosed a personal letter with every one. Sixty percent replied — an unusually high response. When they made graphs of the answers, they found that almost 75 percent were in favor of the timber wolf recovery plan.

Fifth-grade students from Mead School in Wisconsin Rapids, Wisconsin, created posters (far left) and sold wolf tracks (above) to help change people's attitudes about wolves.

Hi,
My name is Matthew Kurz. I'm a 5th grade student from Mead School in Wisconsin Rapids. Our class has been studying wolves. As a special project we decided to send out these surveys. We are hoping that you will help us with our project by taking a few minutes to complete the enclosed form. Send it back to us as soon as possible! Thank you very much for your time.

Sincerely,
Matt Kurz

Students raised over $100 (above) for the Timber Wolf Alliance. This letter (right) was mailed with a survey that polled people's feelings about wolves.

The fifth-graders decided that the positive attitudes were partly due to work by the Timber Wolf Alliance, and they decided to support its activities. They made audio- and videocassettes of wolf songs and poems for the group to use. They made wolf tracks and wolf buttons to sell, and raised more than $100. Using information from their questionnaire, they also wrote letters to their state legislators supporting the wolf recovery plan.

Then they started their own educational project with the younger children in their school. They read stories like "Little Red Riding Hood" aloud, let the children talk out their feelings and then taught them about real wolves. They hope these younger kids will grow up respecting wolves and looking forward to the day when Wisconsin has a stable wolf population once again.

Mead School Survey

The fifth-grade students at Mead School mailed a survey to find out what people think about wolves. People were asked to read several statements and circle their response to each one. Here are two items from the survey.

I think it is a good idea to try and save the timber wolf.

Strongly agree   Agree   No opinion   Disagree   Strongly disagree

I feel that wolves pose a threat to the people that live in northern Wisconsin.

Strongly agree   Agree   No opinion   Disagree   Strongly disagree

After the surveys were completed and returned, the students analyzed the results. They presented their findings in pie charts, bar graphs, and tables. Here are the results from the survey items listed above.

Wolves Are a Threat to People

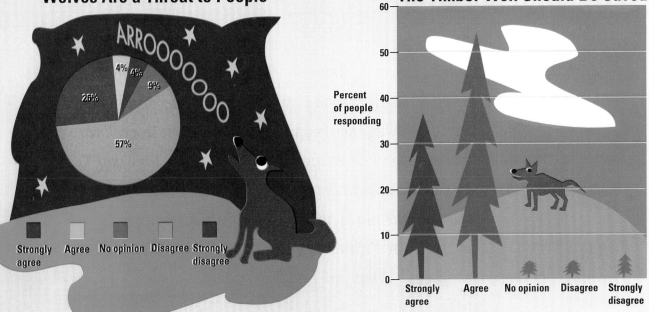

ARROOOOOOO

4% 4% 9%
26%
57%

Strongly agree | Agree | No opinion | Disagree | Strongly disagree

The Timber Wolf Should Be Saved

Percent of people responding

60
50
40
30
20
10
0

Strongly agree | Agree | No opinion | Disagree | Strongly disagree

The Midnight Fox

by Betsy Byars

While his parents take a special trip together, Tom is spending a lonely summer on Aunt Millie and Uncle Fred's farm. His cousin, Hazeline, spends most of her waking hours with Mikey, her boyfriend, leaving Tom to explore the farm and surrounding woods by himself. One day Tom sees a beautiful black fox. He spots her thirteen more times over the next few weeks and feels very protective of her and her cub. Now Uncle Fred wants to get rid of the fox, which has been stealing chickens and turkeys. What can Tom do?

The next morning was hot and dry, and when I looked out my window the air was brown with dust. I could hardly see the forest. It was like the dust had become magnetized by the sun and was rising to meet it.

Happ was lying in the yard under a tree. He had given up his chase at some point during the night and was now in a state of collapse. The heat was already unbearable. The earth had not cooled off during the night and now the sun had already begun to reheat it.

I went downstairs and the only person at the table with any animation was Uncle Fred. Hazeline was sitting with her chin in her hand, sullenly dipping a slice of toast into her coffee and then nibbling at it. Aunt Millie usually sat straight as a broom, but this morning she too was leaning forward on the table. "Sit down and get yourself some cereal."

I sat down and she said, "I swear if we don't get some rain we are all going to dry up and blow away like the crops."

"I'm going to start pumping water from the pond this morning," Uncle Fred said.

"It won't do any good." Aunt Millie turned her napkin over in her lap as if she were looking for the cool side.

"And then this afternoon," Uncle Fred said to me, "you and I'll go after the fox." I could see that it was this thought that had caused his spirits to rise. "Right?"

"Yes." I did not want to go, of course, but I had the idea that if I was there, if I was right at his elbow every minute, there might come a time when I could jar his elbow as he fired his gun and save the fox. It was a noble thought but I knew even then it wasn't going to work.

"In case anyone is interested," Hazeline said in a low voice, "Mikey is not going to marry me."

"What, Hazeline?"

"I said *Mikey's not going to marry me!*" And she slammed down her napkin and left the room.

"What is *that* all about?" Uncle Fred asked.

"Mikey's not going to marry her unless she loses twenty pounds," I said.

"I cannot stand one more thing. I cannot!" Aunt Millie said. "If one more thing happens in this house I just don't know what I'm going to do."

"Now, now. Mikey is going to marry Hazeline. The rain is going to come. And we are going to get the fox that's after your chickens," Uncle Fred said. "Come on, Tom, help me with the pump."

"Well, don't let the boy get a heat stroke out there," Aunt Millie said. "I mean it. That will be absolutely the last straw."

"I'll be all right."

It was afternoon before the pump was working and the muddy water was moving between the small, dusty rows of vegetables.

"Well, that's that. Now, let's take some time off and go into the woods." Uncle Fred paused, then said, "If you're too tired, you don't have to come."

"No, I want to."

He looked pleased. "I think you'll enjoy it."

We went to the house and I waited on the back steps while Uncle Fred went in and got his gun. He came out carrying it, muzzle down, and I could tell just from the way he held it that he knew everything there was to know about that particular gun. I knew that his hands had been over that gun so many times that, blindfolded, he could load it and aim it and probably hit whatever he wanted.

"Let's go."

It was like in an army movie when the sergeant says, "All right, men, let's move out," and all the tired discouraged soldiers get up, dust themselves off, and start walking. I fell in behind Uncle Fred and we went through the orchard — Happ leading the way — and down to the creek. We passed the place where we had found the turkey eggs, passed the place where I had sat and first seen the black fox. There! My eyes found the very spot where I had first seen her coming over the crest of the hill.

Uncle Fred crossed the creek in one leap — the water was that low now — and stepped up the bank. Silently I followed. "Fox tracks," he said, and with the muzzle of his gun he pointed down to the tiny imprints in the sand. I had not even noticed them.

If I had hoped that Uncle Fred was not going to be able to find the black fox, I now gave up this hope once and for all. What it had taken me weeks and a lucky accident to accomplish, he would do in a few hours.

"The fox must be up there in the woods," I said eagerly, knowing she was not, or that if she was, she had gone there only to make a false track.

"Maybe," Uncle Fred said.

"Let's go there then," I said and I sounded like a quarrelsome, impatient child.

"Don't be in too big a hurry. Let's look a bit."

Happ had caught the scent of something and he ran up the creek bank, circled the field, then returned. Uncle Fred walked slowly along the bank. We were now about a half a mile from the fox's den. If we kept on walking up the creek, past the fallen tree, past the old chimney, if we rounded a bend and looked up through the brambles in a certain way, then we could see the fox's den. It seemed to me as I stood there, sick with the heat and with dread, that the fox's den was the plainest thing in the world. As soon as we rounded the bend, Uncle Fred would exclaim, "There it is."

I said again, "Why don't we go up in the woods and look. I think the fox's up there."

"I'm not looking for the fox," he said. "We could chase that fox all day and never get her. I'm looking for the den." He walked a few feet farther and then paused. He knelt and held up a white feather. "One of Millie's chickens," he said. "Hasn't been enough breeze in a week to blow it six inches. Come on."

We walked on along the creek bank in the direction I had feared. I was now overtaken by a feeling of utter hopelessness. My shoulders felt very heavy and I thought I was going to be sick. Usually when something terrible happened, I would get sick, but this time I kept plodding along right behind Uncle Fred. I could not get it out of my mind that the fox's life might depend on me. I stumbled over a root, went down on my knees, and scrambled to my feet. Uncle Fred looked back long enough to see that I was still behind him and then continued slowly, cautiously watching the ground, the woods, everything. Nothing could escape those sharp eyes.

Suddenly we heard, from the woods above, the short high bark I knew so well. The black fox! Uncle Fred lifted his head and at once Happ left the creek bank and dashed away into the woods. He bayed as he caught the scent of the fox, and then his voice, like the sound of a foghorn, was lost in the distant trees.

"That was the fox," I said.

Uncle Fred nodded. Slowly he continued to move up the creek, stepping over logs, rocks, brushing aside weeds, his eyes and the muzzle of his gun turned always to the ground.

We walked up the field and then back to the creek. We crossed the creek and while we were standing there Happ returned. He was hot, dusty, panting. He lay down in the shallow water of the creek with his legs stretched out behind him and lapped slowly at the water.

"Happ didn't get the fox," I said. Every time I spoke, I had the feeling I was breaking a rule of hunting, but I could not help myself. As soon as I had said this, we heard the bark of the fox again. This time it seemed closer than before. Uncle Fred shifted his gun in his hand, but he did not raise it. Happ, however, rose at once to the call, dripping wet, still panting from his last run. Nose to the ground, he headed for the trees.

The sound of his baying faded as he ran deeper into the woods. I knew the fox had nothing to fear from the hound. The fox with her light quick movements could run from this lumbering dog all day. It was Uncle Fred, moving closer and closer to the den with every step, who would be the end of the black fox.

By this time we were only a hundred feet from the entrance to the fox's den. Uncle Fred had crossed the creek again and moved up toward the thicket of trees. From where he was standing, he could have thrown a rock over the trees and it would have landed in the little clearing where I had seen the baby fox play.

He walked past the thicket to a lone tree in the center of the field and stood there for a moment. Then he knocked the creek mud on his shoe off on one of the roots and walked back to me. He turned and walked the length of the thicket. It was like that old game Hot and Cold, where you hide something and when the person gets close to it you say, "You're getting warmer — you're warmer — now you're hot — you're red-hot — you're on fire, you're burning up!" Inside right then I was screaming, "You're burning up."

"Look at that," he said. He pointed with his gun to a pile of earth that had been banked up within the last two months. "Sometimes when a fox makes a den she'll bring the earth out one hole, seal it up, and then use the other hole for the entrance. It'll be around here somewhere."

He moved through the trees toward the den, walking sideways. I could not move at all. I just stood with the sun beating down on my head like a fist and my nose running.

I heard the sound of Happ's barking coming closer. He had lost the fox in the woods but now he had a new scent, older, but still hot. He came crashing through the bushes, bellowing every few feet, his head to the ground. He flashed past me, not even seeing me in his intensity, his red eyes on the ground. Like a charging bull, he entered the thicket and he and Uncle Fred stepped into the small grassy clearing at the same moment.

"Here it is," Uncle Fred called. "Come here."

I wanted to turn and run. I did not want to see Uncle Fred and Happ standing in that lovely secluded clearing, but instead I walked through the trees and looked at the place I had avoided so carefully for weeks. There were the bones, some whitened by the sun, a dried turkey wing, feathers, and behind, the partially sheltered hole. Of course Uncle Fred had already seen that, and as I stepped from the trees he pointed to it with his gun.

"There's the den."

I nodded.

"The baby foxes will be in there."

This was the first time he had been wrong. There was only one baby fox in there, and I imagined him crouching now against the far wall of the den.

"Go back to the house and get me a shovel and sack," Uncle Fred said.

Without speaking, I turned and walked back to the house. Behind me the black fox barked again. It was a desperate high series of barks

that seemed to last a long time, and Happ lunged after the fox for the third time. It was too late now for tricks, for Uncle Fred remained, leaning on his gun, waiting for the shovel and sack.

I went up the back steps and knocked. Usually I just went in the house like I did at my own home, but I waited there till Aunt Millie came and I said, "Uncle Fred wants me to bring him a sack and a shovel."

"Did you get the fox?"

"Uncle Fred found the den."

"If it's in the woods, he'll find it," she said, coming out the door, "but you ought to see that man try to find a pair of socks in his own drawer. Hazeline," she called up to her window, "you want to go see your dad dig out the baby foxes?"

"No."

"I declare that girl is in the worst mood." She walked with me to the shed, put the shovel in my hand, and then pressed a dusty grain sack against me. "Now, you don't be too late."

"I don't think it will take long."

"Are you all right? Your face is beet red."

"I'm all right."

"Because I can make Hazeline take that shovel to her dad."

"I feel fine."

I started toward the orchard with the shovel and sack and I felt like some fairy-tale character who has been sent on an impossible mission, like proving my worth by catching a thousand golden eagles in the sack and making a silver mountain for them with my shovel. Even that did not seem as difficult as what I was really doing.

It must have taken me longer to get back than I thought, for Uncle Fred said, "I thought you'd gotten lost."

"No, I wasn't lost. I've been here before."

I handed him the shovel and let the sack drop to the ground. As he began to dig, I closed my eyes and pressed my hands against my

eyelids, and I saw a large golden sunburst, and in this sunburst the black fox came running toward me.

I opened my eyes and watched Uncle Fred. He dug as he did everything else—powerfully, slowly, and without stopping. His shovel hit a rock and he moved the shovel until he could bring the rock out with the dirt. At my feet the gravelly pile of earth was growing.

I turned away and looked across the creek, and I saw for the fifteenth and last time the black fox. She moved anxiously toward the bushes and there was a tension to her steps, as if she were ready to spring or make some other quick, forceful movement. She barked. She had lost the dog again, and this bark was a high clear call for Uncle Fred and me to follow her.

There was a grunt of satisfaction from Uncle Fred and I turned to see him lift out, on the shovel, covered with sand and gravel, the baby fox.

He turned it onto the sack and the baby fox lay without moving. "He's dead," I said.

Uncle Fred shook his head. "He's not dead. He's just play-acting. His ma taught him to do that."

We both looked down at the little fox without speaking. I knew that if I lived to be a hundred, I would never see anything that would make me feel any worse than the sight of that little fox pretending to be dead when his heart was beating so hard it looked like it was going to burst out of his chest.

I looked over my shoulder and the black fox was gone. I knew she was still watching us, but I could not see her. Uncle Fred was probing the den with his shovel. I said, "I don't think there are any more. She just had one."

He dug again, piled more earth on the pile, then said, "You're right. Usually a fox has five or six cubs."

"I think something happened to the others."

He bent, folded the ends of the sack, and lifted the baby fox. I took the shovel, he the gun, and we started home, the baby fox swinging between us. Happ joined us as we crossed the creek and began to leap excitedly at the sack until Uncle Fred had to hold it shoulder-high to keep it from him.

We walked back to the house without speaking. Uncle Fred went directly to some old rabbit hutches beside the garage. Bubba had once raised rabbits here, but now the cages were empty. Uncle Fred opened one, shook the baby fox out of the sack, and then closed the wire door.

The baby fox moved to the back of the hutch and looked at us. His fur was soft and woolly, but his eyes were sharp. Nervously he went to one corner.

Aunt Millie came out and looked. "Just like a baby lamb," she said. "It's a sweet little thing, isn't it?"

"That's not the way you were talking yesterday," Uncle Fred said.

"Well, I'm not going to have anything after my chickens," she said. "Not *anything*! I'd be after *you* with the broom if you bothered my chickens." They laughed. Her spirits seemed greatly improved now that the fox was doomed, and she called, "Hazeline, come on out here and look at this cute little baby fox."

"No."

Uncle Fred went into the shed, returned, and snapped a lock over the cage latch.

"You think somebody's going to steal your fox?" Aunt Millie laughed.

"I wouldn't put it past a fox to open up an unlocked cage to get her baby."

Aunt Millie shook her head in amazement, then said, "Well, you men have got to get washed up for supper."

We went into the house and I said to Uncle Fred, "What are you going to do with the baby fox?"

"That's my bait. Every hunter alive's got some way to get a fox. They got some special trap or something. Mr. Baynes down at the store makes up a special mixture that he says foxes can't resist. My way is to set up a trap, using the baby fox for bait. I'll sit out on the back porch tonight and watch for her."

"Oh."

"It never fails. That is one bait a fox can't resist."

Meet Betsy Byars

Betsy Byars has written over thirty children's books, but *The Midnight Fox* holds a special place in her heart. "This is my favorite book, because it is very personal," she says. "A great deal of my own children and their activities went into it, and a great deal of myself."

Byars bases most of her stories on real events — family experiences or incidents she reads about in the newspaper. In *The Summer of the Swans,* for example, Sara Godfrey worries about her big feet. Two of Byars's daughters claim that their feet inspired their mother to give Sara this concern.

Now that her four children are adults, Byars has more time for her other great interest: flying. She got her pilot's license in 1984 and says, "I am as proud of that as of anything in my writing career." Byars lives in Clemson, South Carolina, where she continues to write novels for young people.

Meet Ed Martinez

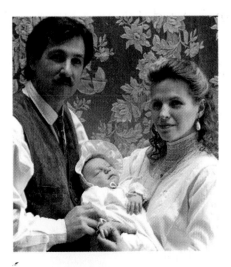

Ed Martinez lives in a 200-year-old house in rural Connecticut with his wife and his son. Oil paints and canvas are his favorite media for illustration, and people are his favorite subject. He and his wife also enjoy painting landscapes in the Connecticut countryside. Martinez has illustrated the books *Little Women* and *Too Many Tamales!*

What Would You Do?

It's Up to You

Aunt Millie wants to save her chickens. Tom wants to save the fox. Is there a way to do both? Discuss how you might save the fox *and* the chickens.

Dear Mom and Dad

If Tom were to write to his parents about his summer on the farm, what do you think he would say? Write a letter that Tom might write about searching for the fox's den with Uncle Fred.

Stalking the Fox!

The fox can't outfox Uncle Fred. He doesn't miss a clue in finding her den. Draw a map of Tom and Uncle Fred's route through the woods, including all the places mentioned in the story and all the clues they find.

Pups and Cubs

In *Wolves* and in *The Midnight Fox* you learned something about the way wolves and foxes raise their young. Make two lists, showing what you've learned about wolf pup rearing and fox cub rearing. Do wolves and foxes raise their young in the same way or differently?

Wildlife – Who Needs It?

by Ann Love and Jane Drake

What would happen if a Malayan pit viper slithered into your kitchen? Your dad would scream, your grandmother'd faint and you'd run for your baseball bat, right? Before you finish off your unwelcome visitor, stop for a minute. The pit viper's venom makes a drug that helps prevent heart attacks in people.

Many wild animals and plants that you might consider creepy, ugly or annoying are valuable. Like the pit viper, they provide much-needed medicines or food for us and for other animals. And all plants and animals add to the variety and beauty of the earth.

The wild world is a rich and important natural pharmacy. Open your family's medicine chest and you'll probably see a bottle of Aspirin or similar pain killer. Did you know that the ingredient that takes away headaches comes from the bark of a riverside willow tree? Aspirin can be made synthetically

A leaping frog unrolls its tongue to make a meal of an unwary fly.

using the chemicals found in the willow, but the heart drug digitalis can be made only from the real plant, the foxglove. Thousands of heart patients owe their lives to this delicate plant. Many hundreds of wild plants and animals contribute crucial ingredients to medicines. Wildlife saves human lives!

Without wild plants we wouldn't have food to eat. Today's food crops are all related to wild plants. About 3000 plants are eaten by people but only seven provide most of our food: wheat, rice, corn, potato, barley, sweet potato and cassava. What would happen if one of these "big seven" was wiped out? Huge numbers of people might become sick or starve.

To prevent this from happening, farmers can crossbreed farm plants with their wild relatives which are immune to many diseases. By protecting *wild* plants, we can keep our *food* crops healthy and preserve the world's future food supply.

Plants and animals also serve as food for other plants and animals. Mosquitoes might drive *you* nuts, but they're food for many amphibians and birds. Scientists see all living things as part of a large natural workshop called an ecosystem. Each creature or plant, no matter how small or ordinary we think it is, plays a vital role in this ecosystem.

The disappearance of one plant or animal can have serious consequences for others. Take the dodo tree and the dodo bird, for example. The dodo tree, whose fruit was the main source of food for the dodo bird, dwindled in numbers when the dodo bird became extinct.

183

Then, with only 13 trees left in the world, an American scientist, Dr. Stanley Temple, discovered why. The dodo tree depended on the dodo bird to eat its seeds. The dodo bird's powerful digestive system cracked open the seed cases so that when the seeds were expelled in the dodo's droppings, they could sprout and form new dodo trees. The two kinds of dodos were interdependent; when the bird became extinct, the tree was threatened with extinction, too.

Not all plants and animals are as useful as the pit viper, foxglove and dodo bird. Some are just plain beautiful. People enjoy watching or photographing them. Wildlife enriches our lives and makes the world a more interesting place.

Pigs, monkeys, and other animals brought to the island of Mauritius by European sailors ate the eggs and young of the dodo, driving it to extinction by 1681. Without the dodo, the dodo tree (left) had no way to plant its seeds.

There Aren't Any Dodoes Anymore

A song by Bob Blue

There was a day when a dodo was a pretty common sight.
We would waddle in the daytime and we'd settle down at night.
But you won't see any dodoes like you could've seen before,
'Cause there aren't any dodoes anymore.

The life of a dodo wasn't glamorous, it's true.
People weren't much impressed by what they saw a dodo do.
Well, there aren't any chances left to try to raise our score,
'Cause there aren't any dodoes anymore.

In the balance of nature, every creature has its role.
From the prowling of the tiger to the digging of the mole.
From the creeping armadillo to the bouncing kangaroo,
Each creature has some special thing to do.

But the doings of the dodo bird will nevermore be done.
No one else could do those doings. Dodo was the only one.
If they really needed doing, there are troubled times in store,
'Cause there aren't any dodoes anymore.

The island of Mauritius, in the southwest Indian Ocean, was once the home of the dodo.

Dear Editor,

Persuasion by Brendan Harrington

What is the problem with bison roaming out of Yellowstone National Park? What should be done about it? Brendan had an opinion and wrote this letter to the editor to persuade others to agree with him. What do you think?

Brendan Harrington
Prescott School
Missoula, Montana

Brendan is the youngest of eleven children. He loves almost all sports. He also likes to write about things that have happened to him. When he wrote this letter in the fifth grade, he decided to write about bison because he has always liked them. Brendan drew the bison below. When he grows up, Brendan would like to become an architect or a doctor.

BRENDAN
HARRINGTON

Dear Editor,

    A controversy in Yellowstone National Park is whether or not bison should be able to roam in and out of park boundaries. Some people think they should be allowed out of the park; others think they should stay in Yellowstone.

    Personally, I think bison should be confined to park limits. Think about it for a minute. If you were a farmer or a rancher, would you want your livelihood ruined because of brucellosis, a disease bison can give to cattle? It ruins people's livelihoods because it makes cattle miscarry their unborn calves, and you can't run a good ranch or farm without healthy cattle. Also, if bison go out of the park, they're not protected by law so they might be shot.

    Two ways that the National Park Service could help solve this problem are by fencing areas where bison roam out and by having people patrol to make sure they don't roam out. People might think that would cost a lot in taxes, but it wouldn't because Yellowstone would only be fencing certain parts of the park.

    In conclusion, I want people to support me by sending letters to Yellowstone suggesting ways to keep bison in Yellowstone or by just writing letters supporting my ideas.

Brendan Harrington

Adiós falcón

escrito por Wenceslao Serra Deliz

Algunas veces en nuestras vidas suceden cosas que parecen dignas de un cuento. Cosas que recordamos como parte de un sueño real y vivido.

Lo que voy a contarte me sucedió a mí. Todo comenzó en Barranquitas, un pueblo amable y hermoso del centro de Puerto Rico, acurrucado entre verdes montañas.

Era la una de la tarde. Hacía fresco, a pesar de que empezaba el mes de julio. Un amigo me llevaba en su carro. Veníamos de trabajar en el pueblo. En la salida, donde la carretera empieza a subir la montaña verde, un niño nos hizo señas. Cuando mi amigo detuvo el carro, el niño nos dijo, alargando la mano: "¡Dos pichones de falcón! ¡A peso cada uno!" Eran dos pajaritos recién nacidos y asustados en un nidito de paja, quizás donde mismo habían nacido. Aún no tenían plumas, y su piel era muy fina, casi transparente. Sus corazones latían con fuerza, como si fueran a salirse de los pechos.

188

Good-bye, Falcon

written by Wenceslao Serra Deliz

Sometimes things happen in our lives that seem worthy of a story. Things that we remember as part of a real and living dream.

What I am going to tell you happened to me. It all began in Barranquitas, a lovely and handsome town nestled between green mountains in the center of Puerto Rico.

It was one o'clock in the afternoon, and cool, even though the month of July had already begun. I was riding in a friend's car. We were returning from our work in town. At the exit where the road begins to climb the green mountain, a boy signaled to us. When my friend stopped the car, the boy held out his hand and said, "Two falcon chicks! For a peso each!" The two scared baby birds were in a straw nest, maybe the same one in which they were born. They didn't have feathers yet, and their skin was very fine, almost transparent. Their hearts beat with such force it seemed they would pop out from their chests.

Los compré y regalé uno a mi amigo. Yo sabía que, a pesar de lo asustados que se veían, los dos pájaros querían crecer y volar un día por el cielo...

Durante todo el camino hablé con mi amigo sobre estos pájaros. El falcón es pariente del guaraguao, y se parece mucho a éste. Vive en todos los campos de Puerto Rico. Prefiere las montañas más cálidas. El color de sus plumas es parecido al barro de las montañas, con manchitas negras. Con sus fuertes garras atrapa lagartijos e insectos para alimentarse. Le gusta volar acompañado de su pareja.

Al llegar a mi casa en la urbanización Las Lomas, del pueblo de Río Piedras, puse el pequeño y transparente pájaro en una jaulita de alambre. Lo dejé en mi cuarto, sobre el escritorio. Al pasar de los días noté que en la pared, en la silla y en parte de la cama había grandes manchas blancuzcas. Ya empezaba a crecer y, como la jaulita resultaba pequeña, había ensuciado todo a su alrededor. Tuve que hacer una jaula más grande para sacarlo al patio, donde estaría desde entonces.

I bought them both and gave one to my friend. I knew that even though they were frightened, the two birds wanted to grow, and one day, to soar through the sky. . . .

For the rest of the trip I talked with my friend about the birds. The falcon is related to and looks very much like the *guaraguao*. Falcons live in the country-side of Puerto Rico and prefer the warmest mountains. Their feathers are colored like the mountain mud, speckled with black. With strong claws they trap small lizards and insects to eat. Falcons like to fly together with their mates.

When I arrived at my home in the housing development of Las Lomas, in the town of Río Piedras, I put the tiny, transparent bird in a little wire cage. I left him in my room on top of my desk. As the days passed I noticed large, whitish stains on the wall, the chair, and part of the bed. The bird had begun to grow and since the little cage was too small, he had soiled everything around him. I had to make a bigger cage and put him out on the patio, where he would stay from then on.

Pasaron las semanas lentamente. Ya iban apareciendo las plumas color barro. Su cuerpo crecía despacio, como crece un niño. Podía notar las pequeñas diferencias de una a otra semana. Es emocionante ver crecer algo vivo: un conejo, un perro, un pajarito o un árbol que hemos sembrado... Todos podemos sentir esa gran alegría si aprendemos a mirar y sentir las cosas vivas que nos rodean.

Al pasar de los meses ya había en la jaula del patio un falcón adulto y hermoso. Pero entonces comencé a notar algo extraño. En sus ojos había una mirada cansada que contrastaba con su belleza de ave salvaje. Sus gritos agudos eran ya una queja interminable. Parecían decir que la jaula donde había crecido le resultaba ya muy pequeña. El mensaje era claro: ya no soportaba el cautiverio, sus ojos necesitaban un mundo de luz, de árboles verdes y de vientos azules...

The weeks dragged by. Already his mud-colored feathers were appearing. His body grew slowly, as a child grows. I noticed small differences from week to week. It is moving to see a living thing grow: a rabbit, a dog, a little bird, or a tree we have planted. . . . All of us can sense this great joy if we learn to see and feel the living things that surround us.

Months passed and soon the cage on the patio held a handsome adult falcon. But then I noticed something strange. A tired look in his eyes clashed with the wild beauty of the bird. His sharp cries were soon an unending complaint. They seemed to say that the cage where he had grown was now much too small. The message was clear: he could no longer endure captivity; his eyes needed a world full of light, of green trees and blue breezes. . . .

Esa misma tarde abrí su jaula, como quien tiende la mano para ayudar a un amigo. El falcón miró sorprendido a su alrededor. No sabía qué hacer en aquel momento nuevo para él. Tuve que tomarlo en mi mano. Sus grandes garras me apretaron asustadas y temblorosas. Lo tiré entonces al aire y voló muy poco, lo suficiente como para posarse en la horqueta de un panapén de una finca vecina. Allí se quedó un largo rato, hasta que llegaron las sombras de la noche.

La noche era como un pájaro de grandes alas negras llenas de nuevas y pequeñas luces. Yo pensaba en un joven falcón que había volado hacia un mundo nuevo. En ese momento comenzaba para él una libertad que alumbraban las estrellas, los cucubanos, y que perfumaban las flores sencillas del moriviví…

That same afternoon I opened his cage, like someone putting out a hand to help a friend. The falcon, surprised, looked all around. He didn't know what to do at that moment, so new for him. I had to take him out with my hand. His great claws grasped me, frightened and trembling. I threw him then into the air and he flew just a bit, enough to perch in the fork of a breadfruit tree on the neighbor's farm. He stayed there a long time, until the night shadows gathered.

The night was like a bird with great black wings full of small new lights. I thought about the young falcon who had flown toward a new world. For him, at that moment, there began a new freedom lit up by the stars and the fireflies, and perfumed by the simple flowers of the *morivivî*. . . .

Al amanecer del día siguiente me despertó el chillido del falcón y el escándalo de sus alas en los árboles. Debía tener mucha hambre. Era un cazador que aún no sabía cazar solo.

Me levanté de la cama. Fui a la nevera y saqué un pedazo de carne. Salí a la calle que daba a la finca y divisé al falcón en lo alto de un árbol. Al verme, comenzó a moverse a las ramas más bajas. Me miró con desconfianza, pues parecía no querer cambiar su libertad por la jaula del patio. Alargué la mano suavemente, dándole a entender que su libertad estaba segura. Se balanceó hábilmente en la rama más baja, abriendo sus grandes alas en el amanecer frío. Tomó rápidamente la carne y voló hacia un alto pino de la finca. Lo miré con alegría y tristeza. Tristeza, porque sabía que pronto no volvería a verlo. Con alegría, porque ya era muy feliz en su mundo verde recién descubierto...

At dawn the next day the falcon's shriek and the racket of his wings in the trees woke me. He must have been hungry. He was a hunter who still didn't know how to hunt alone.

I got out of bed, went to the refrigerator, and took out a piece of meat. I walked out to the road leading to the farm and spied the falcon high up in a tree. When he saw me, he started to move to the lower branches. Looking at me warily, he didn't seem to want to trade his liberty for the cage on the patio. I held out my hand softly, letting him know that his freedom was assured. He balanced deftly on the lowest branch, opening his great wings in the cold dawn. Swiftly, he grabbed the meat and flew toward one of the farm's tall pines. I watched him with joy and sadness. Sadness, because I knew that soon I would no longer see him. With joy, because he was already very happy in his newly discovered, green world. . . .

Desde ese momento, mi amigo decidió comer tres veces al día, como todos nosotros. Y tres veces bajaba desde el pino más alto: por la mañana, al mediodía y al atardecer. Yo le extendía mi mano con un pedazo de carne, cariñosamente. Él lo veía desde la altura, ponía su cuerpo en posición de ataque y salía disparado como una flecha.

Se posaba entonces en mi brazo. Tenía bastante cuidado de no arañarme con sus fuertes garras. Cogía la carne con su pico y volaba otra vez muy alto. Esto sucedía todos los días. Muchas personas iban a verlo, pues se había hecho famoso. Una amistad entre un ave de presa y un hombre es algo que vemos muy pocas veces.

Una tarde pasó algo muy gracioso. En el momento en que le ofrecía su acostumbrada comida, bajó tan abruptamente que no pudo posarse en mi brazo. Agitó sus alas violentamente sobre mi cabeza y sentí que sus garras

From that moment, my friend decided to eat three times a day, like all of us. And three times he would come down from the tallest pine: in the morning, at noon, and at dusk. Affectionately, I offered him a piece of meat from my hand. He saw it from up high and prepared himself for the attack, darting down like an arrow.

Then he landed on my arm. He took care not to scratch me with his strong claws. Grabbing the meat with his beak, he flew back up. Every day this happened. Many people came to see him, as he had become famous. A friendship between a bird of prey and a man is something we see very few times.

One afternoon something funny happened. At the moment that I offered him his usual meal, he descended so abruptly that he couldn't land on my arm. He flapped his wings frantically over my head and I felt his claws sink into my

se hundieron en mi pelo tratando de equilibrar su cuerpo. No me asusté, pues noté que mi amigo hizo un esfuerzo cariñoso por no hacerme daño. A pesar de todo, pude alzar mi brazo y ofrecerle su alimento. Él lo tomó y regresó otra vez a los árboles rumorosos y verdes que lo esperaban…

Un día noté con sorpresa que había venido a comer solamente dos veces. Me preocupé mucho. Después imaginé lo que pasaba, al verlo volar acompañado de una pareja de igual color. Tenía compañía y aprendía a cazar con ella.

Pronto comenzó a bajar solamente una vez. Su compañera lo esperaba en una rama baja del pino. No había duda: ya sabía trabajar para conseguir su alimento y era realmente libre. Pensé que ahora venía a buscar algo de comer sólo para verme y despedirse de mí.

hair in an effort to balance his body. I wasn't afraid because I noticed that my friend made a loving effort not to hurt me. In spite of everything I was able to raise my arm and offer him his meal. He took it and returned again to the murmuring green trees that waited for him.

I was surprised one day when I noticed that he had come to eat only twice. I was very worried. Later, I realized what was happening when I saw him fly by accompanied by a mate of his same color. He had company and was learning to hunt with her.

Soon he began to come down only once a day. His mate waited for him on one of the low branches of the pine tree. There was no doubt: he already knew how to work for his meals and he was truly free. I thought that now he came to get something to eat only to see me and say good-bye.

Después sus esperadas visitas perdieron regularidad. El día que dejó de visitarme me di cuenta que en los últimos días había estado despidiéndose realmente. Mi amigo aprendió a amar la libertad que fue conquistando poco a poco en un esfuerzo diario. Imagino que no resultó fácil para él, pero el resultado final debió ser mucho más feliz que las paredes de su jaula metálica...

Adiós, falcón. Al conocerte supe que era posible tener un amigo del aire, los árboles y los nidos. Aprendí que también los animales pueden sentir miedo ante lo desconocido y sin embargo trabajar y aprender para ser libres. En mi recuerdo siempre eres parte de las montañas donde te conocí. Del cielo donde volaste. De la mañana y de la tarde...

Afterwards, his visits lost regularity. The day he stopped visiting me I realized that in the last few days he had really been saying good-bye. My friend learned to love the freedom that he won bit by bit through daily effort. I don't imagine that it was easy for him, but the final outcome must have been much happier than the walls of his metal cage. . . .

Good-bye, falcon. Knowing you made me realize that it is possible to have a friend from the air, the trees, and the nests. I learned that animals, too, can be afraid of the unknown and still work and learn to be free. In my memory you are always part of the mountains where I met you. Of the sky where you flew. Of the dawn, and of the dusk. . . .

Conoce al autor

Wenceslao Serra Deliz

Criar un falcón fue una experiencia extraordinaria para Wenceslao Serra Deliz. Tanto enriqueció su vida que decidió transformar la experiencia en *Adiós falcón*.

Muchas veces Serra Deliz escribe sobre el tema de Puerto Rico, donde nació y se crió. Las vistas, los sonidos y los cuentos de su tierra natal forman parte de su carácter. Aunque ha vivido en varios lugares en Puerto Rico, diría que es de Quebradillas, un pueblito en la costa noroeste de la isla.

A su padre, quien era ebanista y músico, Serra Deliz le atribuye el desarrollo de sus dotes artísticas. El padre de Serra Deliz murió cuando el autor era todavía un niño, pero su influencia ha durado toda una vida.

Serra Deliz ha escrito varios cuentos y poemas para niños. También le encanta conducir talleres de poesía para escritores jóvenes.

y al artista

Luis Tomás

Los pájaros y el arte eran unos de los primeros intereses de Luis Tomás. De niño en Phoenix, Arizona, criaba palomas como pasatiempo. También le gustaba dibujar los animales en el zoológico de Phoenix. Los padres de Tomás, quienes nacieron en México, le transmitieron el amor que sentían por el arte y la música. Ahora Tomás trabaja como compositor y artista en Arizona. Muchas veces usa un diario para escribir y dibujar sus experiencias y sueños. Él dice: —Puede ser un instrumentito muy poderoso.

Meet the Author

Wenceslao Serra Deliz

Raising a falcon was an extraordinary experience for Wenceslao Serra Deliz. It so enriched his life that he turned that experience into *Adiós falcón*.

When Deliz writes, his subject is often Puerto Rico. Born and raised on the island, the author knows his subject well. The sights, sounds, and tales of his homeland are part of his nature. Though he has lived in many places in Puerto Rico, he considers himself to be from Quebradillas, a small town on the northwest coast of the island.

Deliz credits his father, a cabinetmaker and musician, for helping him develop his artistic gifts. Although Deliz's father died when the author was a boy, he influenced Deliz in lasting ways.

Deliz has written numerous stories and poems for children. He especially enjoys giving poetry workshops for young writers.

and the Illustrator

Luis Tomás

Birds and art were early interests of Luis Tomás's. While growing up in Phoenix, Arizona, he raised pigeons as a hobby. He also enjoyed sketching animals at the Phoenix zoo. Tomás's parents, both born in Mexico, passed on their own love of music and art. Tomás now works as a composer and artist in Arizona. He often uses a journal for writing and drawing his experiences and dreams. "It can be a very powerful little tool," he says.

Set Your Ideas Free

Write a Poem

Bird Ballad

Author Serra Deliz calls his experience with the falcon "worthy of a story," but he could have written the falcon's story in some other form. Write a song or a poem about falcons or about the falcon in this story.

Make a Drawing

Before and After

Scrawny chick becomes majestic adult! Caged hatchling finally soars to freedom! Draw two pictures showing the falcon before and after its release.

How Does Your Falcon Grow?

One cool afternoon in July, Wenceslao Serra Deliz buys a featherless falcon chick. Months later he says good-bye to the grown falcon he calls his friend. What happens to the author in between? Write a series of journal entries that describe his feelings as he watches the falcon grow and realizes that it needs to be free.

To Cage or Not to Cage?

Should birds and other wild animals be brought up in captivity or allowed to remain in the wild? Hold a debate in your class. Use facts and details from the selections you have read to support your ideas.

New Birds
on the BLOCK

Peregrine falcons live in wide-open country near rocky cliffs. So what are they doing in big, crowded cities?

by Claire Miller

When your grandparents were young, plenty of *peregrine* (PAIR-uh-grin) *falcons* lived around the world. They were famous for being the fastest birds of all. (Peregrines can dive like speeding bullets and catch smaller birds in mid-air.)

By the time your *parents* were growing up, the birds were in trouble. Insect poison used on farms and in forests had gotten into their food. The poison, called DDT, made their eggshells thin and weak.

Brian Walton sits on the window ledge of a skyscraper. The young peregrine falcon he's holding will have to learn to hunt for birds above the busy city streets. But it will be safe from DDT, a poison found in the countryside.

Instead of raising babies, the birds found their nests full of scrambled eggs! Without new chicks being hatched, peregrines soon disappeared from most of the world.

To the Rescue

Along came some scientists who wanted to help these endangered birds. They took some of the thin-shelled eggs from peregrine nests. Very carefully, they carried them to their labs. Then they hatched some of the eggs in heated containers called *incubators*.

At first the scientists set the young birds free in places where peregrines once lived. But many of the

"Hey, watch me fly!" this young peregrine seems to say as it flaps its wings. Jerry Craig will feed the peregrines inside this *hack box* every day. When they've learned to hunt for their own food, Jerry will take the box away.

birds were attacked by great horned owls.

Meanwhile, some peregrines discovered the skyscrapers in big cities. The buildings were like cliffs to the birds. And some buildings had window ledges where the birds could lay their eggs.

In the cities, the falcons were safe from the big owls. And there were plenty of pigeons and smaller birds for them to eat. So the scientists figured that cities might be good places to set young peregrines free.

Happy Hacking

To get the young peregrines used to life in a city, the scientists used huge cages called *hack boxes*. They set the boxes high up on buildings and put the birds inside.

"First we wanted the birds to get used to their surroundings," says Jerry Craig, a scientist working in Denver, Colorado. "Then

Wild peregrines rest on cliffs and soar among hills and high mountains. But now they also live among skyscrapers in big cities such as Denver, Colorado (left).

we let them fly free. Lots of people were ready to rescue them from being hit by cars if they landed in the street.

"For a few weeks, the birds came back to the box for their food," he says. "But before long, they learned to catch their own food. We kept feeding them until they could feed themselves completely."

Banding the Babies

Scientists try to keep track of all the peregrines they let go. To do this, they put numbered bands on the birds' legs. The bands are like name tags that help them tell one bird from another.

John Barber works in a skyscraper in Baltimore, Maryland. For many years, peregrines have been raising their babies on one of the building's window ledges. John keeps close watch over the new babies each year.

When the chicks are three weeks old, John crawls out onto the window ledge to put numbered bands on their legs. It doesn't seem to bother him that the ledge is way up on the 33rd floor!

"I'm really glad to be helping these endangered birds," says John. "Some of the falcons I've banded have been found nesting here or in other cities. Others have died from flying into windows or being hit by cars. The bands help us tell which birds these things happened to."

Prime-Time Peregrines

In cities all over America, peregrines are becoming the new birds on the block. In the past two years, for example, 24 young peregrines were let go in Kansas City, Missouri.

The birds were set free from hack boxes on top of the Power and Light Building. From a nearby bank building, a TV camera kept track of the birds. And people who came to the bank could watch the birds on TV.

The people in Kansas City want the birds to stay, so they've put up something new. They attached nesting boxes to smokestacks on the Power and Light Building. TV cameras can keep track of any birds that use the boxes. It's a good way to spy on the birds without disturbing them.

A peregrine parent feeds its hungry youngster.

211

A Wild Sight

It's great fun to watch baby peregrines grow. But the biggest thrills come from watching the adults.

"I always get excited when I see a peregrine gliding on warm air currents high above the buildings," says Pat Redig. He's a scientist from Minnesota who's been working with peregrines for 20 years. "I know that at any second, one of those peregrines might zoom down and grab a bird flying beneath it. What a sight!"

Free of DDT

For peregrines, eating city birds can be good for their health. Take the peregrines that live in Los Angeles, for example. They seem to be better off than the ones living in the nearby countryside.

"The peregrines in our countryside are *still* being hurt by DDT," explains Brian Walton, a bird scientist. "Even though farmers haven't used DDT for 20 years, it is still getting into the bodies of the birds that peregrines eat. So we're still finding a lot of wild peregrines with broken eggs in their nests!

"But city peregrines eat birds that never go near the places that were poisoned with DDT. Since the pigeons don't eat any DDT, the city peregrines don't get it in their bodies. And they lay eggs with strong shells."

Picture-Perfect Peregrines

City peregrines have been making good friends all across the country. For example, the people in Toledo,

This tough peregrine caught a pigeon in midair.

Ohio, think their peregrines are really special. So far, they have the only nesting pair in Ohio.

"Having peregrines in cities like Toledo is great for photographers like me," says Sharon Cummings. "We don't have to climb dangerous cliffs to take action photos of the birds. We just aim our cameras out of office building windows when they fly by or land on a ledge.

"But during nesting season," she says, "*some* people aren't too fond of the birds.

You have to watch where you walk. The ground below their nest is full of their leftovers: bird heads!"

Watch for 'em

Maybe you can get to see some peregrines too. They live in more than 30 cities in North America. When you're in a big city, check with a local bird club, a natural history museum, or a nature center. Find out if peregrines live there. If they do, maybe *you* can catch a glimpse of these new birds on the block.

Like baby falcons in many cities, these will get numbered leg bands. Scientists can then tell the birds apart.

High up on a building, this peregrine falcon peers into a television camera (below). The bird doesn't know that it's the star of a show. People watching the TV set can keep track of everything the peregrine does (left).

Try to See It My Way

Try to See It My Way

CONTENTS

217

THE
HUNDRED PENNY BOX

SHARON BELL MATHIS
Illustrated by Leo & Diane Dillon

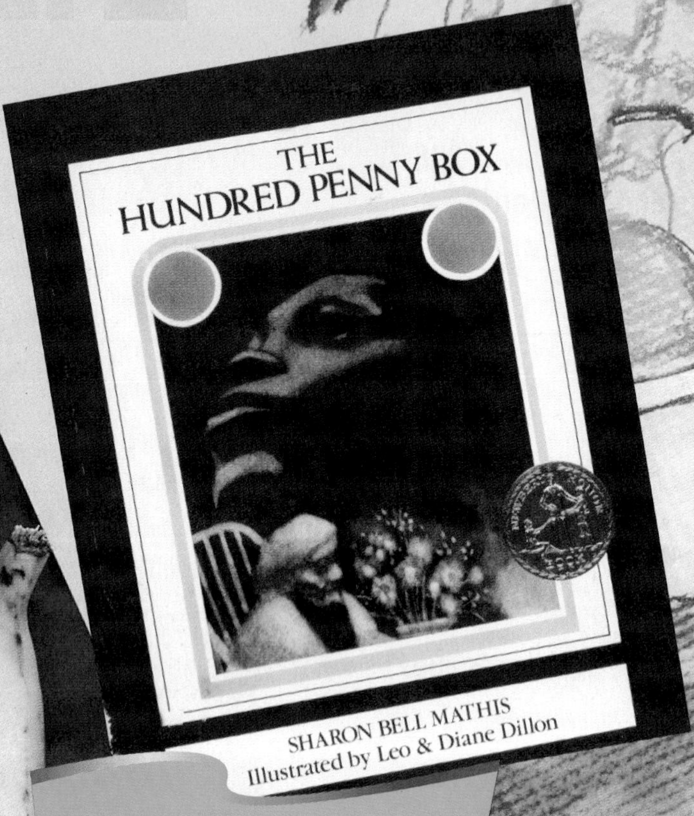

PAPERBACK **PLUS**

The Hundred Penny Box

by Sharon Bell Mathis

In a box of one hundred pennies, Michael's great-great-aunt, Aunt Dew, keeps the stories of her one hundred years

In the same book . . .

More about Aunt Dew's family tree, pennies through history, and another seasoned storyteller

TRY SOME NEW POINTS OF VIEW

Hello, My Name Is Scrambled Eggs
by Jamie Gilson
Will Tuan Nguyen, newly arrived from Vietnam, be Americanized by his American friend?

A Llama in the Family
by Johanna Hurwitz
Instead of the mountain bike Adam is hoping for, his mother buys a llama to start a new business.

Stealing Home
by Mary Stolz
When his great-aunt visits, Thomas is afraid that his life of fishing and baseball with his grandfather will change.

The Facts and Fictions of Minna Pratt
by Patricia MacLachlan
Minna wishes that her mother, a writer, and her father, a psychologist, would act normal, like the parents of her friends.

In Two Worlds: A Yup'ik Eskimo Family
by Aylette Jenness
An Eskimo family tries to observe its ancient customs while living in a world of modern conveniences.

Red-Dirt Jessie
by Anna Myers
Jessie is sure that taming a half-wild dog as a pet will cheer up her father.

PAPERBACK PLUS

Dear Mr. Henshaw
by Beverly Cleary

Leigh Botts writes to his favorite author . . . and finds out about himself.

In the same book . . .

Much more, including Beverly Cleary and her readers, trucks, and monarch butterflies

Winner of the Newbery Award

Beverly Cleary

Dear Mr. Henshaw

Illustrated by Paul O. Zelinsky

Meet the Author of *In the Year of the Boar and Jackie Robinson*

Bette Bao Lord

At age 10

The story of Shirley Temple Wong's arrival in America from China is based on Bette Bao Lord's own childhood. She remembers sailing into San Francisco in the autumn of 1946: "Only yesterday, resting my chin on the rails of the S.S. *Marylinx,* I peered into the mist for *Mei Guo*, beautiful country. It refused to appear. Then, within a blink, there was the Golden Gate, more like the portals to heaven than the arches of a man-made bridge." From California the family made its way to New York.

"I arrived in Brooklyn, New York, on a Sunday," she recalls. "On Monday I was enrolled at P. S. 8. By putting up ten fingers, I found myself sentenced to the fifth grade. It was a terrible mistake. By American reckoning, I had just turned eight. And so I was the shortest student by a head or two in class."

Like Shirley, Lord persevered and learned English. For a short time, she dreamed of winning a Nobel Prize in chemistry. But she went on to a career helping to promote understanding between China and the United States, and for several years she taught and performed modern dance.

Lord "stumbled into writing" by deciding to tell the story of her sister Sansan, "who grew up in China [and] was reunited with the family after a separation of sixteen years." Much later she wrote about her own early life in the United States. The result was her first book for children, *In the Year of the Boar and Jackie Robinson,* in which "China's Little Ambassador" is a chapter.

In 1985

Meet the Illustrator

Drawing the illustrations for *In the Year of the Boar and Jackie Robinson* brought back a lot of memories for Winson Trang. Like Shirley, the heroine of the story, Trang was born in Asia and came to the United States knowing no English. Trang arrived in San Francisco in 1979 when he was 15 years old.

Trang had to travel a long and dangerous route to get to the United States. He left his homeland, Vietnam, in 1975 at the end of a long war. With a cousin, he traveled by train to China, the country where his grandparents were born. Then he traveled by boat to Hong Kong, where he lived in a refugee camp for a year before relatives helped him gain passage to the United States.

Other members of Trang's family reached the United States by different routes, sometimes narrowly avoiding disaster. His mother and sisters were on a boat that capsized. Out of a total of four hundred passengers, they were among the ninety who survived.

Trang learned English quickly and, after college, attended art school. Working as a translator of Chinese, he began to find work as a freelance illustrator. One of his assignments was *Child of the Owl*, by Laurence Yep.

Trang offers his own story as encouragement to young people interested in a career as an illustrator. "Keep at it," he says. "Hang on until you get your opportunity!"

*In China her family calls her
Sixth Cousin or sometimes
Bandit. But just before Bandit
and her mother sail to America
to join her father, she changes her
name to Shirley Temple Wong.
The time of her arrival is 1947.
In China it's the Year of the Boar.
The place is Brooklyn, New
York. And Shirley is about to
face a major challenge: her first
day in an American school.*

China's Little Ambassador

Nine o'clock sharp the very next morning,
Shirley sat in the principal's office at P. S. 8.
Her mother and the schoolmistress were
talking. Shirley didn't understand a word.
It was embarrassing. Why hadn't she, too,
studied the English course on the records
that Father had sent? But it was too late
now. She stopped trying to understand.
Suddenly, Mother hissed, in Chinese.
"Stop that or else!"

Shirley snapped her head down. She
had been staring at the stranger. But she
could not keep her eyes from rolling up
again. There was something more foreign
about the principal than about any other
foreigner she had seen so far. What was it?

In the Year of the Boar and Jackie Robinson

by Bette Bao Lord

It was not the blue eyes. Many others had them too. It was not the high nose. All foreign noses were higher than Chinese ones. It was not the blue hair. Hair came in all colors in America.

Yes, of course, naturally. The woman had no eyelashes. Other foreigners grew hair all over them, more than six Chinese together. This woman had none. Her skin was as bare as the Happy Buddha's belly, except for the neat rows of stiff curls that hugged her head.

She had no eyebrows, even. They were penciled on, and looked just like the character for man, 人. And every time she tilted her head, her hair moved all in one piece like a hat.

"Shirley."

Mother was trying to get her attention. "Tell the principal how old you are."

Shirley put up ten fingers.

While the principal filled out a form, Mother argued excitedly. But why? Shirley had given the correct answer. She counted just to make sure. On the day she was born, she was one year old. And two months later, upon the new year, she was two. That was the Year of the Rabbit. Then came the Dragon, Snake, Horse, Sheep, Monkey, Rooster, Dog and now it was the year of the Boar, making ten. Proof she was ten.

Mother shook her head. Apparently, she had lost the argument. She announced in Chinese, "Shirley, you will enter fifth grade."

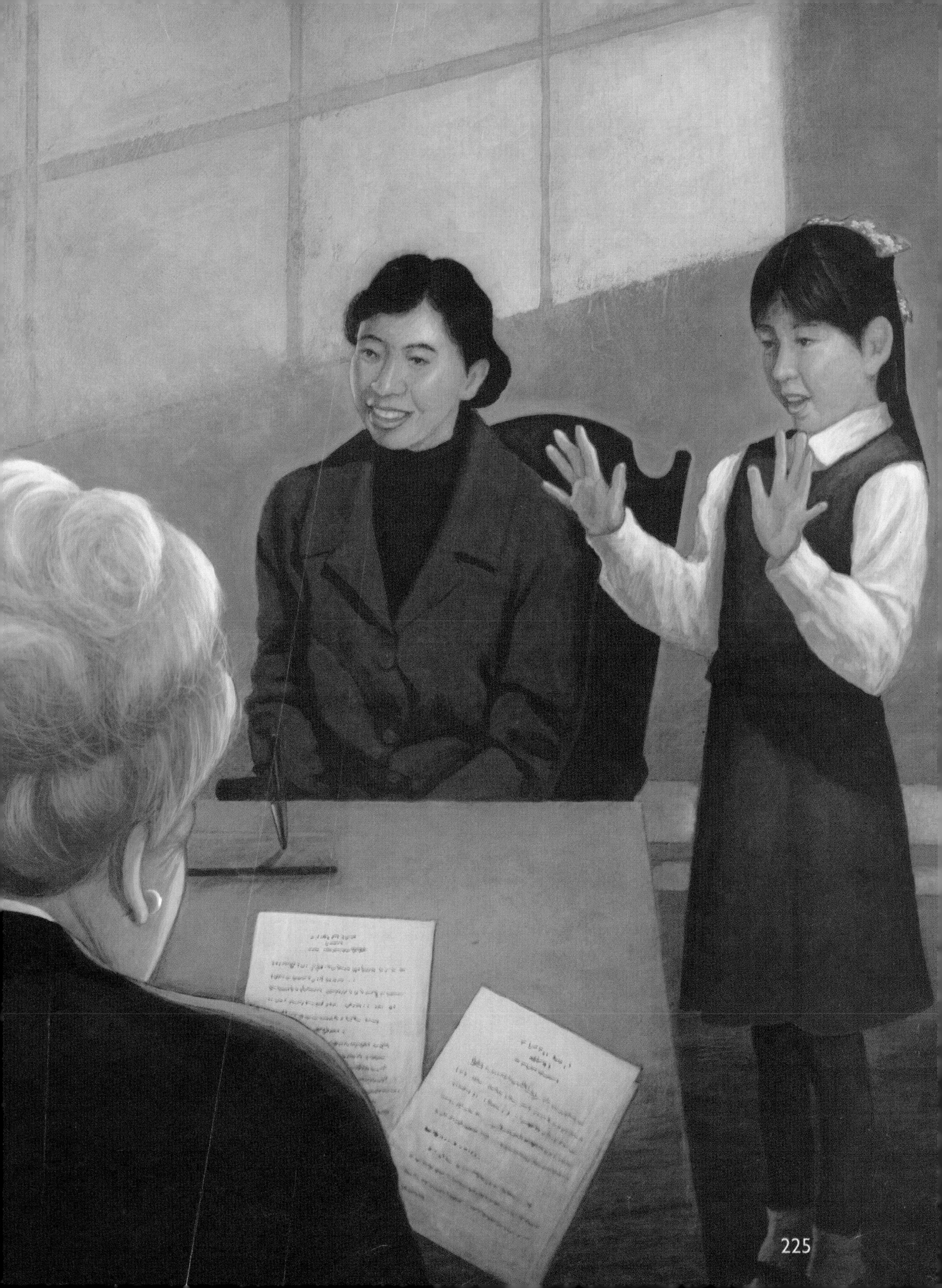

"Fifth? But, Mother, I don't speak English. And besides, I only completed three grades in Chungking."

"I know. But the principal has explained that in America everyone is assigned according to age. Ten years old means fifth grade. And we must observe the American rules, mustn't we?"

Shirley nodded obediently. But she could not help thinking that only Shirley had to go to school, and only Shirley would be in trouble if she failed.

Mother stood up to leave. She took Shirley by the hand. "Remember, my daughter, you may be the only Chinese these Americans will ever meet. Do your best. Be extra good. Upon your shoulders rests the reputation of all Chinese."

All five hundred million? Shirley wondered.

"You are China's little ambassador."

"Yes, Mother." Shirley squared her shoulders and tried to feel worthy of this great honor. At the same time she wished she could leave with Mother.

Alone, the schoolmistress and Shirley looked at each other. Suddenly the principal shut one eye, the right one, then opened it again.

Was this another foreign custom, like shaking hands? It must be proper if a principal does it, Shirley thought. She ought to return the gesture, but she didn't know how. So she shut and opened both eyes. Twice.

This brought a warm laugh.

The principal then led her to class. The room was large, with windows up to the ceiling. Row after row of students, each one unlike the next. Some faces were white, like clean plates; others black like ebony. Some were in-between shades. A few were spotted all over. One boy was as big around as a water jar. Several others were as thin as chopsticks. No one wore a uniform of blue, like hers. There were sweaters with animals on them, shirts with stripes and shirts with squares, dresses in colors as varied as Grand-grand Uncle's paints. Three girls even wore earrings.

While Shirley looked about, the principal had been making a speech. Suddenly it ended with "Shirley Temple Wong." The class stood up and waved.

Amitabha! They were all so tall. Even Water Jar was a head taller than she. For a fleeting moment she wondered if Mother would consider buying an ambassador a pair of high-heeled shoes.

"Hi, Shirley!" The class shouted.

Shirley bowed deeply. Then, taking a guess, she replied, "Hi!"

The teacher introduced herself and showed the new pupil to a front-row seat. Shirley liked her right away, although she had a most difficult name, Mrs. Rappaport. She was a tiny woman with dainty bones and fiery red hair brushed skyward. Shirley thought that in her previous life she must have been a bird, a cardinal perhaps. Yet she commanded respect, for no student

talked out of turn. Or was it the long mean pole that hung on the wall behind the desk that commanded respect? It dwarfed the bamboo cane the teacher in Chungking had used to punish Four Hands whenever he stole a trifle from another.

Throughout the lessons, Shirley leaned forward, barely touching her seat, to catch the meaning, but the words sounded like gurgling water. Now and then, when Mrs. Rappaport looked her way, she opened and shut her eyes as the principal had done, to show friendship.

At lunchtime, Shirley went with the class to the school cafeteria, but before she could pick up a tray, several boys and girls waved for her to follow them. They were smiling, so she went along. They snuck back to the classroom to pick up coats, then hurried out the door and across the school yard to a nearby store. Shirley was certain they should not be there, but what choice did she have? These were now her friends.

One by one they gave their lunch money to the store owner, whom they called "Mr. P." In return, he gave each a bottle of orange-colored water, bread twice the size of an ear of corn oozing with meat balls, peppers, onions, and hot red gravy, and a large piece of brown paper to lay on the icy sidewalk and sit upon. While they ate, everyone except Shirley played marbles or cards and traded bottle caps and pictures of men swinging a stick or wearing one huge glove. It was the best lunch Shirley had ever had.

And there was more. After lunch, each of them was allowed to select one item from those displayed under the glass counter. There were paper strips dotted with red and yellow sugar tacks, chocolate soldiers in blue tin foil, boxes of raisins and nuts, envelopes of chips, cookies as big as pancakes, candy elephants, lollipops in every color, a wax collection of red lips, white teeth, pink ears and curly black mustaches. Shirley was the last to make up her mind. She chose a hand, filled with juice. It looked better than it tasted, but she did not mind. Tomorrow she could choose again.

But when she was back in her seat, waiting for Mrs. Rappaport to enter the classroom, Shirley's knees shook. What if the teacher found out about her escapade? There would go her ambassadorship. She would be shamed. Her parents would lose face. All five hundred million Chinese would suffer. Round and round in her stomach the meat balls tumbled like pebbles.

Then Mrs. Rappaport came in. She did not look pleased. Shirley flinched when the teacher went straight to the long mean pole. For the first time her heart went out to Four Hands. She shut her eyes and prayed to the Goddess of Mercy. Oh Kwan Yin, please don't let me cry! She waited, listening for Mrs. Rappaport's footsteps to become louder and louder. They did not. Finally curiosity overcame fear and she looked up. Mrs. Rappaport was using the pole to open a window!

The lessons continued. During arithmetic, Shirley raised her hand. She went to the blackboard and wrote the correct answer. Mrs. Rappaport rewarded her with a big smile. Shirley opened and shut her eyes to show her pleasure. Soon, she was dreaming about candy elephants and cookies the size of pancakes.

Then school was over. As Shirley was putting on her coat, Mrs. Rappaport handed her a letter, obviously to be given to her parents. Fear returned. Round and round, this time like rocks.

She barely greeted her mother at the door.

"What happened?"

"Nothing."

"You look sick."

"I'm all right."

"Perhaps it was something you ate at lunch?"

"No," she said much too quickly. "Nothing at all to do with lunch."

"What then?"

"The job of ambassador is harder than I thought."

At bedtime, Shirley could no longer put off giving up the letter. Trembling, she handed it to Father. She imagined herself on a boat back to China.

He read it aloud to Mother. Then they both turned to her, a most quizzical look on their faces.

"Your teacher suggests we take you to a doctor. She thinks there is something wrong with your eyes."

235

See It Shirley's

Draw a Picture

In a Class by Herself

Think about Shirley's classroom on her first day of school. Which people and objects stand out? Draw a picture of Shirley's classroom as Shirley sees it.

Write a Letter

Dear Fourth Cousin

How would Shirley describe her first day of school to her favorite cousin back in China? Write a letter that Shirley might write, telling how she feels about being in America.

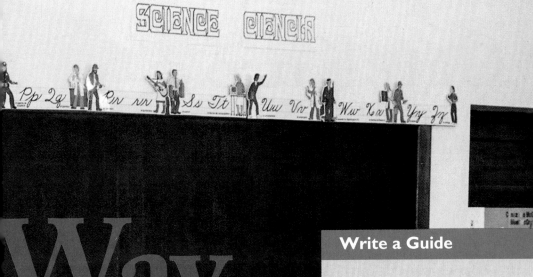

Way

Write a Guide

What a Wink Means

Strange poles, unusual food, people shutting and opening their eyes . . . Shirley is surrounded by hundreds of new details. Write a guidebook for Shirley, explaining some of the items and customs of her school and classroom.

Compare and Contrast

In the Same Boat

Think about a time when you were a newcomer in a group. How did you feel? What did you notice? Have a discussion comparing your "new kid" experience with Shirley's.

My Cat, Kuro

A Description by Mark Aoyama

To someone else, Kuro might look like any other black cat. But to Mark, Kuro is very special indeed. Mark wrote this description to help other people "see" Kuro as he does.

Mark Aoyama
North Beach Elementary School
Seattle, Washington

Mark was in the fifth grade when he wrote this description of his special cat. In addition to writing, Mark likes to read, play soccer, draw, make things, and play video games. Someday Mark would like to be an artist or a designer of video games.

My Cat, Kuro

My cat, Kuro, which is Japanese for "Blackie," is part Persian and part Siamese. Anyway, that's what we think. He is as black and as shiny as polished obsidian. And he is as big as a French poodle. When he lies on our kitchen floor, he stretches out like a bungee cord until he reaches three-and-one-half feet from the tip of his front paws to the tip of his back paws.

Kuro did not always look like a beautiful fur scarf. He came to live with us when my mom found him wandering around where she works. He had no collar and no place to live. When she brought him home, he was dirty and had fleas and ringworm fungus. He only weighed nine pounds, and his ribs poked out from his sides. Now he is round and sleek, weighing in at fourteen pounds, four ounces.

There are lots of ways Kuro communicates with us by making different sounds. When he needs to go outside or wants food, he makes a loud, hollow "Mroowuu." But, when you're holding the container of catnip, he makes a high-pitched, pleading, three-syllabled "Merow-erow-erow." When Kuro wants to come in from outside, he rubs his paws against the kitchen window, making a squeaking noise on the glass. He always says "hello" as he comes through the door, a sweet little chirplike "Brrrip."

Kuro has yellowish-green eyes, but he can only see out of one of them because of a congenital cataract. This doesn't keep him from catching a large assortment of birds, rats, and mice. Kuro is very proud of these "presents," which he leaves for us. He must feel as if he has caught dinner for our family.

Except when catching little furry things, Kuro is lazy. Most of his day is spent sleeping, eating, sleeping, watching television, sleeping, looking out the window, sleeping, and sitting under the bushes.

I like to nuzzle Kuro's soft, thick fur. That's how I know where he's been last. If he smells like

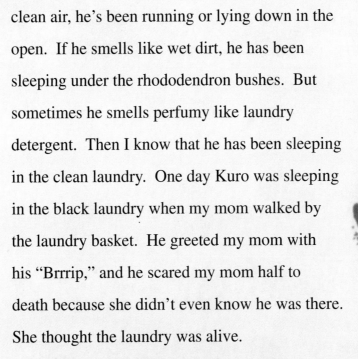

clean air, he's been running or lying down in the open. If he smells like wet dirt, he has been sleeping under the rhododendron bushes. But sometimes he smells perfumy like laundry detergent. Then I know that he has been sleeping in the clean laundry. One day Kuro was sleeping in the black laundry when my mom walked by the laundry basket. He greeted my mom with his "Brrrip," and he scared my mom half to death because she didn't even know he was there. She thought the laundry was alive.

My cat has a superfriendly personality. Although he shows no mercy to rodents, he is very loving to our family members. Kuro will jump into my mother's arms from the floor when he wants to be held.

If my mom hadn't brought Kuro home when he was a stray, he probably wouldn't be alive now. I love Kuro, and I can't imagine what the world would be like without him.

HOANG ANH
A VIETNAMESE-AMERICAN BOY

BY DIANE HOYT-GOLDSMITH / PHOTOGRAPHS BY LAWRENCE MIGDALE

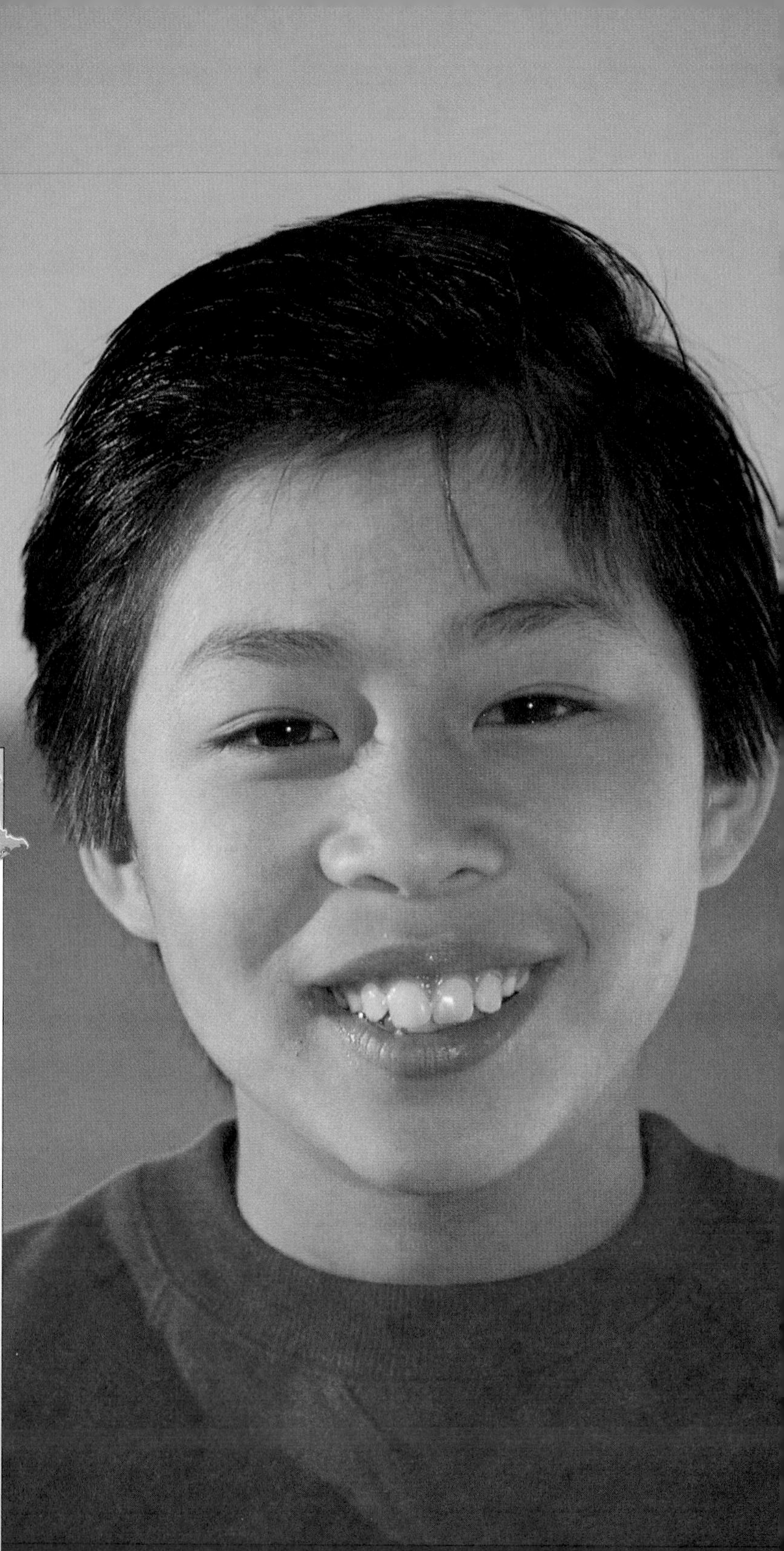

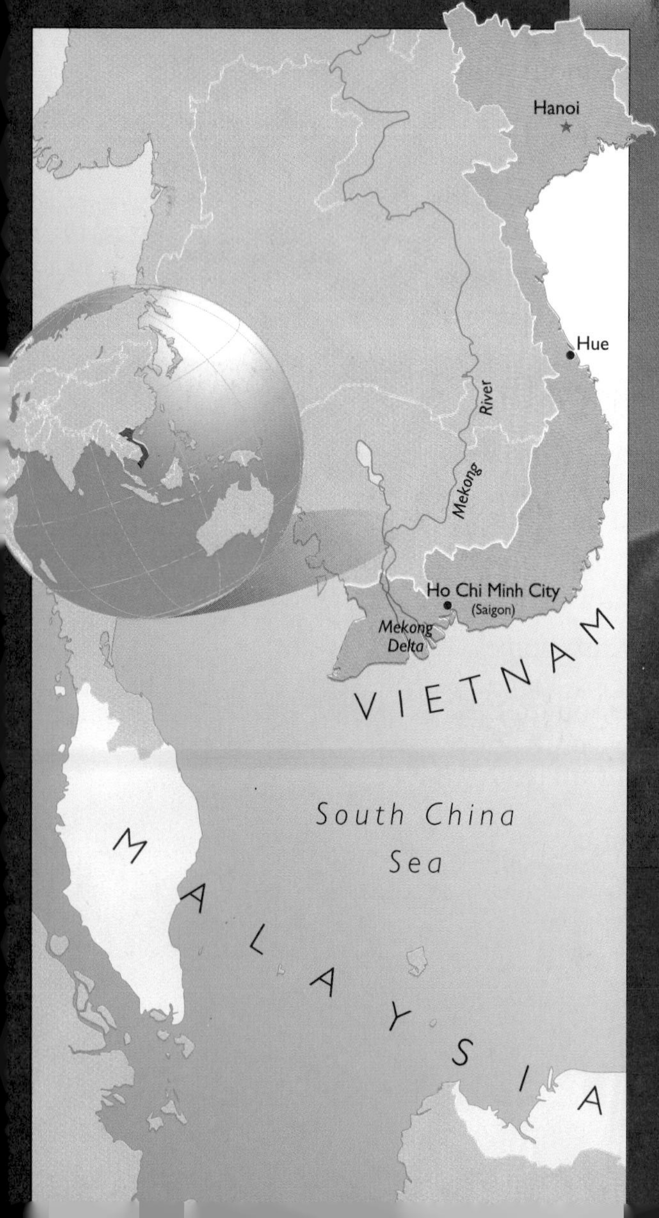

Hanoi ★

Hue ●

Mekong River

VIETNAM

Ho Chi Minh City ●
(Saigon)

Mekong Delta

South China Sea

M A L A Y S I A

Vietnam is located on the eastern side of the

Indochinese Peninsula, in Southeast Asia. In

1978 Hoang Anh's family fled Vietnam. They

first went to Malaysia, which lies to the south-

west of Vietnam, across the South China Sea.

Hoang Anh

A Vietnamese-American Boy

by Diane Hoyt-Goldsmith

My name is Hoang Anh Chau *(WONG ON CHOH)*. I live in the town of San Rafael, California. In our home, we speak two languages: Vietnamese and English. I came to this country with my family when I was just a baby. We are all refugees from Vietnam, here to begin a new life. My parents, my older brothers, my sister, and I are new citizens of the United States. We are Vietnamese-Americans.

My father, Thao Chau *(TAU CHOH)*, is a fisherman. On days when the weather is good, he gets up at three o'clock in the morning. He goes to his boat and heads out to the ocean. Working hard all day, my father visits the places where he has set traps to catch crabs and eels. Usually, he doesn't get home until long after dark. My father learned to be a fisherman in Vietnam.

Hoang Anh's father raises the wire crab trap with a winch and cable that is powered by electricity. The white plastic cup in the center holds the bait.

Happy that the morning's catch was good, Hoang Anh helps his father put the crabs into a tall barrel. His father will take the crabs to a fish market in San Francisco, where they will be sold.

My parents came from a small town called Kieng Giang *(KEENG JANG)* on the Mekong *(MAY-KONG)* Delta in the southern part of Vietnam. In that region, there are many rice farms. My father, like his father before him, owned a tractor and earned a living by plowing the fields for farmers.

But in 1977, my parents made a decision that changed their lives. They decided to leave Vietnam.

My father had been a soldier in the South Vietnamese army since 1971. For years, he had fought alongside the Americans against the Communist forces led by North Vietnam. During the war, many of my father's friends and relatives were killed. He watched as the war destroyed homes, farms, and towns. He saw that his way of life was changing forever.

244

Unable to defeat the Communists, the United States sent its soldiers home in 1973. Two years later, the Communists of North Vietnam took control of the entire country. The new government acted harshly toward people like my father who had fought against them. My parents were frightened for their own safety. They worried about the future. They wanted to raise their children in a better place.

The Communist government of Vietnam, however, would not allow people to leave the country. So my parents planned secretly to escape from Vietnam and seek a new life of safety and freedom in the United States. In doing so, they would become refugees.

To carry out his plan, my father sold his tractor and bought a small fishing boat. He learned to fish, working in the waters of the Gulf of Thailand. He had a plan to escape, but he did not want the Vietnamese government to become suspicious. He watched and waited for the right time.

Then one day in 1978, my parents gathered together some food and clothing for a long journey. They said goodbye to their parents and their friends. In the dark of the night, my parents brought their four young children on board the small fishing boat. With his family and twenty-four other refugees hidden below the deck, my father sailed away from the shores of Vietnam.

He pretended it was just another day of fishing. But when the little boat reached the open water, he did not stop to put out the crab traps. Sailing west and south, he kept on going toward the island nation of Malaysia.

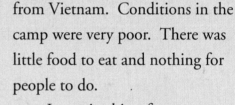

A news clipping shows the Chau family shortly after their arrival in the United States. Hoang Anh, on his mother's lap, is still a small baby. His father and a brother sit on the couch and his aunt stands in the doorway behind.

My brothers and sister were much too young to realize what was happening. They had no idea of the danger they were in. The small, overcrowded boat faced many hardships on the journey. It could have been lost at sea. It could have been swamped in a terrible storm. The passengers could have run out of food and water before reaching land again. Worst of all, sea pirates could have discovered the boat and taken everybody's belongings and even their lives.

But my family was lucky. After two days and two nights on the ocean, they reached Malaysia safely. For more than a year, they lived in a camp for refugees. It was filled with many other people who had fled from Vietnam. Conditions in the camp were very poor. There was little food to eat and nothing for people to do.

It was in this refugee camp in Malaysia that I was born. In spite of the poor conditions there, I was a very healthy baby. When I was a few months old, a church in Oregon sponsored my family, and we emigrated to the United States.

I have read in books that over a million people fled from Vietnam after the war because they were frightened about what the country would be like under a Communist government. Many of these "boat people" made it to safety, as my family did. But many more were shipwrecked and had to be rescued by passing boats. Some were discovered by the Communist government and sent back to Vietnam. The most unfortunate people were those who met pirate ships. They were robbed, beaten, kidnapped, sold as slaves, or even tossed overboard. As a result many refugees have just disappeared completely.

Sometimes, when I help my father at the docks, I look at his fishing boat and think about his daring escape. The boat that carried my family away from Vietnam was ten feet shorter in length, yet it brought thirty people to a new life. My parents were very brave to have taken such risks to bring us all to the United States.

Hoang Anh's father fishes from this boat. It is much larger than the boat that brought his family and many other refugees out of Vietnam.

Ma! Don't Throw That Shirt Out

by Jack Prelutsky

Ma! Don't throw that shirt out,
it's my all-time favorite shirt!
I admit it smells peculiar,
and is stained with grease and dirt,
that it's missing half its buttons,
and has got so many holes
that it might have been infested
by a regiment of moles.

Yes! I know that I've outgrown it,
that it's faded and it's torn,
I can see the sleeves are frazzled,
I'm aware the collar's worn,
but I've had that shirt forever,
and I swear that I'll be hurt
if you dare to throw that shirt out —
IT'S MY ALL-TIME FAVORITE SHIRT!

REFLECTION

by Shel Silverstein

Each time I see the Upside-Down Man
Standing in the water,
I look at him and start to laugh,
Although I shouldn't oughtter.
For maybe in another world
Another time
Another town,
Maybe HE is right side up
And I am upside down.

LIKE JAKE AND ME

by Mavis Jukes · pictures by Lloyd Bloom

The rain had stopped. The sun was setting. There were clouds in the sky the color of smoke. Alex was watching his stepfather, Jake, split wood at the edge of the cypress grove. Somewhere a toad was grunting.

"Jake!" called Alex.

Jake swung the axe, and wood flew into the air.

"Jake!" Alex called again. "Need me?" Alex had a loose tooth in front. He moved it in and out with his tongue.

Jake rested the axe head in the grass and leaned on the handle. "What?" he said. He took off his Stetson hat and wiped his forehead on his jacket sleeve.

Alex cupped his hands around his mouth. "Do . . . you . . . need . . . me . . . to . . . help?" he hollered. Then he tripped over a pumpkin, fell on it, and broke it. A toad flopped away.

Jake adjusted the raven feather behind his hatband. "Better stay there!" he called. He put his hat back on. With powerful arms, he sunk the axe blade into a log. It fell in half.

"Wow," thought Alex. "I'll never be able to do that."

Alex's mother was standing close by, under the pear tree. She was wearing fuzzy woolen leg warmers, a huge knitted coat with pictures of reindeer on the back, and a red scarf with the name *Virginia* on it. "I need you," she said.

Alex stood up, dumped the pumpkin over the fence for the sheep, and went to Virginia.

"I dropped two quarters and a dime in the grass. If I bend down, I may never be able to get up again," she said. Virginia was enormous. She was pregnant with twins, and her belly blocked her view to the ground. "I can't even see where they fell."

"Here!" said Alex. He gave her two quarters. Then he found the dime. He tied her shoe while he was down there.

"Thanks," said Virginia. "I also need you for some advice." She pointed up. "Think it's ready?"

One of the branches of the pear tree had a glass bottle over the end of it. Inside were some twigs and leaves *and* two pears. In the spring, Virginia had pushed the bottle onto the branch, over the blossoms. During the summer, the pears had grown and sweetened inside the bottle. Now they were fat and crowding each other.

The plan was that when the pears were ripe, Virginia would pull the bottle from the tree, leaving the fruit inside. Then she'd fill the bottle with pear nectar and trick her sister, Caroline. Caroline would never guess how Virginia got the pears into the bottle!

"Shall we pick it?" asked Virginia.

"Up to you!" said Alex.

Months ago, Virginia had told him that the pears, and the babies, would be ready in the fall. Alex looked away at the hills. They were dusky gray. There were smudges of yellow poplars on the land. Autumn was here.

Alex fiddled with his tooth. "Mom," he asked, "do you think the twins are brothers or sisters?"

"Maybe both," said Virginia.

"If there's a boy, do you think he'll be like Jake or like me?"

"Maybe like Jake *and* you," said Virginia.

"Like Jake *and* me?" Alex wondered how that could be possible.

"Right," said Virginia.

"Well, anyway," said Alex, "would you like to see something I can do?"

"Of course," she said.

Alex straightened. Gracefully he lifted his arms and rose up on his toes. He looked like a bird about to take off. Then he lowered his

arms and crouched. Suddenly he sprang up. He spun once around in midair and landed lightly.

Virginia clapped. "Great!"

Alex did it again, faster. Then again, and again. He whirled and danced around the tree for Virginia. He spun until he was pooped. Jake had put down the axe and was watching.

"Ballet class!" gasped Alex. "Dad signed me up for lessons, remember?"

"Of course I remember," said Virginia. "Go show Jake!"

"No," panted Alex. "Jake isn't the ballet type."

"He might like it," said Virginia. "Go see!"

"Maybe another time," said Alex. He raced across the field to where Jake was loading his arms with logs. "Jake, I'll carry the axe."

"Carry the axe?" Jake shook his head. "I just sharpened that axe."

Alex moved his tooth with his tongue and squinted up at Jake. "I'm careful," he said.

Jake looked over at the sheep nosing the pumpkin. "Maybe another time," he told Alex.

Alex walked beside him as they headed toward the house. The air was so cold Jake was breathing steam. The logs were stacked to his chin.

Virginia stood under the pear tree, watching the sunset. Alex ran past her to open the door.

Jake thundered up the stairs and onto the porch. His boots were covered with moss and dirt. Alex stood in the doorway.

"Watch it!" said Jake. He shoved the door open farther with his shoulder, and Alex backed up against the wall. Jake moved sideways through the door.

"Here, I'll help you stack the wood!" said Alex.

"Watch it!" Jake came down on one knee and set the wood by the side of the woodstove. Then he said kindly, "You've really got to watch it, Alex. I can't see where I'm going with so big a load."

Alex wiggled his tooth with his tongue. "I just wanted to help you," he said. He went to Jake and put his hand on Jake's shoulder. Then he leaned around and looked under his Stetson hat. There was bark in Jake's beard. "You look like a cowboy in the movies."

"I have news for you," said Jake. "I *am* a cowboy. A real one." He un-snapped his jacket. On his belt buckle was a silver longhorn steer. "Or was one." He looked over at Alex.

Alex shoved his tooth forward with his tongue.

"Why don't you just pull out that tooth?" Jake asked him.

"Too chicken," said Alex. He closed his mouth.

"Well, everybody's chicken of something," said Jake. He opened his jacket pocket and took out a wooden match. He chewed on the end of it and looked out the windows behind the stove. He could see Virginia, still standing beneath the tree. Her hands were folded under her belly.

Jake balled up newspaper and broke some sticks. He had giant hands. He filled the woodstove with the wadded paper and the sticks and pushed in a couple of logs.

"Can I light the fire?" Alex asked.

"Maybe another time," said Jake. He struck the match on his rodeo belt buckle. He lit the paper and threw the match into the fire.

Just then Alex noticed that there was a wolf spider on the back of Jake's neck. There were fuzzy babies holding on to her body. "Did you know wolf spiders carry their babies around?" said Alex.

"Says who?" asked Jake.

"My dad," said Alex. He moved his tooth out as far as it would go. "He's an entomologist, remember?"

"I remember," said Jake.

"Dad says they only bite you if you bother them, or if you're squashing them," said Alex. "But still, I never mess with wolf spiders." He pulled his tooth back in with his tongue.

"Is that what he says, huh," said Jake. He jammed another log into the stove, then looked out again at Virginia. She was gazing at the landscape. The hills were fading. The farms were fading. The cypress trees were turning black.

"I think she's pretty," said Alex, looking at the spider.

"I do, too," said Jake, looking at Virginia.

"It's a nice design on her back," said Alex, examining the spider.

"Yep!" said Jake. He admired the reindeer coat, which he'd loaned to Virginia.

257

"Her belly sure is big!" said Alex.

"It has to be big, to carry the babies," said Jake.

"She's got an awful lot of babies there," said Alex.

Jake laughed. Virginia was shaped something like a pear.

"And boy! Are her legs woolly!" said Alex.

Jake looked at Virginia's leg warmers. "Itchy," said Jake. He rubbed his neck. The spider crawled over his collar.

"She's in your coat!" said Alex. He backed away a step.

"We can share it," said Jake. He liked to see Virginia bundled up. "It's big enough for both of us. She's got to stay warm." Jake stood up.

"You sure are brave," said Alex. "I like wolf spiders, but I wouldn't have let that one into my coat. That's the biggest, hairiest wolf spider I've ever seen."

Jake froze. "Wolf spider! Where?"

"In your coat getting warm," said Alex.

Jake stared at Alex. "What wolf spider?"

"The one we were talking about, with the babies!" said Alex. "And the furry legs."

"Wolf spider!" Jake moaned. "I thought we were talking about Virginia!" He was holding his shoulders up around his ears.

"You never told me you were scared of spiders," said Alex.

"You never asked me," said Jake in a high voice. "Help!"

"How?" asked Alex.

"Get my jacket off!"

Alex took hold of Jake's jacket sleeve as Jake eased his arm out. Cautiously, Alex took the jacket from Jake's shoulders. Alex looked in the coat.

"No spider, Jake," said Alex. "I think she went into your shirt."

"My shirt?" asked Jake. "You think?"

"Maybe," said Alex.

Jake gasped. "Inside? I hope not!"

"Feel anything furry crawling on you?" asked Alex.

"Anything *furry* crawling on me?" Jake shuddered. "No!"

"Try to get your shirt off without squashing her," said Alex. "Remember, we don't want to hurt her. She's a mama."

"With babies," added Jake. *"Eek!"*

"And," said Alex, "she'll bite!"

"Bite? Yes, I know!" said Jake. "Come out on the porch and help me! I don't want her to get loose in the house!"

Jake walked stiffly to the door. Alex opened it. They walked out onto the porch. The sky was thick gray and salmon colored, with blue windows through the clouds.

"Feel anything?" asked Alex.

"Something . . ." said Jake. He unsnapped the snaps on his sleeves, then the ones down the front. He opened his shirt. On his chest was a tattoo of an eagle that was either taking off or landing. He let the shirt drop to the floor.

"No spider, back or front," reported Alex.

They shook out the shirt.

"Maybe your jeans," said Alex. "Maybe she got into your jeans!"

"Not my *jeans!*" said Jake. He quickly undid his rodeo belt.

"Your boots!" said Alex. "First you have to take off your boots!"

"Right!" said Jake. He sat down on the boards. Each boot had a yellow rose and the name *Jake* stitched on the side. "Could you help?" he asked.

"Okay," said Alex. He grappled with one boot and got it off. He checked it. He pulled off and checked the sock. No spider. He tugged on the other boot.

"You've got to pull harder," said Jake, as Alex pulled and struggled. "Harder!"

The boot came off and smacked Alex in the mouth. "Ouch!" Alex put his tongue in the gap. "Knocked my tooth out!" He looked in the boot. "It's in the boot!"

"Yikes!" said Jake.

"Not the spider," said Alex. "My tooth." He rolled it out of the boot and into his hand to examine it.

"Dang," said Jake. "Then hurry up." Alex dropped the tooth back into the boot. Jake climbed out of his jeans and looked down each leg. He hopped on one foot to get the other sock off.

"She won't be in your sock," said Alex. "But maybe — "

"Don't tell me," said Jake. "Not my shorts!"

Alex stared at Jake's shorts. There were pictures of mallard ducks on them. "Your shorts," said Alex.

"I'm afraid to look," said Jake. He thought he felt something creeping just below his belly button.

"Someone's coming!" said Alex. "Quick! Give me your hat! I'll hold it up and you can stand behind it."

"Help!" said Jake in a small voice. He gave Alex the hat and quickly stepped out of his shorts. He brushed himself off in the front.

"Okay in the back," said Alex, peering over the brim of the hat.

Jake turned his shorts inside out, then right side in again. No spider. When he bent over to put them on, he backed into his hat, and the raven feather poked him. Jake howled and jumped up and spun around in midair.

"I didn't know you could do ballet!" said Alex. "You dance like me!"

"I thought I felt the spider!" said Jake. He put on his shorts.

"What on *earth* are you doing?" huffed Virginia. She was standing at the top of the stairs, holding the bottle with the pears inside.

"We're hunting for a spider," said Jake.

"Well!" said Virginia. "I like your hunting outfit. But aren't those *duck*-hunting shorts, and aren't you cold?"

"We're not hunting spiders," explained Jake. "We're hunting *for* a spider."

"A big and hairy one that *bites!*" added Alex.

"A wolf spider!" said Jake, shivering. He had goose bumps.

"Really!" said Virginia. She set the bottle down beside Jake's boot. "Aha!" she cried, spying Alex's tooth inside. "Here's one of the spider's teeth!"

Alex grinned at his mother. He put his tongue where his tooth wasn't.

Jake took his hat from Alex and put it on.

"Hey!" said Virginia.

"What?" said Jake.

"The spider!" she said. "It's on your hat!"

"Help!" said Jake. "Somebody help me!"

Alex sprang up into the air and snatched the hat from Jake's head.

"Look!" said Alex.

"Holy smoke!" said Jake.

There, hiding behind the black feather, was the spider.

Alex tapped the hat brim. The spider dropped to the floor. Then off she swaggered with her fuzzy babies, across the porch and into a crack.

Jake went over to Alex. He knelt down. "Thanks, Alex," said Jake. It was the closest Alex had ever been to the eagle. Jake pressed Alex against its wings. "May I have this dance?" Jake asked.

Ravens were lifting from the blackening fields and calling. The last light had settled in the clouds like pink dust.

Jake stood up holding Alex, and together they looked at Virginia. She was rubbing her belly. "Something is happening here," she told them. "It feels like the twins are beginning to dance."

"Like Jake and me," said Alex. And Jake whirled around the porch with Alex in his arms.

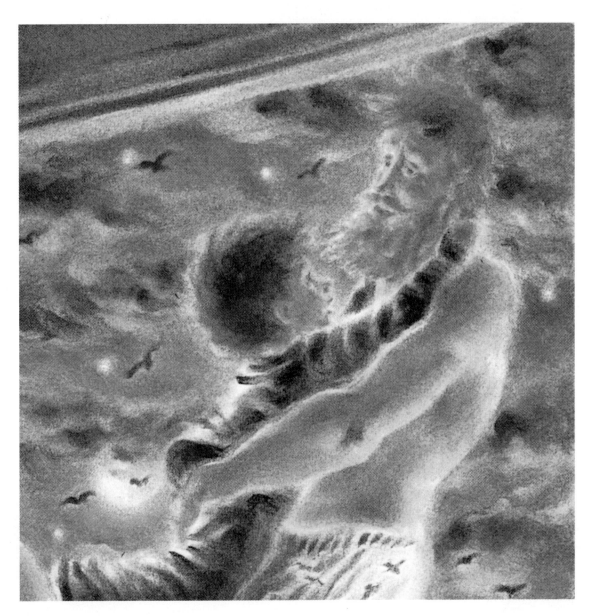

263

Meet the Author
Mavis Jukes

Mavis Jukes's experiences with one of her own stepsons inspired her to write *Like Jake and Me.* As in the story, a shared "act of courage" brought Jukes and her stepson closer. She dared Cannon, her nine-year-old stepson, to tap-dance in front of a theater full of people. He dared her to join him, and together they danced "like two dopes" across the stage. "I'll never forget it, ever," says Jukes, "because it was the first time Cannon had ever held my hand."

Mavis Jukes also has two daughters. The older one sparked Jukes's switch from a career in law to writing. "One day I wrote a story for her," Jukes remembers. "When I saw what I had written, I realized I was a writer."

Jukes thinks that there are lots of people who simply don't realize that they are writers. And she wants to encourage them: "If you love to tell stories, if you love to hear stories, if you love words and how people speak them, you may be a writer. If you notice things — bees changing places on flowers, a plastic bag blowing down the street in the dark . . . you may be a writer. If you love movies and music, you may be a writer."

Jukes has written many award-winning books for young readers. *Like Jake and Me* was a 1985 Newbery Honor book. You might also enjoy *Blackberries in the Dark* and *No One Is Going to Nashville.*

Meet the Illustrator
Lloyd Bloom

When Lloyd Bloom illustrates a book, he responds to it with a special style that brings out the best in the author's story. Sometimes he creates black-and-white drawings, other times colorful paintings. For *Like Jake and Me,* Bloom went even further, discovering a new way of painting with pastels that brings Mavis Jukes's story vividly to life.

Bloom has been working at his art ever since he was a teenager in New York City. He has studied many kinds of art, including painting, drawing, and sculpture. In addition to *Like Jake and Me,* Bloom has illustrated many other books for young people. Some of them include *Grey Cloud,* by Charlotte Towner Graeber; *Arthur, For the Very First Time,* by Patricia MacLachlan; and *A Man Named Thoreau,* by Robert Burleigh.

SPIN OUT YOUR IDEAS

Illustrate a Scene

Picture This

Mavis Jukes's colorful descriptions help readers visualize the story. When you read *Like Jake and Me*, what pictures came to *your* mind? Draw something in the story that isn't already illustrated, or draw another view of something that is. Use the story's descriptions as your guide.

Hold a Discussion

To Each His Own

Jake and Alex have different reactions to the wolf spider. Discuss the way each of them responds. Then talk about things that scare other people but don't scare you.

What's in a Title?

Think about the title of the selection *Like Jake and Me*. Why do you think Mavis Jukes gave her story that name? Write a paragraph telling what the title means to you.

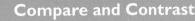

I AM NOT SCARED OF THESE!

Live and Learn

Think about *Like Jake and Me* and *In the Year of the Boar and Jackie Robinson*. Shirley and Alex each go through learning experiences. Have a discussion about what each of these main characters learns. How are Shirley and Alex alike and how do they differ?

Try to See It . . . .

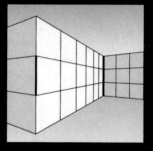

The Long and Short of It   Are the dark lines in this picture the same length? Perspective makes your brain say *no*, but what does your ruler say?

Parallel Lines?   The short hash marks on these long lines make them appear to veer away from each other. But do they really? Lift the bottom edge of your book and look across the picture from the lower left corner — and get a straight answer!

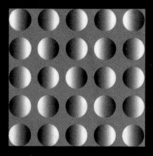

Shading and Shape   The sun provides constant "overhead lighting," which your brain uses to help define shapes. Here, light is hitting the circles from different sides, so your brain can't really "decide" on their shape. If you turn the picture 90 degrees to the left or right, however, the light comes from "above." Then you can see an X of either concave (inward) or convex (outward) circles.

Which Is It?   This vase was made for England's Queen Elizabeth II and Prince Philip. When you look at it, what do you see? A vase with an irregular shape — or the profiles of Elizabeth (right) and Philip (left)? Your brain can recognize both, but not at the same time. Either the vase or the profiles could be the background — or the foreground — so they jump back and forth before your eyes.

. . . If You Can!

Artists and architects use light, color, shape — and the way your brain works — to fool and delight your eyes!

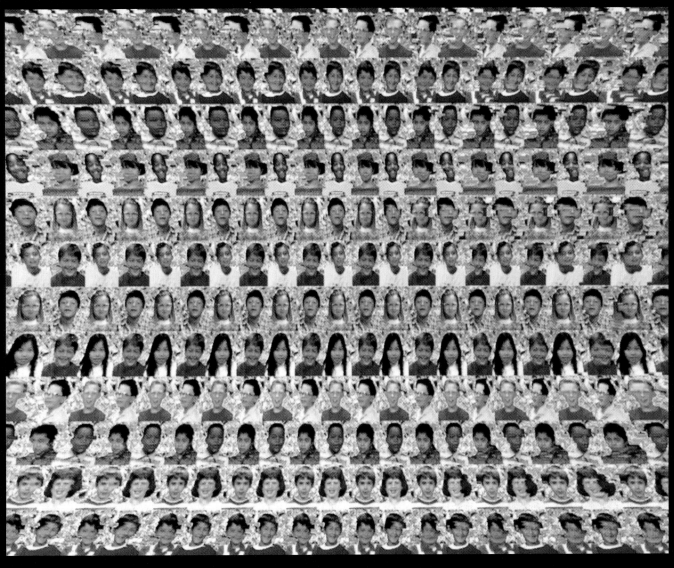

Patience Makes Perfect Explore the exciting world of three-dimensional imaging. When you stare "through" the repeating patterns, a new, 3-D image gradually appears. Try it — but don't look "at" the new image or it'll disappear!

An Artistic Breakthrough   The artist of this mural on a water tank in Sacramento, California, used a nearly photographic painting technique called *trompe l'oeil* ("fool the eye") to make this superhero appear to smash through the wall.

Which Way Is Up? Dutch graphic artist M. C. Escher called this visual riddle "Relativity." The whole picture is confusing, but look at each staircase separately and it makes perfect sense.

Building Art It reflects the street, neighboring buildings, and the sky. The architect designed this skyscraper in downtown Winnipeg, Manitoba, to both stand out and disappear in its environment.

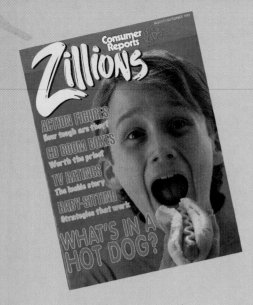

The goal of advertisers is to make you see things their way. The "Bug Squad," a monthly feature in *Zillions* magazine, helps you see through the words – and numbers – advertisers use to pitch their clients' products.

HI, GANG! IT'S **ME**, THE OL' INSECTOR, YOUR HOST FOR A NEW QUIZ SHOW, **THE GAME OF NUMBERS!** FROM YOUR LETTERS, IT'S OBVIOUS THAT BUG SQUAD MEMBERS ARE **BUGGED** BY AD CLAIMS THAT **DON'T "ADD UP"**!

From the files of the NOT-SO SECRET **BUG SQUAD**

So many DIFFERENT pain relievers can't be preferred by "3 out of 4 doctors"!
Anonymous
Riverview, Michigan

I hate when ads say their products have a "lifetime guarantee."
Alexis Allen
Brigantine, New Jersey

3 OUT OF **4 DOCTORS** PREFER THE PAIN RELIEF IN **BRAINOL!**

3 OUT OF **4 DOCTORS** PREFER **SUFFERIN …**

3 OUT OF **4 DOCTORS** PREFER **ZAPERIN …**

IT'S TIME TO PLAY **EXPLAIN THAT NUMBER-CLAIM!** WELL, GANG, HOW CAN DIFFERENT BRANDS **CLAIM THE EXACT SAME THING?**

Me, Mop, and the Moondance Kid

BY WALTER DEAN MYERS

Mop, T.J., and T.J.'s brother, Moondance, once lived together at the Dominican Academy, a home for orphans. T.J. and Moondance have been adopted, but Mop — and Taffy, the Academy llama — face an uncertain future if the Academy closes. Meanwhile, the Elks, the kids' baseball team, is trying hard to get into the play-offs. The team has lots of boosters: Marla, the coach; Sister Carmelita of the Academy; and Peaches, a neighborhood character. But the team also has its doubters. Mr. Treaster, a rival coach, keeps laughing at the Elks. T.J. and Moondance's adoptive father, once a professional ballplayer, is growing impatient. And T.J. is beginning to doubt himself.

Saturday was the day of the Pumas' game and I was really excited. Dad asked three times when the game was going to start. I was in a good mood, but it didn't last too long. When me and Moondance got to the Academy to pick up Mop, we got some bad news about Taffy. The zoo didn't want her after all.

"What will they do with her?" Moondance asked.

Sister Carmelita shrugged. "Maybe we can find a farm that will take her," she said. "There are a lot of llama farms out west."

"Let's get to the game," Mop said. "We'll talk about Taffy later."

We had to play the Pumas, and then we had to play the Hawks. If we beat the Pumas, then we would have second place and be in the play-offs against the first-place team which we knew already was going to be the Eagles. If we lost to the Pumas, we could still get into the play-offs by beating the Hawks.

"We want to beat the Pumas," Marla said when we got to the field. "If we do, then we can relax a little bit for the last game before the play-offs."

275

"We're not going to win the play-offs against no Eagles," Evans said. "They too good."

"We have a chance in a short series," Marla said. "We just have to win two games out of the three."

"How we gonna win two games when we ain't never won once against them?" Evans said.

"We're better than we were when we first played them," Marla said. "And we'll prove it."

Mike pitched for us and the Pumas scored five runs in the first inning. I wasn't playing. Marla had Lo Vinh playing third base instead of me.

"Why aren't you playing third base?" Dad had shown up shortly after the game started. "That kid they have out there now doesn't look that good."

"I don't know," I said. "Maybe Marla just wants to let him play for a while."

Dad's jaw tightened a little. And then he went up into the stands to watch the game.

By the third inning the score was 15 to 3 and I knew we were going to lose. Dad was right about Lo Vinh not being too good at third base. But then he hurt his hand and Marla brought in Jennifer! You ever see Jennifer play? If the ball goes two feet away from her, she won't even go for it.

Brian got mad and threw his glove down and Marla told him if he did that again, he would come out of the game.

"Hey, Marla, you got a great squad there!" Joe Treaster had shown up and was leaning against the fence. "I hope they make the play-offs!"

"So do I," Marla said.

A guy came down to the field and said he thought Marla should put Moondance on third base and put Jennifer in the outfield.

"You go back into the stands and I will run this team!" Marla said in this real loud voice.

"Tell him, baby!" Mr. Treaster yelled again.

In the fifth inning we scored two runs and everybody got happy again. Marla switched Brian from short to pitcher and put Mike on short-stop. We were still way behind though.

In the top of the sixth Brian struck out the first Puma and Mop made a diving catch of a pop foul for the second out. The next two batters bunted balls down the third base line toward Jennifer. She didn't even try to run in for them. Brian got so mad he threw his glove at her. That's when Marla took him out of the game.

Brian's father was yelling at Marla. Mr. Treaster was yelling at her and laughing. I looked around to see what my Dad was doing and I saw him talking to Sister Carmelita.

"Hey! T.J.! Wake up!"

I turned and saw that Marla was pointing at me. I got my glove and went over to her.

She switched Mike back to pitcher, brought Joey DeLea in to play shortstop and put me in right field.

"Come on, guys," Marla said. "Let's prove we can stop them when we have to."

Mike loaded the bases by walking the next batter. Then their best hitter got up. He swung at the first pitch.

I could hear the crack of the bat and saw the ball coming right out to me. It looked like it was growing bigger as it came.

I went running in for it. I knew I was going to catch it. It came down and down. I was banging my glove with my fist. I was all ready to catch it.

It was a little higher than I thought.

I went back two steps and reached up as far as I could. The ball flew just over my glove. It bounced over the fence for an automatic double.

Everybody in the infield was throwing their gloves down and looking at me. Everybody.

Even from where I was standing, way in the outfield, all by myself, I could see Dad shaking his head. I knew what he was thinking. He was wondering how come he had such a lousy kid playing ball.

They scored one more run and then we got up. When I went in, I saw Marla talking to everybody. Then when I got to the bench they all said things like "Nice try" and "You almost had it." But nobody looked at me and I knew that Marla had told them to say that.

We didn't score that inning, but neither did the Pumas during the top of the seventh.

I got up in the last of the seventh. There were two outs and I missed the first two pitches. Then I bunted at the next ball and hit it but it went foul. Then the umpire called me out because of a rule about a foul bunt on the third strike being an out.

The Pumas won, 18 to 5.

After the game I didn't even want to go near Dad. He came over to where me and Jennifer were packing up the bases in the old blue duffel bag that we carried our stuff in and went up to Marla.

"Tough loss," he said.

"They're all tough losses, Mr. Williams," Marla said.

"Titi said that you might actually make the play-offs." Dad shifted his weight from one foot to the other. "I can't see how you're going to win."

I pushed home plate as hard as I could down to the bottom of the bag.

"I don't know who this Titi is," Marla said. "But he might have also told you that we scored some runs against this team. If we had another pitcher besides Brian, if Moondance could throw the ball over the plate, for example, we would have a chance of at least being respectable."

"Why don't you let Titi help?" Dad said. "She used to be the best pitcher in our league."

"In the first place, I don't know this Titi," Marla said. "And I think it's a little late with the play-offs starting next week."

"You don't know Sister Carmelita?" Dad asked.

"Sister Carmelita?"

"Yeah, way back before she was a nun she used to play Little League ball right here in Lincoln Park," Dad said. "We used to call her Titi then. And she could *pitch*!"

Okay, so Sister Carmelita used to be a pitcher. But do you know who really helped Moondance turn out to be a good pitcher? Peaches! Okay, Peaches *and* Sister Carmelita.

Marla talked to Sister Carmelita and asked if she could help Moondance. Sister Carmelita said that she didn't know, but she would try. So we all went out to the playground the next day and Dad put the Sunday comics on the ground for the plate. Moondance started pitching to Mop.

Zip! Zip! Zip!

He could throw that ball over the plate so fast it wasn't even funny.

Zip! Zip! Zip!

Marla shook her head.

"Let's see how you hold the ball, Moondance." Sister Carmelita looked at how Moondance held the ball in his hand.

"Like this," Moondance said, holding the ball up.

Sister Carmelita held his hand still and moved the ball a little. "Try it that way," she said. "Don't let it touch your palm. It's a little trickier, but I think you can do it."

The first ball that Moondance threw went right over Mop's head.

"Follow through!" Sister Carmelita called out. "Bring your arm all the way down."

Zip! Whack!

That's the way the ball went. It went even faster than it did the first time he was throwing.

Zip! Whack!

The next ball went over Mop's head, but after that the ball was going right into the glove.

Zip! Whack!

Zip! Whack!

"T.J., stand at the plate." Marla handed me a bat.

No way I wanted to stand there with the bat. I looked at Marla to see if she really meant for me to stand there, but she had already gone over to sit on one of the benches. Dad was leaning against the backstop and Sister Carmelita was standing near Moondance out at the mound. It was as if they were watching a show or something.

I looked at Moondance and he looked at me. He had his tongue out and was wiping off his pitching hand. Mop got down on her knees and put one hand behind her back.

"Throw it past him, Moondance!" she yelled. "He can't hit!"

"Don't swing, T.J.," Marla called out. "I just want to see his control." Zip!

The ball went outside and against the backstop. Dad looked at Moondance and one eyebrow went up. Mop got the ball and threw it back to Moondance. Sister Carmelita was talking to him, but I couldn't hear what she was saying.

You know how I felt? A little nervous. Even though I didn't have to swing at the ball, you get a little nervous when Moondance throws it with all of his might.

Zip!

The ball went outside and past Mop's glove again.

"Give him a target, Mop!"

"I am giving him a target!" Mop yelled back as she picked the ball up again.

"C'mon, Son." Dad made a fist and held it up toward Moondance. "Bring it high and tight."

I didn't know what that meant, but I saw the next ball go flying outside again.

"Stand on the other side, T.J."

That's what Marla said.

"No!" That's what I said. Moondance was throwing the balls just where she wanted me to stand.

"You're not scared of the ball, are you?" Dad asked.

"No," I said.

I went to the other side. I wasn't scared of the ball. I mean, if the ball and me were in a dark room together, I wouldn't be nervous or anything. I was afraid of being *hit* by the ball.

Moondance wound up and threw the ball. I dropped the bat and got ready to duck in case it came toward me, but it didn't. It went on the other side.

"Moondance, are you afraid of hitting him?" Marla got off the bench and started toward us.

"I don't want to hit anybody," Moondance said.

"Don't worry about it, just throw the ball to Hop," Dad said.

"That's Mop, *M-O-P*." Mop gave Dad a look.

"If you just aim for Mop's glove, you won't be that close to him," Marla said. "You can almost do it with your eyes closed."

I got away from the plate. He wasn't throwing the ball at me with his eyes closed.

"Just keep your eye on the glove," Sister Carmelita said. "Take your time."

Moondance looked at Mop's glove and kept his eyes right on it. He wound up and threw the ball again.

Zip!

Fast as anything, but outside. I think they were right. He didn't want to hit me.

Then Dad caught and Mop got up to bat. Same thing. Moondance didn't want to throw the ball near anybody.

Dad said he would talk to him and I saw Moondance look a little sad. Sometimes Dad says things that sound good, or at least okay, but deep down you know they're not. He said he would talk to Moondance, that everything would be okay. But you could tell by the way he said it that he wasn't happy with the way Moondance pitched. I could tell it and Moondance could tell it too.

It's bad when you mess up and people aren't happy with you. Like when I missed the fly ball and everybody on the team threw their gloves down. But I think it's even worse when you do something good, like Moondance did, and somebody isn't happy with you because you didn't do it good enough. Especially when that somebody is your dad.

Still, Sister Carmelita had helped Moondance a little, and we didn't even know that Peaches was going to help too.

When we got home, Dad got out all these pictures of him playing baseball. He looked great. I imagined myself doing some of the things he did.

WILLIAMS'S HOMER SPURS ASU WIN!

"That's when we won the national championship," Dad said. "We made every paper in the state of Arizona every day that week!"

"That's where I first met him," Mom said. "All he ever talked about then was playing baseball. All he ever did was play baseball too. I think he married me because I could keep score."

Then he showed us the pictures of himself when he played for Kansas City.

"It must be hard to be a great baseball player," I said.

"Sometimes," Dad said. "It's even harder not to be a great ballplayer."

WALTER DEAN MYERS
AUTHOR

Walter Dean Myers likes to write for young people. He hopes they will see themselves in his stories. Myers says, "When kids find . . . a good character who makes them say look, here I am in this book, this guy feels the same way I do — it's reassuring."

Myers used some of his own experiences in writing *Me, Mop, and the Moondance Kid*. Like T.J., he was raised by adoptive parents. At the age of three, he went to live with the Dean family in the Harlem section of New York City. There he found a close community that helped him believe in himself. Many of Myers's more than thirty books draw on those early years.

You can follow the further adventures of T.J. and his friends in *Mop, Moondance, and the Nagasaki Knights*. Read what happens when the Elks face a baseball team from Japan.

ANTHONY WOOLRIDGE
ILLUSTRATOR

A lifelong resident of Virginia, Anthony Woolridge has been drawing and painting since the age of six. His grandfather, a farmer who raised chickens, pigs, and goats, encouraged Woolridge's interest in nature. "I wasn't the play-around-in-the-city type," Woolridge recalls. He had something else in common with T.J., Mop, and Moondance, however. He grew up with friends of many cultures. He remembers what it was like to be part of a group of "different people finding a common goal."

Put Your Ideas in Play!

What Did He Mean?

At the end of the selection, Mr. Williams says, "It's even harder not to be a great ballplayer." What do you think he means? Share your thoughts in a small group or with the class.

I Remember . . .

When T. J. and his family return home after the game, Mr. Williams shows photographs from his days as a baseball player. If T. J. were to create a scrapbook of his own, what would he put in it? Brainstorm some ideas. Then put together a scrapbook for T. J.

I'll Trade You!

Make a baseball card for each of your favorite characters in *Me, Mop, and the Moondance Kid*. Draw a picture of each character and write his or her name on one side of the card. Write a brief description of the character on the back of the card.

Great Expectations

Think about the characters in *Me, Mop, and the Moondance Kid, Like Jake and Me,* and *In the Year of the Boar and Jackie Robinson.* T. J., Alex, and Shirley all try to please someone by behaving in a certain way. Write a few sentences explaining what each character is trying to do and why. Then write about a time when you tried to live up to someone else's expectations.

We Could Be Friends

by Myra Cohn Livingston

We could be friends
Like friends are supposed to be.
You, picking up the telephone
Calling me

to come over and play
or take a walk,
finding a place
to sit and talk,

Or just goof around
Like friends do,
Me, picking up the telephone
Calling you.

Narcissa

by Gwendolyn Brooks

Some of the girls are playing jacks.
Some are playing ball.
But small Narcissa is not playing
Anything at all.

Small Narcissa sits upon
A brick in her back yard
And looks at tiger lilies,
And shakes her pigtails hard.

First she is an ancient queen
In pomp and purple veil.
Soon she is a singing wind.
And, next, a nightingale.

How fine to be Narcissa,
A-changing like all that!
While sitting still, as still, as still
As anyone ever sat!

Felita

by Nicholasa Mohr

A wonderful thing happened this new school year. Gigi, Consuela, Paquito, and I were all going into the fourth grade, and we were put in the same class. It had never happened before. Once I was in the same class with Consuela, and last year Gigi and Paquito were together. But this — it was too good to be true! Of course knowing Gigi and I were in the same class made me the happiest.

Our teacher, Miss Lovett, was friendly and laughed easily. In early October, after we had all settled into our class and gotten used to the routine of school once more, Miss Lovett told us that this year our class was going to put on a play for Thanksgiving. The play we were going to perform was based on a poem by Henry Wadsworth Longfellow, called "The Courtship of Miles Standish." It was about the Pilgrims and how they lived when they first landed in America.

We were all so excited about the play. Miss Lovett called for volunteers to help with the sets and costumes. Paquito and I agreed to help with the sets. Consuela was going to work on makeup. Gigi had not volunteered for anything. When we asked her what she was going to do, she shrugged and didn't answer.

Miss Lovett said we could all audition for the different parts in the play. I was really interested in being Priscilla. She is the heroine. Both Captain Miles Standish and the handsome, young John Alden are in love with her. She is the most beautiful maiden in Plymouth, Massachusetts. That's where the Pilgrims used to live. I told my friends how much I would like to play that part. Everyone said I would be perfect . . . except Gigi. She said that it was a hard part to do, and maybe I wouldn't be able to play it. I really got annoyed and asked her what she meant.

"I just don't think you are right to play Priscilla. That's all," she said.

"What do you mean by right?" I asked. But Gigi only shrugged and didn't say another word. She was beginning to get on my nerves.

Auditions for the parts were going to start Tuesday. Lots of kids had volunteered to audition. Paquito said he would try out for the brave Captain Miles Standish. Consuela said she was too afraid to get up in front of everybody and make a fool of herself. Gigi didn't show any interest in the play and refused to even talk to us about it. Finally the day came for the girls to read for the part of Priscilla. I was so excited I could hardly wait. Miss Lovett had given us some lines to study. I had practiced real hard. She called out all the names of those who were going to read. I was surprised when I heard her call out "Georgina Mercado." I didn't even know Gigi wanted to try out for Priscilla. I looked at Gigi, but she ignored me. We began reading. It was my turn. I was very nervous and kept forgetting my lines. I had to look down at the script a whole lot. Several other girls were almost as nervous as I was. Then it was Gigi's turn. She recited the part almost by heart. She hardly looked at the script. I noticed that she was wearing one of her best dresses. She had never looked that good in school before. When she finished, everybody clapped. It was obvious that she was the best one. Miss Lovett made a fuss.

"You were just wonderful, Georgina," she said, "made for the part!" Boy, would I have liked another chance. I bet I could have done better than Gigi.

Why hadn't she told me she wanted the part? It's a free country, after all. She could read for the same part as me. I wasn't going to stop her! I was really angry at Gigi.

After school everyone was still making a fuss over her. Even Paquito had to open his stupid mouth.

"Oh, man, Gigi!" he said. "You were really good. I liked the part when John Alden asked you to marry Captain Miles Standish and you said, 'Why don't you speak for yourself, John?' You turned your head like this." Paquito imitated Gigi and closed his eyes. "That was really neat!" Consuela and the others laughed and agreed.

I decided I wasn't walking home with them.

"I have to meet my brothers down by the next street," I said. "I'm splitting. See you." They hardly noticed. Only Consuela said goodbye. The rest just kept on hanging all over Gigi. Big deal, I thought.

Of course walking by myself and watching out for the tough kids was not something I looked forward to. Just last Friday Hilda Gonzales had gotten beat up and had her entire allowance stolen. And at the beginning of the term Paquito had been walking home by himself and gotten mugged. A bunch of big bullies had taken his new schoolbag complete with pencil and pen case, then left him with a swollen lip. No, sir, none of us ever walked home from school alone if we could help it. We knew it wasn't a safe thing to do. Those mean kids never bothered us as long as we stuck together. Carefully I looked around to make sure none of the bullies were in sight. Then I put some speed under my feet, took my chances, and headed for home.

Just before all the casting was completed, Miss Lovett offered me a part as one of the Pilgrim women. All I had to do was stand in the background like a zombie. It wasn't even a speaking part.

"I don't get to say one word," I protested.

"Felicidad Maldonado, you are designing the stage sets and you're assistant stage manager. I think that's quite a bit. Besides, all the speaking parts are taken."

"I'm not interested, thank you," I answered.

"You know" — Miss Lovett shook her head — "you can't be the best in everything."

I turned and left. I didn't need to play any part at all. Who cared?

Gigi came over to me the next day with a great big smile all over her face. I just turned away and made believe she wasn't there.

"Felita, are you taking the part of the Pilgrim woman?" she asked me in her sweetest voice, just like nothing had happened.

"No," I said, still not looking at her. If she thought I was going to fall all over her like those dummies, she was wasting her time.

"Oh," was all she said, and walked away. Good, I thought. I don't need her one bit!

At home Mami noticed something was wrong.

"Felita, what's the matter? You aren't going out at all. And I haven't seen Gigi for quite a while. In fact I haven't seen any of your friends."

"Nothing is the matter, Mami. I just got lots of things to do."

"You're not upset because we couldn't give you a birthday party this year, are you?" Mami asked. "You know how hard the money situation has been for us."

My birthday had been at the beginning of November. We had celebrated with a small cake after dinner, but there had been no party.

"No. It's not that," I said and meant it. Even though I had been a little disappointed, I also knew Mami and Papi had done the best they could.

"We'll make it up to you next year, Felita, you'll see."

"I don't care, Mami. It's not important now."

"You didn't go having a fight with Gigi or something? Did you?"

"Now why would I have a fight with anybody!"

"Don't raise your voice, miss," Mami said. "Sorry I asked. But you just calm down."

The play was going to be performed on the day before Thanksgiving. I made the drawings for most of the scenery. I made a barn, a church, trees and grass, cows, and a horse. I helped the others make a real scarecrow. We used a broom and old clothes. Paquito didn't get the part of Captain Miles Standish, but he made a wonderful fence out of cardboard. It looked just like a real wooden fence. Consuela brought in her mother's old leftover makeup. She did a good job of making up everybody.

By the time we set up the stage, everything looked beautiful. Gigi had tried to talk to me a few times. But I just couldn't be nice back to her. She acted like nothing had happened, like I was supposed to forget she hadn't told me she was going to read for the part! I wasn't going to forget that just because she was now Miss Popularity. She could go and stay with all her newfound friends for all I cared!

The morning of the play, at breakfast, everybody noticed how excited I was.

"Felita," Papi exclaimed, "stop jumping around like a monkey and eat your breakfast."

"She's all excited about the school play today," Mami said.

"That's right. Are you playing a part in the play?" Papi asked.

"No," I replied.

"But she's done most of the sets. Drawing and designing. Isn't that right, Felita?"

"Mami, it was no big deal."

"That's nice," said Papi. "Tell us about it."

"What kind of sets did you do?" Johnny asked.

"I don't know. Look, I don't want to talk about it."

"Boy, are you touchy today," Tito said with a laugh.

"Leave me alone!" I snapped.

"Okay." Mami stood up. "Enough. Felita, are you finished?" I nodded. "Good. Go to school. When you come back, bring home a better mood. Whatever is bothering you, no need to take it out on us." Quickly I left the table.

"Rosa," I heard Papi say, "sometimes you are too hard on her."

"And sometimes you spoil her, Alberto!" Mami snapped. "I'm not raising fresh kids."

I was glad to get out of there. Who needs them, I thought.

The play was a tremendous hit. Everybody looked wonderful and played their parts really well. The stage was brilliant with the color I had used on my drawings. The background of the countryside, the barn, and just about everything stood out clearly. Ernesto Bratter, the stage manager, said I was a good assistant. I was glad to hear that, because a couple of times I'd had to control my temper on account of his ordering me around. But it had all worked out great.

No doubt about it. Gigi was perfect as Priscilla. Even though the kids clapped and cheered for the entire cast, Gigi got more applause than anybody else. She just kept on taking a whole lot of bows.

Afterward Miss Lovett had a party for our class. We had lots of treats. There was even a record player and we all danced. We had a really good time.

Of course Priscilla, alias Gigi, was the big star. She just couldn't get enough attention. But not from me, that was for sure. After the party Gigi spoke to me.

"Your sets were really great. Everybody said the stage looked wonderful."

"Thanks." I looked away.

"Felita, are you mad at me?"

"Why should I be mad at you?"

"Well, I did get the leading part, but . . ."

"Big deal," I said. "I really don't care."

"You don't? But . . . I . . ."

"Look," I said, interrupting her, "I gotta go. I promised my mother I'd get home early. We have to go someplace."

I rushed all the way home. I didn't know why, but I was still furious at Gigi. What was worse was that I was unhappy about having those feelings. Gigi and I had been real close for as far back as I could remember. Not being able to share things with her really bothered me.

We had a great Thanksgiving. The dinner was just delicious. Abuelita brought her flan. Tío Jorge brought lots of ice cream. He always brings us kids a treat when he visits. Sometimes he even brings each one of us a small gift — a nature book or crayons for me and puzzles or sports magazines for my brothers. He's really very nice to us. One thing about him is that he's sort of quiet and doesn't talk much. Papi says that Tío Jorge has been like that as far back as he can remember.

Abuelita asked me if I wanted to go home with her that evening. Boy, was I happy to get away from Mami. I just couldn't face another day of her asking me questions about Gigi, my friends, and my whole life. It was getting to be too much!

It felt good to be with Abuelita in her apartment. Abuelita never questioned me about anything really personal unless I wanted to talk about it. She just waited, and when she sensed that I was worried or something, then she would ask me. Not like Mami. I love Mami, but she's always trying to find out every little thing that happens to me. With my abuelita sometimes we just sit and stay quiet, not talk at all. That was nice too. We fixed the daybed for me. And then Tío Jorge, Abuelita, and I had more flan as usual.

"Would you like to go to the park with me this Sunday?" Tío Jorge asked me.

"Yes."

"We can go to the zoo and later we can visit the ducks and swans by the lake."

"Great!" I said.

Whenever Tío Jorge took me to the zoo, he would tell me stories about how he, Abuelita, and their brothers and sisters had lived and worked as youngsters taking care of farm animals. These were the only times I ever heard him talk a whole lot.

"It's not just playing, you know," he would say. "Taking care of animals is hard work. Back on our farm in Puerto Rico we worked hard, but we had fun too. Every one of us children had our very own favorite pets. I had a pet goat by the name of Pepe. He used to follow me everywhere." No matter how many times he told me the same stories, I always enjoyed hearing them again.

"Well." Tío Jorge got up. "It's a date then on Sunday, yes?"

"Yes, thank you, Tío Jorge."

"Good night," he said and went off to bed.

Abuelita and I sat quietly for a while, then Abuelita spoke.

"You are getting to be a big girl now, Felita. You just turned nine years old. My goodness! But I still hope you will come to bed with your abuelita for a little while, eh?"

I got into bed and snuggled close to Abuelita. I loved her the best, more than anybody. I hadn't been to stay with her since the summer, and

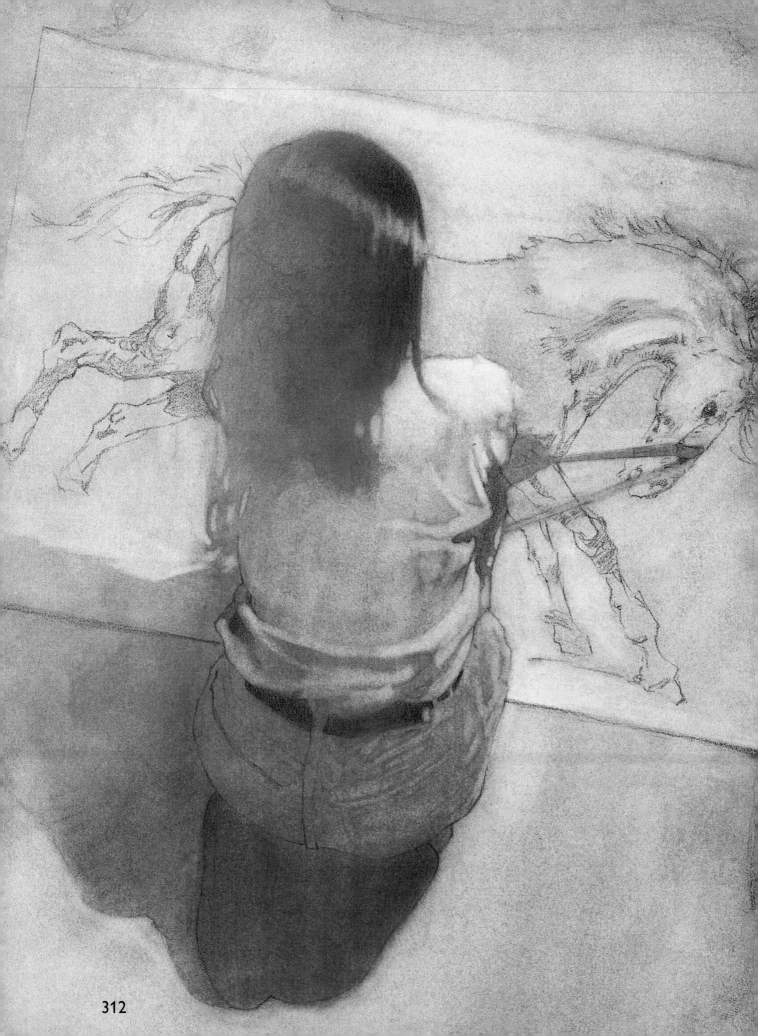

somehow this time things felt different. I noticed how tired Abuelita looked. She wasn't moving as fast as she used to. Also I didn't feel so little next to her anymore.

"Tell me, Felita, how have you been? It seems like a long time since we were together like this." She smiled her wonderful smile at me. Her dark, bright eyes looked deeply into mine. I felt her warmth and happiness.

"I'm okay, Abuelita."

"Tell me about your play at school. Rosa tells me you worked on the stage sets. Was the play a success?"

"It was. It was great. The stage looked beautiful. My drawings stood out really well. I never made such big drawings in my life. There was a farm in the country, a barn, and animals. I made it the way it used to be in the olden days of the Pilgrims. You know, how it was when they first came to America."

"I'm so proud of you. Tell me about the play. Did you act in it?"

"No." I paused. "I didn't want to."

"I see. Tell me a little about the story."

I told Abuelita all about it.

"Who played the parts? Any of your friends?"

"Some."

"Who?"

"Well, this boy Charlie Martinez played John Alden. Louie Collins played Captain Miles Standish. You don't know them. Mary Jackson played the part of the narrator. That's the person who tells the story. You really don't know any of them."

I was hoping she wouldn't ask, but she did.

"Who played the part of the girl both men love?"

"Oh, her? Gigi."

"Gigi Mercado, your best friend?" I nodded. "Was she good?"

"Yes, she was. Very good."

"You don't sound too happy about that."

"I don't care." I shrugged.

"But if she is your best friend, I should think you would care."

"I . . . I don't know if she is my friend anymore, Abuelita."

"Why do you say that?"

I couldn't answer. I just felt awful.

"Did she do something? Did you two argue?" I nodded. "Can I ask what happened?"

"Well, it's hard to explain. But what she did wasn't fair."

"Fair about what, Felita?"

I hadn't spoken about it before. Now with Abuelita it was easy to talk about it.

"Well, we all tried out for the different parts. Everybody knew what everybody was trying out for. But Gigi never told anybody she was going to try out for Priscilla. She kept it a great big secret. Even after I told her that I wanted to try for the part, she kept quiet about it. Do you know what she did say? She said I wasn't right for it . . . it was a hard part and all that bunch of baloney. She just wanted the part for herself, so she was mysterious about the whole thing. Like . . . it was . . . I don't know." I stopped for a moment, trying to figure this whole thing out. "After all, I am supposed to be her best friend . . . her very best friend. Why shouldn't she let me know that she wanted to be Priscilla? I wouldn't care. I let her know my plans. I didn't go sneaking around."

"Are you angry because Gigi got the part?"

It was hard for me to answer. I thought about it for a little while. "Abuelita, I don't think so. She was really good in the part."

"Were you as good when you tried out for Priscilla?"

"No." I looked at Abuelita. "I stunk." We both laughed.

"Then maybe you are not angry at Gigi at all."

"What do you mean?"

"Well, maybe you are a little bit . . . hurt?"

"Hurt?" I felt confused.

"Do you know what I think? I think you are hurt because your best friend didn't trust you. From what you tell me, you trusted her, but she didn't have faith in you. What do you think?"

"Yes." I nodded. "Abuelita, yes. I don't know why. Gigi and I always tell each other everything. Why did she act like that to me?"

"Have you asked her?"

"No."

"Why not? Aren't you two speaking to each other?"

"We're speaking. Gigi tried to be friendly a few times."

"Don't you want to stay her friend?"

"I do. Only she came over to me acting like . . . like nothing ever happened. And something did happen! What does she think? That she can go around being sneaky and I'm going to fall all over her? Just because she got the best part, she thinks she's special."

"And you think that's why she came over. Because she wants to be special?"

"I don't know."

"You should give her a chance. Perhaps Gigi acted in a strange way for a reason."

"She wasn't nice to me, Abuelita. She wasn't."

"I'm not saying she was. Or even that she was right. *Mira*, Felita, friendship is one of the best things in this whole world. It's one of the few things you can't go out and buy. It's like love. You can buy clothes, food, even luxuries, but there's no place I know of where you can buy a real friend. Do you?"

I shook my head. Abuelita smiled at me and waited. We were both silent for a long moment. I wondered if maybe I shouldn't have a talk with Gigi. After all, she had tried to talk to me first.

"Abuelita, do you think it's a good idea for me to . . . maybe talk to Gigi?"

"You know, that's a very good idea." Abuelita nodded.

"Well, she did try to talk to me a few times. Only there's just one thing. I won't know what to say to her. I mean, after what's happened and all."

"After so many years of being close, I am sure you could say 'Hello, Gigi. How are you?' That should be easy enough."

"I feel better already, Abuelita."

"Good," Abuelita said. "Now let's you and I get to sleep. Abuelita is tired."

"You don't have to tuck me in. I'll tuck you in instead." I got out of bed and folded the covers carefully over my side. Then I leaned over her and gave her a kiss. Abuelita hugged me real tight.

"My Felita has become a young lady," she whispered.

I kept thinking of what Abuelita had said, and on Monday I waited for Gigi after school. It was as if she knew I wanted to talk. She came over to me.

"Hello, Gigi," I said. "How are you?"

"Fine." Gigi smiled. "Wanna walk home together?"

"Let's take the long way so we can be by ourselves," I said.

We walked without saying anything for a couple of blocks. Finally I spoke.

"I wanted to tell you, Gigi, you were really great as Priscilla."

"Did you really like me? Oh, Felita, I'm so glad. I wanted you to like me, more than anybody else. Of course it was nothing compared to the sets you did. They were something special. Everybody liked them so much."

"You were right too," I said. "I wasn't very good for the part of Priscilla."

"Look." Gigi stopped walking and looked at me. "I'm sorry about . . . about the way I acted. Like, I didn't say anything to you or the others. But, well, I was scared you all would think I was silly or something. I mean, you wanted the part too. So, I figured, better not say nothing."

"I wouldn't have cared, Gigi. Honest."

"Felita . . . it's just that you are so good at a lot of things. Like, you draw just fantastic. You beat everybody at hopscotch and kick-the-can. You know about nature and animals, much more than the rest of us. Everything you do is always better than . . . what I do! I just wanted this part for me. I wanted to be better than you this time. For once I didn't wanna worry about you. Felita, I'm sorry."

I was shocked. I didn't know Gigi felt that way. I didn't feel better than anybody about anything I did. She looked so upset, like she was about to cry any minute. I could see she was miserable and I wanted to comfort her. I had never had this kind of feeling before in my whole life.

"Well, you didn't have to worry. 'Cause I stunk!" We both laughed with relief. "I think I was the worst one!"

"Oh, no, you weren't." Gigi laughed. "Jenny Fuentes was the most awful."

"Worse than me?"

"Much worse. Do you know what she sounded like? She sounded like this. 'Wha . . . wha . . . why don't you . . . speeek for your . . . yourself *Johnnnn*?" Gigi and I burst into laughter.

"And how about that dummy, Louie Collins? I didn't think he read better than Paquito."

"Right," Gigi agreed. "I don't know how he got through the play. He was shaking so much that I was scared the sets would fall right on his head."

It was so much fun, Gigi and I talking about the play and how we felt about everybody and everything. It was just like before, only better.

Meet Nicholasa Mohr

Nicholasa Mohr has been putting pictures and words together since she was a child. "From the moment my mother handed me some scrap paper, a pencil, and a few crayons," she remembers, "I discovered that by making pictures and writing letters I could create my own world."

Mohr grew up as a member of a Puerto Rican family in New York City's Hispanic neighborhood, *El Barrio*. The world of *El Barrio*, however, seldom appeared in the books Mohr read while growing up. "I had never really seen myself, my brothers, or my family in those books," she recalls. Later, Mohr was inspired to re-create the world of her childhood in books she wrote herself.

Mohr worked as an artist until an editor saw her creative word-picture "graffiti" and asked her to try writing stories. Since then she has written four children's books and has illustrated two of them. Felita's story continues in the book *Going Home.*

Meet Kevin Beilfuss

When Kevin Beilfuss (pronounced *BAIL fyoos*) was growing up, he loved sports. His favorite sport is softball — he now helps coach a girls' softball team — but football comes in a close second. When he isn't playing ball or working on his illustrations, Beilfuss plays chess. "It's a great way to take a break and exercise your mind at the same time," he says. In the future, Beilfuss hopes to add sculpture and children's book illustration to his fine-arts experience.

Act on Your Ideas

Between Friends

How did the misunderstanding between Felita and Gigi get started? How could it have been cleared up earlier? Discuss these questions in small groups. Then compare your solutions with those of other groups.

Don't Call Us, We'll Call You

According to Felita and Gigi, the auditions for the Thanksgiving play were as entertaining as the play itself. Take the parts of students in Felita's class, and role-play the auditions. Don't be afraid to ham it up!

322

Through Gigi's Eyes

All through the selection, Felita fumes over Gigi's playing Priscilla in the class play. How does Gigi feel about the way Felita is behaving? Write a dramatic monologue or letter in which Gigi explains her feelings to her own *abuelita*.

Way to Go!

In each of the selections in this theme, one or more characters overcome a problem. List the characters and the problems they solve. Who do you think does the best job solving his or her problem? Write a persuasive argument explaining your opinion.

Living with a Hearing Impairment

by the Westridge Young Writers Workshop

KIDS EXPLORE the Gifts of Children with Special Needs

WESTRIDGE YOUNG WRITERS WORKSHOP

WRITTEN BY KIDS!

Gena Perry at home with her two sisters, Michaela and Brianna

Gena (right) with her friend Christy

In Gena's Own Words

Would you like to get to know me better? I would like to get better acquainted with you, too! It's easy to do — just talk to me. I have noticed that sometimes people are afraid to talk to me because they know that I am hearing impaired. They are worried that I won't understand them. Don't worry, if I don't understand something you say, I will ask you about it.

It helps if you stand where I can see your face (it's hard to read your lips when all I can see is the back of your head!). Also, if you stand with the sun or a bright light behind your head, sometimes shadows get on your face and it is hard to see your mouth. You don't need to talk really slow or really loud. Especially, please don't exaggerate how you enunciate each word. All those things distort the words you are saying. Remember, I am used to reading lips just the way people really talk, so that is what is easiest for me to lip read.

Because I am hearing impaired, people often wonder if I can talk. Believe me, I can! In fact, sometimes my dad says I talk too much! My voice sounds a little different though. My friends say it sounds like I have a foreign accent. If you don't understand what I say, it's no big deal. Just ask me. But please include me in your conversation.

Sometimes when everybody is talking at once, I won't be able to lip read it all, and I will have to ask you what was said. *Please* don't say, "I'll tell you later," and then forget to do it. That drives me crazy! More than anything, just treat me like you would treat any other friend. I'd love to be friends with you.

Gena talking with the young authors who wrote this chapter

Questions & Answers About Hearing Impairment

We found out many things about being hearing impaired by asking questions.

What does it mean to be hearing impaired?

Some people believe that "hearing impaired" and "deaf" mean the same thing. Other people told us that when you are deaf you can't hear anything, but if you are hearing impaired you can hear something, although it might sound like just a whisper. In our book we have chosen to use the term hearing impaired because that is how Gena refers to herself.

Some people who are hearing impaired cannot understand spoken conversation without the help of a hearing aid. They may hear some sounds without the hearing aid, but these sounds are too faint to be understood.

There are many types and degrees of hearing loss. Try plugging your ears and having a friend whisper something to you. What you hear is kind of what it's like to have a hearing loss.

With other types of hearing loss, you can't hear certain frequencies. You might not hear the high tones of sounds or you might not hear the low tones. For example, you wouldn't hear all the notes of a song. Or in a conversation, you would hear silences where the tones you couldn't hear should be.

How do you become hearing impaired?

You can become hearing impaired from many different things. Most commonly people are born with a hearing impairment. If a baby has a lot of ear infections, he or she might get a hearing impairment. A person might become hearing impaired by listening to very loud music or going to a rock concert and sitting too close to the loud speaker. Adults might get a hearing loss from operating noisy machines every day at their jobs. Many people lose their hearing naturally from old age.

How long does it take to tell that a person is hearing impaired?

A person can be tested for a hearing loss in a short amount of time. If a baby is not learning to speak, does not react to loud noises, or doesn't seem to notice when someone calls his or her name, it might be a sign of hearing loss. Adults might find out later in life that they lost some of their hearing and not even know when it happened.

Gena doing her homework

Gena answering students' questions.

Do hearing impaired people ever get their hearing back?

Hearing impaired people usually do not get their hearing back and are hearing impaired their whole lives. There are some things that can be done to help hearing impaired people hear a little better. They might have surgery, or they might wear hearing aids to help make the sounds louder in their ears.

Can hearing impaired people talk?

Hearing impaired people can talk, but it takes a lot of work to learn how. Imagine trying to learn another language without ever being able to hear someone say the words correctly. Hearing impaired people that do talk sound a little different from people who can hear. Some people sound like they have foreign accents, and some exaggerate the sounds in words.

Many hearing impaired people spend a lot of time with voice therapists who help them learn to speak by watching and touching.

A hearing impaired person can feel how words are sounded by touching their teacher's throat or their own throat while they talk. Some hearing impaired people choose not to talk and prefer to use sign language or another form of communication.

What is sign language?

Sign language is a language made up of hand movements, gestures, and facial expressions. Each letter of the alphabet is signed in a different way. Just as Spanish and Japanese are complete languages, American Sign Language (ASL) is a language in itself, with thousands of signs for different words. There are many places where you can take a class and learn sign language. Check in your phone book under "Deaf" or "Hearing Impaired" to see what organizations are in your area.

How do you talk to hearing impaired people?

If they can read lips, you talk to hearing impaired people just as you would to a hearing person. If the person cannot read lips, then you could spell out what you want to say using hand signs, act out what you want to say, learn American Sign Language, or write a note.

What are some of the things that make life easier for hearing impaired people?

There are many things that help hearing impaired people. Many hearing impaired people have doorbells that flash a light instead of ringing when someone is at the door.

There are also phones that flash a light when the phone rings, and alarm clocks that light up instead of make noise.

To watch television, hearing impaired people use a system called closed captioning. A program that is closed captioned runs a special symbol on the screen to tell hearing impaired people they can use close captions. A special box called a decoder box prints the words spoken on the show at the bottom of the TV screen. This way a hearing impaired person can watch the show and read the words as they are spoken. We found out that as of 1993, new televisions have this decoder box built right inside the television. In fact, if you have a newer television, you could try this to see what it is like.

CATASTROPHE!

CATASTROPHE!

CONTENTS

THE POWER OF NATURE

PAPERBACK **PLUS**

Head for the Hills!

by Paul Robert Walker

On May 31, 1889, the people of Johnstown, Pennsylvania, had almost no warning when the dam above their town burst.

In the same book . . .

More about modern-day dams and how to build an embankment dam of your own

Books to Explore

Clouds of Terror
by *Catherine A. Welch*
An 1870s Minnesota farm family faces catastrophe in the form of swarms of grasshoppers.

The Disaster of the *Hindenburg:* The Last Flight of the Greatest Airship Ever Built
by *Shelley Tanaka*
A fourteen-year-old cabin boy recalls the wonders and the tragic end of the *Hindenburg.*

Earthquake! A Story of Old San Francisco
by *Kathleen Kudlinski*
It is April 18, 1906. San Francisco is struck by a devastating earthquake and fire. Can Phillip save the family's horses and himself?

Spill! The Story of the *Exxon Valdez*
by *Terry Carr*
An account of a crude-oil catastrophe in Alaska's Prince William Sound

Hurricane!
by *Jules Archer*
These devastating storms cause loss of life and destruction of property. Can they be prevented?

The *Titanic*
by *Deborah Kent*
The tragic, ironic story of the "unsinkable" *Titanic*'s first — and last — voyage

PATRICIA LAUBER

VOLCANO
The Eruption and Healing of Mount St. Helens

PAPERBACK **PLUS**

Volcano: The Eruption and Healing of Mount St. Helens
by Patricia Lauber

A chronicle of the explosion of Mount St. Helens, the resulting devastation, and nature's remarkable, continuing recovery

In the same book . . .
Human stories from Mount St. Helens, and fact and folklore about volcanoes

While watching a sitcom on TV, Dan Hatch and his friend Arthur have heard tornado warnings for their town of Grand Island, Nebraska. Now even Minerva, Dan's cat, is acting nervous. Dan's mom has gone to check on Mrs. Smiley, an elderly neighbor, and his dad is away at Grandma and Grandpa Hatch's farm. That leaves the two boys alone to look after Dan's baby brother, Ryan. They have a flashlight and blankets in case of an emergency, but there has never been a wind as strong as this one!

NIGHT OF THE TWISTERS

BY IVY RUCKMAN

"Whooeeeee!" Arthur exclaimed. "Sounds like my bull-roarer outside!"

I hurried downstairs with the emergency stuff and set it on the bathroom counter. Minerva went with me, scurrying across my feet on the steps, acting the way she does when she wants attention.

I picked her up by the middle, smoothed down her stripes, and balanced her on the glass door of the shower. Usually she'll do a tightrope act for me, but she only yowled and jumped off. After giving me her mean jungle look, she sat down to dig at her ear.

"You got a flea in there?" I asked, bending to give her a good scratching.

She didn't like that, either.

Upstairs, Arthur was hooting and hollering again. I decided I was missing all the good parts, so I hurried up the two short flights of steps, with Minerva dashing ahead of me.

Sometime in there, in the middle of all that comedy on the screen, the siren began. Now, *that* is a very sobering sound. It's unlike anything else, having its own built-in chill factor.

I thought of Mom first. She'd hear it and come back, I told myself.

Then I thought of Dad and how far the farm was from town. They wouldn't even hear the siren out there.

In half a second, I was at the phone, dialing 555–2379.

Four rings. Then I heard Grandma's voice.

"Grandma!" I shouted into the phone. "Where have you been? There's a tornado just north of G. I. The siren's going, can you hear it?"

339

A voice said something, but it sounded so far away.

"Talk louder, Grandma! I can't hear you."

The voice faded away entirely. I wasn't even sure it was Grandma's now.

"There's a tornado coming! Can you hear me?"

Finally, there wasn't anything on the line but the sound of another phone ringing very faintly, as if it were in New York or someplace far away. I couldn't figure it out.

By then, Arthur was standing next to me. I was just about to hand him the phone when, abruptly, the siren stopped. It didn't taper off, it just quit, as if someone snipped it with scissors. Except for the TV, everything around us suddenly seemed very still.

"Hey," he said, raising his eyebrows, "they changed their minds."

I hung up the phone. I didn't know what was happening.

"Maybe they got their weather signals crossed," he suggested happily. "They could, you know. I read a book once about that happening, where this whole fleet of fishing boats put out to sea . . . " he rattled on.

I ran to the door, thinking I might see Mom pulling into the driveway, but no luck.

"It's quit blowing," I called over my shoulder to Arthur.

Sure enough, the wind had died down. Maybe the storm wouldn't amount to anything after all.

That nice comforting thought had hardly entered my mind when the siren blared forth again. With a jolt, I remembered what Mom had told us to do.

"We always turn on the radio," Arthur said, already on his way to the kitchen. "You want me to? I'll get the weather station."

I was hardly listening. I hurried down the bedroom hallway to Ryan's room at the end. I hated like everything to get him up. He'd cry. I knew he'd wake up and cry. Without Mom, Arthur and I would have him screaming in our ears the whole time.

When I saw him in his crib, peacefully sleeping on the side of his face, his rear end in the air, I just didn't have the heart to wake him up. I'd wait a minute or two. Mom would be back. Anyway, it's blowing over, I told myself, it won't last.

Quietly, I closed the door behind me.

That's when the lights started flickering.

In the hallway, I practically had a head-on with Arthur, who was coming at me real fast. The look on his face scared me.

"There's no . . . there's no . . . "

"*What?*"

"There's no radio reception anymore. It just went dead! This guy . . . He kept saying, 'Tornado alert, tornado alert!' Then it went dead."

We rushed back to the living room. The TV was flashing these big letters that filled the entire screen: CD . . . CD . . . CD . . .

"What's it mean?" Arthur cried.

"Civil Defense Emergency!" I whirled around. "I'm getting Ryan!"

The lights flickered again.

At the same time we heard these really strange sounds that stopped us in our tracks. They were coming from the bathroom and the kitchen. Sucking sounds. The drains were sucking! I felt this awful pulling in my ears, too, as if there were vacuums on both sides of my head.

"I've got to go home!" Arthur cried all of a sudden, bolting for the door.

I ran after him. "You're not — you can't!" I grabbed the back of his T-shirt, hauled him around, and pushed him toward the stairs. "Get *down* there. I have to get Ryan! Now *go!*"

I don't know what I'd have done if he hadn't minded me. We were catching the fear from each other, and even though the siren was screaming on and off again, so I didn't know what it was telling us, I knew we had to take cover fast.

The lights went out for good just before I reached Ryan's room.

I smashed face first into Ryan's butterfly mobile. That's how I knew I was at the crib. I felt for him, got my hands under his nightshirt and diaper, rolled him over. I lifted him, but we didn't get far. He was caught in the mobile, his arm or his head . . . I couldn't see . . . I couldn't get him loose. . . .

"Mom!" I yelled, though I knew she wasn't there.

I tried to lay him down again, but he was so tangled, part of him was still up in the air. He started to cry.

"Wait, Ryan, I'll get you out!" But I couldn't.

Finally, holding him with my left arm, I climbed onto the side of the crib. My right hand followed the string up the mobile, way up to the hook. I yanked it loose. The whole thing came crashing down on top of us as I jumped backward off the crib.

The plastic butterfly poking me was poking Ryan, too, but I didn't care. The tornado was close, and I knew it. Both my ears had popped, and I had this crazy fear that those drains, sucking like monsters now, would get us if the storm didn't.

Arthur was at the bottom of the stairs, waiting. Thank God he'd found the flashlight! I jumped the last half-flight to the floor.

"Hurry!" I screamed. I swung into the doorway of the bathroom, with Arthur right behind me. We crouched under the towel rack.

"Shine it here, on Ryan," I gasped. "He's caught in this thing." By now Ryan was kicking and screaming, and his eyes were big in the light.

Once we got the mess of strings free of Ryan's sweaty nightshirt, Arthur kicked the mobile against the wall by the toilet.

"I have to go home!" he cried. "They won't go to the basement. Mama never does."

The beam of light bounced around the blackness of the bathroom as Arthur scrambled to his feet, but I grabbed and held on to him.

"You can't go! It's here! Can't you feel it?"

The siren quit again as I pulled him back down and threw my leg over him. The flashlight clattered to the floor and rolled away from us.

We heard it next. The lull. The deadliest quiet ever, one that makes you think you might explode. The heat in that room built until I couldn't get my breath.

Then I began to hear noises. A chair scraping across the kitchen floor upstairs.

"Your mom's back!" Arthur said, pushing at my leg.

I knew it wasn't my mother moving the chair.

The noises got worse. It seemed as if every piece of furniture was moving around up there . . . big, heavy things, smashing into each other.

A window popped.

Crash! Another.

Glass, shattering — everywhere — right next to us in the laundry room.

I pulled a towel down over Ryan and held him tight. If he was still crying, I didn't know it because I was *feeling* the sucking this time. It was like something trying to lift my body right up off the floor.

Arthur felt it, too. "Mother of God!" He crossed himself. "We're going to die!"

Ten seconds more and that howling, shrieking tornado was upon us.

"The blanket!" I screamed at Arthur's ear.

He pulled it down from the countertop and we covered ourselves, our hands shaking wildly. I wasn't worrying about my mom then or my dad or Mrs. Smiley. Just us. Ryan and Arthur and me, huddled together there on the floor.

The roaring had started somewhere to the east, then came bearing down on us like a hundred freight trains. Only that twister didn't move on. It stationed itself right overhead, making the loudest noise I'd ever heard, whining worse than any jet. There was a tremendous crack, and I felt the wall shudder behind us. I knew then our house was being ripped apart. Suddenly chunks of ceiling were falling on our heads.

We'll be buried! was all I could think.

At that moment, as plain as anything above that deafening roar, I heard my dad's voice: *The shower's the safest place.*

I didn't question hearing it. Holding Ryan against me with one arm, I began crawling toward the shower stall. I reached back and yanked at Arthur's shirt. Somehow we got inside with the blanket. Another explosion, and the glass shower door shattered all over the bathroom floor.

We pulled the blanket over our heads and I began to pray. Out loud, though I couldn't hear my own voice: "God help us, God help us." I said it over and over, into Ryan's damp hair, my lips moving against his head. I knew Arthur was praying, too, jammed there into my side. I could feel Ryan's heart beating through his undershirt against mine. *My* heart was thanking God for making me go back for him, but not in words. Outside those places where our bodies touched, there was nothing but terror as the roar of that tornado went on and on. I thought the world was coming to an end, *had* come to an end, and so would we, any minute.

Then I felt Ryan's fat fingers close around one of mine. He pulled my hand to his mouth and started sucking on my finger. It made me cry. The tears ran down my cheeks and onto his head. With the whole world blowing to pieces around us, Ryan took my hand and made me feel better.

Afterward, neither Arthur nor I was able to say how long we huddled there in the basement shower.

"A tornado's forward speed is generally thirty to fifty miles an hour," the meteorologist had told us.

Our tornado's forward speed was zero. It parked right there on Sand Crane Drive. Five minutes or ten, we couldn't tell, but it seemed like an hour. Roaring and humming and shrieking, that twister was right on top of us. I'll never be that scared again as long as I live. Neither will Arthur.

Meet IVY RUCKMAN

On June 3, 1980, tornadoes smashed through the town of Grand Island, Nebraska. Ivy Ruckman had been there only three weeks earlier, visiting a cousin. When she learned about the disaster, "the goose bumps wouldn't go away," she said. So Ruckman decided to write about it. She pored over newspaper accounts and spent two weeks in Grand Island, interviewing townspeople.

"In the end," she said, "my best interviews were with elementary school students." The result of those interviews and all her research is the book *Night of the Twisters*.

A native of Nebraska, Ruckman now makes her home in Salt Lake City, Utah. She is also the author of *No Way Out* and *What's an Average Kid Like Me Doing Way Up Here?*

Meet JULIE DOWNING

Julie Downing grew up just west of "Tornado Alley," in Colorado. Skiing, hiking, and acting were among her favorite activities. By the time she was in her teens, Downing was expanding her artistic interests by teaching art to neighborhood children. A college course in book illustration convinced her to pursue a career as an illustrator. Downing has illustrated trolls in *A Ride on the Red Mare's Back*, by Ursula K. Le Guin, and baseball players in Matt Christopher's *Supercharged Infield*.

353

Brace Yourself for a BRAINSTORM!

Write a Dialogue

Brother to Brother

Ryan Hatch was just a baby during the night of the twisters. What questions do you think he might ask his brother when he is older? With a partner, write and act out Ryan's questions and Dan's answers about that night.

Create a Picture

As You See It

What pictures come to mind from reading *Night of the Twisters*? Draw, paint, or use other art materials to show your favorite scene in the selection.

Tornado Talk

Think about Arthur's words and actions during the tornado. What advice would you give Arthur and his family about what to do the next time a twister strikes?

Front-Page News

How might the newspapers of Grand Island, Nebraska, have covered the terrible event of June 3, 1980? Use information from the selection to write a newspaper article about the tornado, answering the questions *who*, *what*, *when*, *where*, *why*, and *how*.

TORNADO!

by Arnold Adoff

On April 3, 1974, a
powerful tornado struck Xenia,
Ohio. The tornado was part of a
"once-in-a-century" outbreak of 148
twisters that roared through thirteen
states. By the following day, three hundred
people had been killed and 5400 injured.
Arnold Adoff was living in the nearby
town of Yellow Springs when the
Xenia tornado struck.

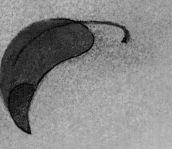

if you hold

your self
      tight together
and listen

      you can hear the danger

if you hold
your self
      tight together
and listen

      afraid can be full
         of life

  my feet are hot

  and my hands
      are
      ice

      and
      wet

  and my hands
  are
      holding
      my
      hands

inside the house

inside
  the noise
we seem
  too small
for
the
  wild
  wind

  dark
  time
and
the
 clock has
  stopped
but
 it
 is
 tornado
  time

it moved

                down the main street
                and along the railroad
                                tracks
all across the
                        flat
new section
of the town

new streets of houses
old streets

up the highway
to the college

to the end

                                they

                        figured
                that in
                        80
                seconds
                        it was here
                                had been
                and gone
                        away

NATURAL FORCES:
FOUR BIG ONES

Hurricane

Hurricanes form over warm tropical seas. Wind speeds may reach as high as 220 miles an hour, powerful enough to drive a board through a tree trunk.

Names of hurricanes are drawn from alphabetical lists. When a killer storm hits land, its name is taken off the lists forever.

Cross Section of a Hurricane

Cumulonimbus clouds

Eye wall   Eye wall

Eye

Earthquake

In January 1994 a killer earthquake struck Los Angeles, California. It leveled buildings, sparked numerous fires, and toppled some of the many freeway overpasses in the Los Angeles area.

In 1811 and 1812, a series of enormous earthquakes rocked the midwestern and eastern United States. How enormous? People felt some of the shocks over one thousand miles away. The ground sank to form an eighteen-mile-long lake in northwestern Tennessee, and the Mississippi River flowed backward for a time.

Fire

About 90 percent of forest fires in the United States are started by people. Lightning is the second leading cause.

Even a quarter mile away from a blazing fire, the air temperature can be a blistering 120°F.

The most devastating fire in the history of the United States occurred on October 8, 1871, in Peshtigo, Wisconsin. Over 1500 people died in the blaze when hot, dry winds turned a forest fire into a firestorm. Firestorms, also known as "blowup" fires, are huge columns of fire. They are pushed upward by strong air currents that can scatter burning debris for miles around the firestorm itself.

Flood

Cross Section of a Flood Plain

Flood plain

Flood level

Levee   **Average water level**   Levee

Farmers like to cultivate the rich land of a river's flood plain. Consequently, flood damage to property can be extensive if levees fail.

Worldwide, floods kill more people every year than tornadoes, hurricanes, lightning, or windstorms.

Flash floods happen quickly, with little or no warning. In the western United States, flash floods often sweep through canyons during sudden rainstorms.

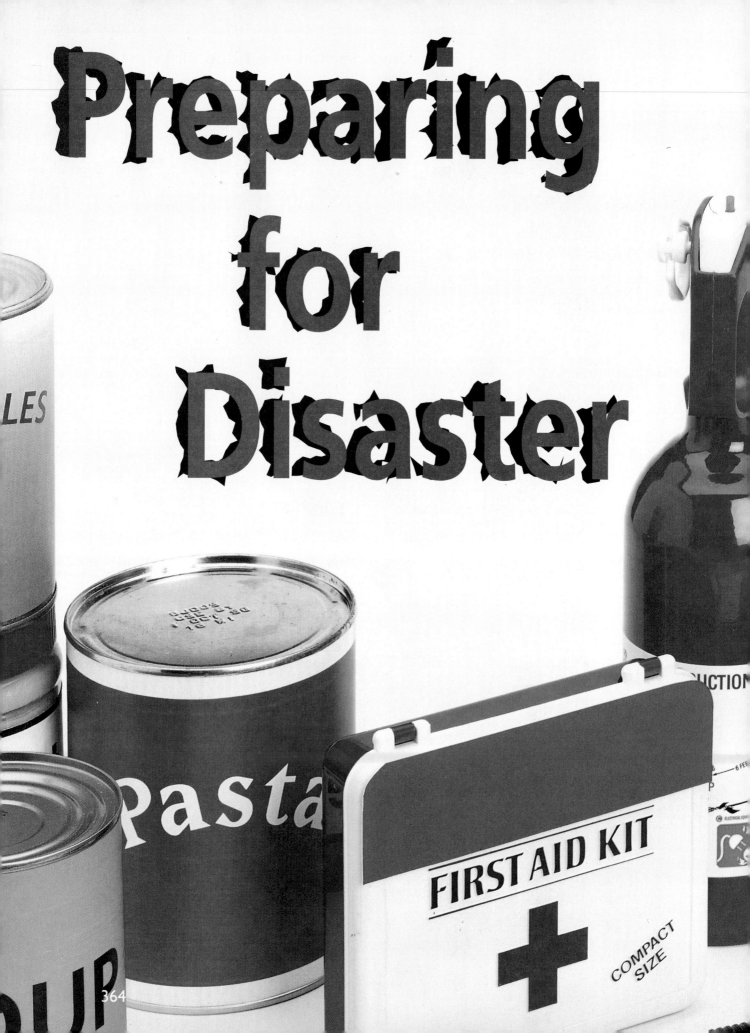

Preparing for Disaster

Plan and Get Ready

American Red Cross

...erned about. They can happen in most states . . .
...f your household complete

Earthqua...
anytime ...
each of t...
Plan.

you ...

Bedr...

Livi...

Ot...

Are You Ready for an Earthquake?

Here's what you can do to prepare for such an emergency

☐ Prepare a Home Earthquake Plan

✓ Select a place everyone would meet following an earthquake.

✓ Designate an out-of-town family member or friend to be your family contact person . . . so that each of you can call him or her to say you're safe or to relay messages.

✓ Conduct periodic earthquake drills . . . and review your Home Earthquake Plan now and then.

✓ Make these simple improvements around your home—
  • Strap the water heater to a wall.
  • Bolt bookcases and other tall, heavy furniture to the wall.
  • Put bolts or latches on cabinet doors.

✓ Take a First Aid/CPR course from your local Red Cross chapter.

☐ Prepare an Earthquake Safety Kit

✓ Assemble an Earthquake Safety Kit containing—
  • First aid kit
  • Fire extinguisher
  • Canned food and a can opener
  • Bottled water
  • Sturdy shoes and work gloves
  • Extra blankets and trash bags
  • Essential medications
  • Battery-powered radio, a flashlight, and extra batteries

✓ Also include in the kit written instructions on how to turn off your home's utilities.

☐ When the shaking begins . . .

✓ If you are inside, go only a few steps to a safety spot you have already picked. It could be a heavy desk or table you could crouch under (and

hold on to) to be safe from falling objects . . . or just an inside corner of a room. Pick a spot away from windows, bookcases, or tall, heavy furniture that could fall on you.

✓ If you live in a high-rise building, don't be surprised if the fire alarms and sprinklers go off during a quake.

✓ If you are outside, find a clear spot away from buildings, trees, and power lines.

✓ If you are in a car, drive to a clear spot (as above) and stay in the car until the shaking stops.

☐ After the shaking stops . . .

✓ Be prepared for aftershocks.

✓ Check people for injuries. Give first aid.

✓ Inspect your home for damage.

✓ Listen to the radio for instructions.

✓ Go to a Red Cross shelter if your home is unsafe.

About
SEYMOUR SIMON

Seymour Simon has written science books about nearly everything under the sun — and beyond! But the author of nonfiction titles like *Our Solar System* and *Storms* doesn't just write books that stick to "the facts." He has also written two series of fiction books. One is about a whiz kid named Chip Rogers, who uses his computer to solve mysteries. The other is about a boy named Einstein Anderson, whose science skills help him solve problems.

These characters sound a lot like Seymour Simon himself, who went to the Bronx High School of Science and was president of the Junior Astronomy Club. Did Simon have any other hobbies besides science when he was a boy? "I've always written — even while I was a high school student," he says. And he had another boyhood interest that should surprise no one: reading science fiction.

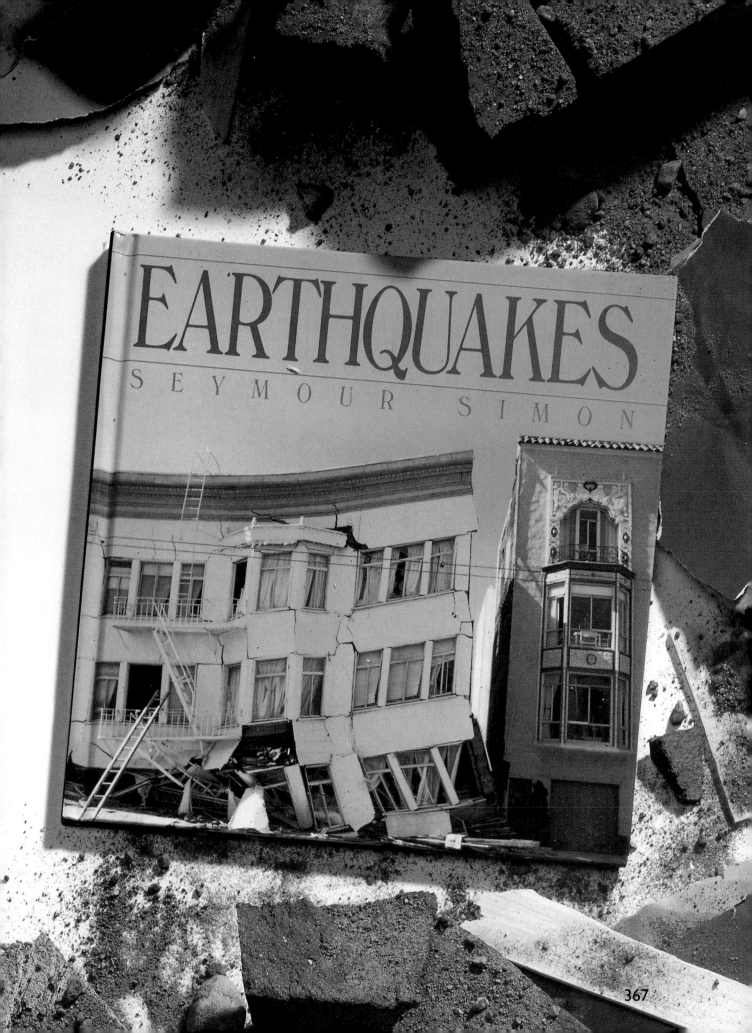

EARTHQUAKES

BY SEYMOUR SIMON

The earth beneath our feet usually feels solid and firm. Yet a million times each year — an average of once every thirty seconds — somewhere around the world the ground shakes and sways. We call this an earthquake.

Most earthquakes are too small to be noticed by people; only sensitive scientific instruments record their passage. But hundreds of quakes every year are strong enough to change the face of the land. A medium-sized earthquake near Seattle, Washington, bent these railroad tracks into twisted ribbons of steel. A larger earthquake can cause enormous destruction.

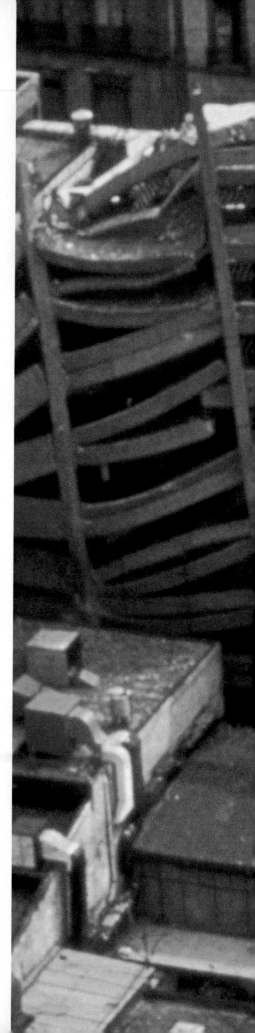

On the morning of September 19, 1985, a major earthquake struck Mexico City. It killed about ten thousand people and injured at least another twenty thousand. Hundreds of buildings were destroyed, including homes and stores, hotels and hospitals, and schools and businesses. This multilevel parking garage (left side of photo) collapsed like a house of cards, while some of the neighboring buildings suffered only slight damage.

371

BLOCKS AT REST   STRESS BUILDS UP   THE ENERGY IS RELEASED
                      ALONG THE FAULT

Most earthquakes take place in the earth's crust, a five- to thirty-mile-deep layer of rocks that covers the earth. Cracks in the rocks, called faults, run through the crust. The rocks on one side of a fault push against the rocks on the other side, causing energy to build up. For years, friction will hold the rocks in place. But finally, like a stretched rubber band, the rocks suddenly snap past each other. The place where this happens is called the focus of an earthquake.

From the focus, the energy of the quake speeds outward through the surrounding rocks in all directions. The shocks may last for less than a second for a small quake to several minutes for a major one. Weaker shocks, called aftershocks, can follow a quake on and off for days or weeks.

Sections of the crust have slipped past each other along two fault lines and offset this ridge in Wyoming (left). This kind of sideways movement is called a strike-slip fault.

Sometimes one side of a fault will slip higher than the other. This is what happened along this highway in the Mojave Desert of California (right). This kind of up-and-down movement is called a dip-slip fault.

Four out of five of the world's earthquakes take place along the rim of the Pacific Ocean, a zone called the Pacific Ring of Fire. Alaska, California, Mexico, the west coasts of Central and South America, and the east coasts of China, Japan, and New Zealand are all located within the Pacific Ring of Fire. Another major earthquake zone stretches through Italy, Greece, and Turkey to the Middle East and into Asia.

In the United States, almost half of the quakes each year occur in southern California. In other sections of the United States, earthquakes are rare. About the only places that have never recorded an earthquake are the southern parts of Florida, Alabama, and Texas.

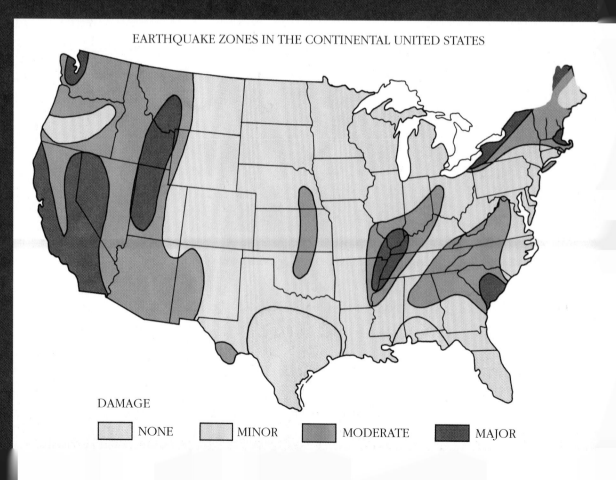

EARTHQUAKE ZONES IN THE CONTINENTAL UNITED STATES

DAMAGE

NONE   MINOR   MODERATE   MAJOR

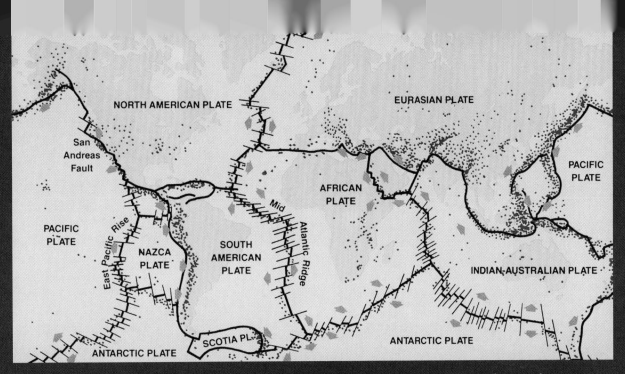

This map shows the plates in the earth's crust. The red dots indicate places where earthquakes have occurred.

Why do most earthquakes in the United States occur in California? The answer lies deep within the earth. The earth's solid rocky crust floats on the mantle, an 1,800-mile-thick layer of very heavy, melted rock that moves up and down and around. Over the years, these movements have cracked the crust like an eggshell into a number of huge pieces called plates.

The plates float slowly about on the mantle up to four inches a year. As the plates move, they run into or pull away from each other, producing enormous strains in the rocks along their edges. The United States and Canada are riding on the North American plate, which is slowly moving into the Pacific plate. The colliding plates are what causes most of the earthquakes along the West Coast. But earthquakes can occur anywhere there are stresses in underlying rocks.

375

The San Andreas Fault is the boundary line between the North American and the Pacific plates. It winds seven hundred miles through southern California to just north of San Francisco, where it dives under the Pacific Ocean. Along the way, it slashes under houses and dams, across deserts and farms, and through towns and cities where more than 20 million people live. Dozens of small- to medium-sized quakes occur along this fault each year. Scientists think that a huge, deadly earthquake will strike along the San Andreas Fault by the end of this century.

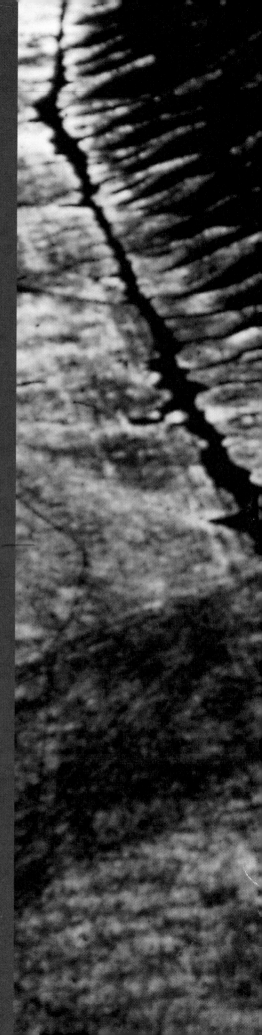

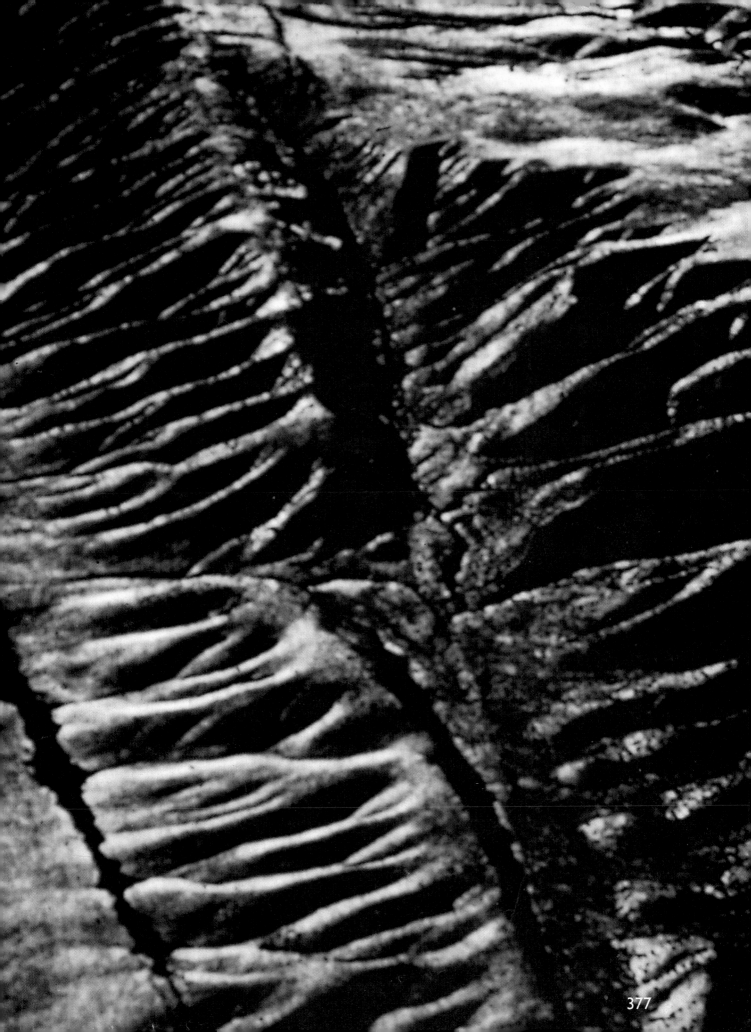

The 1906 San Francisco earthquake was one of the most violent earthquakes ever recorded. The gigantic quake was felt over an area of 375,000 miles, more than twice the size of California. More than three thousand people lost their lives in the quake and the following fires. This view (above) shows San Francisco in flames hours after the quake. The fires alone destroyed 28,000 buildings in the city.

This fence (right) was broken and offset eight feet by the movement of the San Andreas Fault during the 1906 earthquake. Besides the widespread strike (side-to-side) slip along the fault, there was also a dip (up-and-down) slip of as much as three feet in some places.

How do you measure and compare the sizes of earthquakes? The size cannot be judged solely by the damage to buildings or the number of people killed. That's because a medium quake close to a large city will cause more destruction than will a larger quake in an unpopulated area.

Seismographs are the instruments that scientists use to measure earthquake shocks. A modern seismograph (below) can record a tiny earth tremor thousands of miles away. The tremor shows as a wiggly line traced on a turning drum. The bigger the quake, the larger the wiggle.

There are hundreds of seismograph stations all over the world that time the arrival of earthquake waves. Scientists use the measurements to find an earthquake's force, its focus underground, and its epicenter, the place on the ground just above the focus.

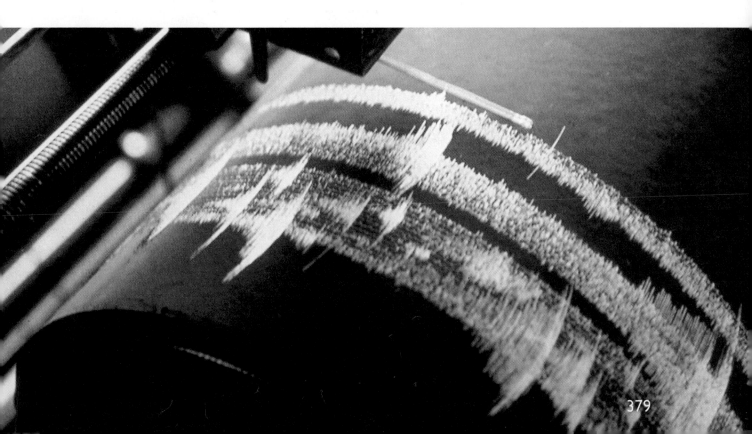

Scientists use the Richter Scale to measure an earthquake's magnitude, the amount of energy it releases. Each number on the Richter Scale stands for an earthquake that is ten times more powerful than the number below it. You would hardly notice a magnitude-2 quake, but a magnitude-3 quake is ten times greater and easily felt by everyone. The scale has no upper end, but any quake that registers 6 or more is considered a major quake.

The Armenian earthquake of December 7, 1988, measured 6.9 and was followed, four minutes later, by a 5.8 aftershock. Dozens of other quakes occurred in the area over the next months. The quake and aftershocks caused tens of thousands of deaths and injuries, terrible destruction, and made half a million people homeless.

381

Scientists use another scale to measure the effects of an earthquake. The Mercali Intensity Scale uses observations of the quake damage to rate it on a scale ranging from I, where the effects are scarcely noticeable, to XII, where damage is total and the ground heaves in waves. Usually, the intensity is greatest near the center of the quake and smaller the farther away from the center. But other factors, such as the soil in the area and the construction of the buildings, are also important.

For example, the earthquake that shook the San Francisco area in October 1989 (during the World Series) measured 7.1 on the Richter Scale. On the Mercali scale, it measured X to XI in the Marina district, where the houses are built on loose soil, but only VI or VII in other parts of the city, where the houses suffered much less damage.

Sand sometimes bubbles up during earthquakes, gushing water and soil like miniature mud volcanoes. These "sand boils" are particularly dangerous to buildings. In places where water is close to the surface, sandy layers turn into quicksand and structures crumble. During the 1989 San Francisco quake, sand boils erupted in basements, yards, and beneath houses all over the Marina district.

These apartment houses in Niigata, Japan, tumbled as a result of an earthquake in 1964. The leaning buildings were caused when the soil beneath the foundations turned to quicksand. About a third of the city sunk by as much as six feet when the soil dropped away.

On the afternoon of Good Friday, March 27, 1964, Anchorage, Alaska, was shaken apart by the most violent earthquake ever recorded in the United States. It measured 8.4 on the Richter Scale. Government Hill Elementary School was split in two when the ground beneath it dropped. Houses began sliding apart, cracks in the pavement opened and closed like huge jaws, the ground rolled in huge waves. In the first three days after the quake, three hundred aftershocks shook the buildings that remained standing.

The Good Friday earthquake brought another type of destruction along the coastline. The focus of the quake was deep beneath the waters of Prince William Sound in the Gulf of Alaska. The quake acted like a giant paddle churning the waters.

Huge quake-formed sea waves, called tsunamis, battered the land for hours. An entire section of the waterfront at the port of Seward cracked off and slid into the ocean. Boats were overturned, buildings broke apart, and everything was left in a tangled mess.

The tsunamis moved across the Pacific at speeds of hundreds of miles an hour, reaching as far as Hawaii and even Japan, four thousand miles away.

Scientists have learned much about earthquakes and their effects. They can measure even the slightest movements along faults. But we need to know much more about earthquakes before we can predict weeks or even days in advance when a big one will hit. Until then, proper building design can help lessen their effects. We now know that houses in earthquake-prone areas should be built on solid rock and not on sand, for example. In California and Japan, new houses are designed to be earthquake-resistant.

It also helps to know what to do when an earthquake strikes. If you are indoors, get under a heavy table, desk, or bed. Stay away from windows, mirrors, or high cabinets. If you are in a high building, stay out of the elevators and stairways. If you are outdoors, move away from high buildings, walls, power poles, or any other tall objects. If possible, move to an open area. Above all, remain calm and don't worry. The chances of your being hurt in a quake are very, very slight.

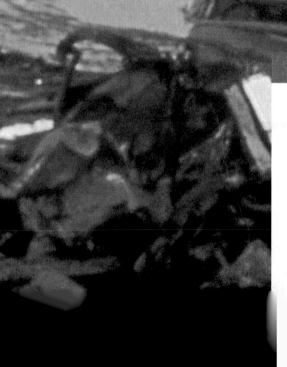

EARTHSHAKING IDEAS!

Have a Discussion

Shake, Rattle, and Roll

Would your knees *shake*? Would your teeth *rattle*? Would the floor *roll* beneath your feet? If you've never experienced an earthquake, meet with a few classmates and discuss how it might feel to be in one. If you have been through an earthquake, discuss how it *did* feel.

Broadcast a Report

Eyewitness at the Epicenter

Cover an earthshaking catastrophe . . . live! Prepare a news report describing one of the earthquakes mentioned in the selection. Use an audio or video recorder to interview classmates acting as eyewitnesses. Then broadcast your report for the rest of the class.

It's Your Fault

Make waves by creating your own earthquake. Use clay to make a three-dimensional model that shows what happens along a fault line during an earthquake. Use the diagram on page 372 to help you out.

Demolition Derby

If an earthquake were to compete against a tornado in a demolition derby, which natural disaster would win? Find out by making a chart that compares and contrasts the damage done by earthquakes and tornadoes.

VOLCANOES

A Research Report by Alida Verduzco

Would you want to live near a volcano? When she researched volcanoes for her report, Alida learned that volcanic eruptions can have good effects as well as bad.

Alida Verduzco

Olive Street Elementary School
Porterville, California

"The hardest part was gathering all the facts," Alida said after she wrote this report in the fifth grade. "I had to decide which parts of the books were useful. But I felt proud when I was finished, and I learned many things about volcanoes that I didn't know."

Alida has also written legends and essays. She enjoys drawing, coloring, doing arts and crafts activities, and playing sports. She has thought about becoming a lawyer, a math teacher, an artist, or a scientist.

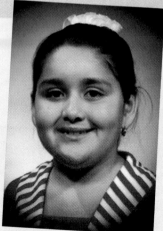

CD-ROM
ENCYCLOPEDIA
M–Z

Volcanoes

Volcanoes have caused some of the world's worst disasters, but they can be helpful as well as harmful to people and other living things. They can hurt and even kill, but they can also help things grow. Knowing what volcanoes are and how they are formed makes it easier to understand what a volcano can do.

Volcanoes are openings in the earth's crust. Lava flows out of these openings in the earth's crust. Not only lava comes out but sometimes gases, ash, dust, and rocks called volcanic bombs come shooting out.

The crust of the earth is the top layer. The crust is like the peel of an orange, but in some places it is very thick and in some places it is very thin. In some places it is so thin that the crust is cracked. Most volcanoes are formed along lines where the earth's crust is thin.

Underneath the crust, there is a layer called the mantle. The rock in the mantle of the earth is very hot and even melts. This rock is called magma. The magma also contains gases.

This magma tries to bubble over like boiling water that tries to run out of the top of a pan. But the magma cannot escape easily because of the earth's crust. So the magma pushes out of the part of the earth's crust that is thin and cracked like the shell of an egg. The moving magma then makes the sections of the crust either move away from each other or smash together until there is an opening. Then the magma escapes through the opening.

When it comes out of the opening, it is not called magma anymore, but instead it is called lava. When the lava cools, it sometimes creates an upside-down cone shape. But not all volcanoes become cone-shaped.

Volcanoes can kill many living things. When a volcano erupts, it throws out many gases and ash that poison the air that people, animals, and plants need to breathe. Also, the lava that the volcano throws out may burn and kill people.

Volcanoes can also destroy buildings and sometimes even whole cities. A volcano in Italy that killed many people and buried a city was Vesuvius, which erupted in the year 79.

Volcanoes can also help living things. When the lava cools down on the land, it works as fertilizer for plants and crops. Also, the lava material is used to build roads and other things. In some places people even use underground steam near volcanic areas for energy. In Reykjavik, Iceland, many people heat their homes with hot water piped from underground.

In conclusion, volcanoes are openings in the earth's crust that have lava, ash, dust, rock fragments, and gases shooting out of them. They can hurt people and other living things when they erupt, but they can also be helpful.

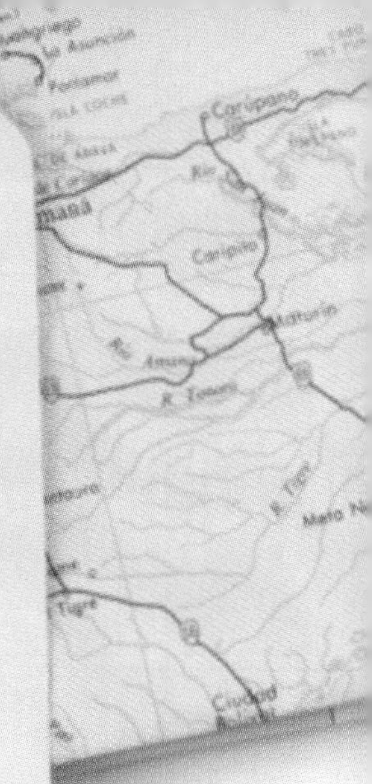

Bibliography

Cashman, Katharine V. "Volcano." World Book Encyclopedia. 1994 ed.

Knapp, Brian. Volcano. Austin: Steck, 1990.

Thompson, Brenda and Cynthia Overbeck. Volcanoes: A First Fact Book. Minneapolis: Lerner, 1977.

Wood, Jenny. Volcanoes: Fire from Below. Milwaukee: Gareth Stevens, 1991.

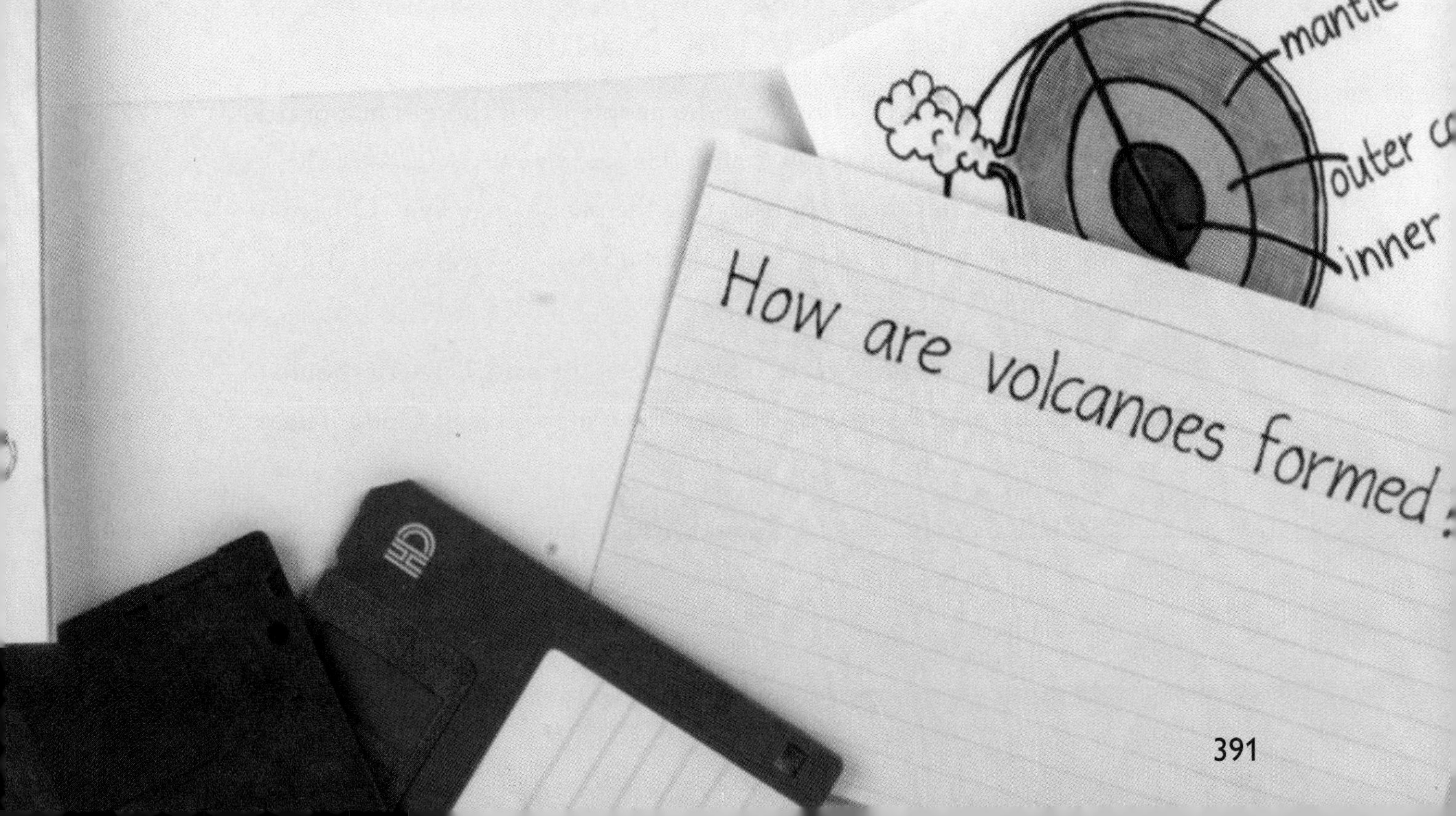

crust
mantle
outer c
inner

How are volcanoes formed

KEEPERS OF THE EARTH
Native American Stories and Environmental Activities for Children

Michael J. Caduto and Joseph Bruchac
Foreword by N. Scott Momaday
Illustrations by John Kahionhes Fadden and Carol Wood

HOW THUNDER AND EARTHQUAKE MADE OCEAN

told by Joseph Bruchac

THUNDER lived at Sumig.

One day he said, "How shall the people live if there is just prairie there? Let us place the ocean there." He said to EARTHQUAKE, "I want to have water there, there so that the people may live. Otherwise they will have nothing to live on." He said to EARTHQUAKE, "What do you think?"

EARTHQUAKE thought. "That is true," he said. "There should be water there. Far off I see it. I see the water. It is at Opis. There are salmon there and water."

"Go," said THUNDER. "Go with Kingfisher, the one who sits there by the water. Go and get water at Opis. Get the water that is to come here."

Then the two of them went. Kingfisher and EARTHQUAKE went to see the water. They went to get the water at Opis. They had two abalone shells that THUNDER had given to them. "Take these shells," THUNDER had said. "Collect the water in them."

First Kingfisher and EARTHQUAKE went to the north end of the world. There EARTHQUAKE looked around. "This will be easy," he said. "It will be easy for me to sink this land." Then EARTHQUAKE ran around. He ran around and the ground sank. It sank there at the north end of the world.

Then Kingfisher and EARTHQUAKE started for Opis. They went to the place at the end of the water. They made the ground sink behind them as they went. At Opis they saw all kinds of seals and salmon. They saw all the kinds of animals and fish that could be eaten there in the water at Opis. Then they took water in the abalone shells.

"Now we will go to the south end of the world," said EARTHQUAKE. "We will go there and look at the water. THUNDER, who is at Sumig, will help us by breaking down the trees. The water will extend all the way to the south end of the world. There will be salmon and fish of all kinds and seals in the water."

Now Kingfisher and EARTHQUAKE came back to Sumig. They saw that THUNDER had broken down the trees. Together the three of them went north. As they went together they kept sinking the ground. The Earth quaked and quaked and water flowed over it as Kingfisher and EARTHQUAKE poured it from their abalone shells. Kingfisher emptied his shell and it filled the ocean halfway to the north end of the world. EARTHQUAKE emptied his shell and it filled the ocean the rest of the way.

As they filled in the ocean, the creatures which would be food swarmed into the water. The seals came as if they were thrown in in handfuls. Into the water they came, swimming toward shore. EARTHQUAKE sank the land deeper to make gullies and the whales came swimming through the gullies where the water was deep enough for them to travel. The salmon came running through the water.

Now all the land animals, the deer and elk, the foxes and mink, the bear and others had gone inland. Now the water creatures were there. Now THUNDER and Kingfisher and EARTHQUAKE looked at the ocean. "This is enough," they said. "Now the people will have enough to live on. Everything that is needed is in the water."

So it is that the prairie became ocean. It is so because THUNDER wished it so. It is so because EARTHQUAKE wished it so. All kinds of creatures are in the ocean before us because THUNDER and EARTHQUAKE wished the people to live.

ABOUT JOSEPH BRUCHAC

Joseph Bruchac is a storyteller and poet who carries on the traditions of his Native American heritage. He is a member of the Abenaki, or "People of the Dawn Land," who live in the northeastern United States and in parts of Quebec, Canada. Bruchac discovered his love for writing while he was in college. He has been writing and teaching creative writing ever since.

As a teacher and a writer, Bruchac hopes to convey Native American traditions of respect for the earth and the natural world. His goal is "to share my insights into the beautiful and all too fragile world of human life and living things." "How Thunder and Earthquake Made Ocean" first appeared in *Keepers of the Earth: Native American Stories and Environmental Activities for Children,* by Joseph Bruchac and Michael J. Caduto. Look for another story from that book, "Old Man Coyote and the Rock," in the next theme, "From the Prairie to the Sea."

THE STORY OF THE
Challenger
DISASTER

by Zachary Kent

In Concord, New Hampshire, people arose with a feeling of high expectation. It was January 28, 1986, and the space shuttle *Challenger* was scheduled to blast into orbit that day. Traveling on the spacecraft was a Concord schoolteacher named Christa McAuliffe. Although American military pilots, scientists, and even politicians had shuttled into space before, McAuliffe would be the first private citizen in the United States to make the thrilling flight.

Late in the morning excited students filled the Concord High School auditorium to witness the shuttle launch on television. Many showed their festive mood by wearing party hats and blowing noisemakers. Newsmen and camera crews lined the walls to record the happy scene.

Above: *Challenger*'s first landing at Edwards Air Force Base   Right: Christa McAuliffe teaching class in Concord, New Hampshire

Watching the television screen, the students loudly joined in, calling out the final countdown. "...Three...two...one...lift-off!" they shouted as the rockets boosted the shuttle from the launchpad. Sudden cheers and clapping rang throughout the room. Students unfurled a banner that read, "We're with U Christa." The noise continued as the *Challenger* arched up through the air, leaving a thick trail of smoke behind it. With pride and wonder these young people watched their teacher speed toward space.

In another moment an unexpected flash burst across the screen. "Shut up, everyone!" yelled a teacher who realized something was wrong. The auditorium fell into silence as a television voice announced, "The vehicle has exploded." Young faces stared in disbelief as smiles turned to tears. No one ever dreamed that such a horrible thing could happen. Later, in grief, Principal Charles Foley told reporters, "We were enjoying the entire event. We were celebrating with her. Then it stopped. That's all. . . . It just stopped."

As the tragedy sank in, weeping students and teachers returned to their classrooms. Within an hour Principal Foley sent everyone home. Outside the school, a reporter approached one student, Rusty Spalding, for his reaction to the explosion. "Shocked, very shocked," the young man revealed with tears in his eyes. "I felt as if my whole body blew up inside when I saw that. And I can just never be as shocked as I am now."

That afternoon millions of people across the nation shared in those sad feelings. In a stunning instant, a time of joy and triumph turned into a nightmare. In its twenty-five years of space exploration, the United States had never

A somber newsboy displays the *Concord Monitor*'s account of the disaster.

CONCORD ⬢ MONITOR

City, NASA Look For Answers

Virgil "Gus" Grissom (left), Edward H. White (center), and Roger B. Chaffee were killed when fire engulfed their *Apollo 1* spacecraft during a launch test on January 27, 1967.

suffered a worse disaster than the loss of the shuttlecraft *Challenger* and its seven-member crew.

America's earliest astronauts well understood the dangers of flying into space. Veteran astronaut Walter Schirra, Jr., remarked, "We felt we were flying in the safest machine you could put together. But the potential was always there. . . . It's a risky business."

After Alan B. Shepard, Jr., became the first American in space on May 5, 1961, the program of the National Aeronautics and Space Administration (NASA) advanced without a major misfortune. The successes of the *Mercury* and *Gemini* space flights left America unprepared when tragedy first struck on January 27, 1967. On that day Virgil "Gus" Grissom, Edward H. White, and Roger B. Chaffee trained for the first mission in NASA's *Apollo* program. The three pilots sat in their space capsule atop a *Saturn* rocket on the Cape Canaveral, Florida, launchpad. Minutes into their training exercise Gus

Neil Armstrong walks on the moon.

Grissom's frantic voice called mission control. "Fire! We've got a fire in the cockpit!" In another fourteen seconds a second voice, probably Roger Chaffee's, cried, "We've got a bad fire! Let's get out. . . . We're burning up!" Smoke and flames poured from the capsule. By the time technicians could come to their aid, the three astronauts had died of burns and suffocation.

The *Apollo* tragedy, caused when faulty wiring sent sparks into the capsule's pure oxygen air, halted America's space program for over twenty months. When the *Apollo* flights finally continued, they led to *Apollo 11*'s successful landing on the moon on July 20, 1969. "That's one small step for man, one giant leap for mankind," announced Neil Armstrong as he became the first human to set foot on the moon. In that wonderful moment Americans regained their confidence in NASA's projects.

Americans were not the only ones to risk their lives while exploring space. In the history of its space program the Soviet Union suffered two tragic accidents. On April 24, 1967, the *Soyuz 1* space capsule crashed on reentry. Its parachute failed to open and cosmonaut Vladimir Komarov died. Then on June 29, 1971, cosmonauts Georgi Dobrovolsky, Vladislav Volkov, and Viktor Patsayev met sudden death during the reentry of *Soyuz 11*. The returning capsule lost pressure due to a faulty seal, and the three brave men suffocated. created a spacecraft that allowed orbiting astronauts to return to Earth by landing like an airplane on an airstrip. This reusable,

UNDAUNTED, NASA BELIEVED IT COULD SOLVE WHATEVER PROBLEMS THE AMERICAN SPACE PROGRAM ENCOUNTERED.

Undaunted, NASA believed it could solve whatever problems the American space program encountered. NASA readied itself for the next big step in space exploration. In 1972 President Richard Nixon authorized the development of the space shuttle. During the next nine years scientists and engineers thick-bodied "shuttle" measured 120 feet long from nose to tail and 80 feet across its delta-shaped wings. When the space shuttle *Columbia* first blasted into orbit on April 12, 1981, piloted by John Young and Robert Crippen, it marked the start of a bold new era in space flight. The shuttle proved

its worth in successive flights by launching communications satellites from its 60- by 15-foot cargo bay. Its scientific equipment conducted valuable ecological and industrial experiments such as mapping Earth's flood and air pollution areas and mixing chemical elements in the zero gravity of space.

On April 4, 1983, NASA successfully launched its second shuttle, *Challenger*. More streamlined than the *Columbia*, *Challenger* soon proved itself the workhorse of the shuttles. Though the *Discovery* and the *Atlantis* later joined the fleet, time after time NASA returned to use *Challenger*. Landing again and again at Edwards Air Force Base in California, *Challenger* presented a glorious sight. On its second trip on June 18, 1983, *Challenger* carried America's first woman into space, Sally Ride. Guion Bluford, the country's first black astronaut, flew with the crew on *Challenger's* third mission.

In the summer of 1984 President Ronald Reagan announced that the first person in the nation's Space Flight Participant Program would be a teacher. In a flurry of excitement more than eleven thousand American educators applied for the position. Giving each application careful consideration, NASA narrowed its choices to ten finalists. On July 19, 1985, at a White House ceremony Vice-President George Bush named thirty-six-year-old Christa McAuliffe to be the "first private citizen passenger in the history of space flight." Overcome by her selection McAuliffe thanked him saying, "It's not often that a teacher is at a loss for words."

Overnight all of America wanted to learn about the lucky social studies teacher and follow her activities. One NASA official told reporters, "Her enthusiasm is a very infectious thing. She's a natural for the mission." Her friends and pupils agreed. "She's the kind of person who could come back and relate it meaningfully to her

Christa McAuliffe and her children respond to well-wishers during a parade in Concord, New Hampshire.

students," revealed Concord High School Principal Foley. In her application McAuliffe had stated her desire to keep a flight journal that would "humanize the technology of the Space Age" for students. She believed her experiences as a pioneer space traveler might one day be compared with those of the pioneers who journeyed West in Conestoga wagons. "I really hope the students get excited about the Space Age because they see me as an ordinary person up there in space," she told an interviewer.

On her return home to Concord, the town welcomed McAuliffe with a parade. Newspapers throughout New Hampshire ran feature stories about her. Camera crews visited the modest house where she lived with her lawyer husband, Steven, and their two children. Through it all McAuliffe remained enthusiastic. "I just can't believe people are so excited and proud," she cheerfully exclaimed.

At last the time arrived for McAuliffe to begin her training at the Johnson Space Center in Houston, Texas. Saying good-bye to her children was difficult.

"I don't want her to go in space, because I just want her to stay around my house," five-year-old Caroline had said. "See ya later, alligator," Christa McAuliffe lovingly called to her daughter as she left for the airport. Within her baggage was a stuffed toy frog named Fleegle, which she had promised her nine-year-old son Scott she would carry into space for him.

At the Johnson Space Center NASA workers prepared McAuliffe for her *Challenger* mission. Day after day she studied training manuals to learn about life in orbit. She read about procedures for dealing with space accidents and about emergency landings. Wearing NASA's bright blue flight suit, she experienced weightlessness in a space agency training jet and spent many other hours aloft. At meals she sometimes ate specially packaged foods just as she would in space. She also spent time becoming friends with her fellow crew members.

The six people joining Christa McAuliffe on *Challenger*'s tenth voyage into space were skilled pilots and knowledgeable scientists representing a cross section of America.

Christa experiences weightlessness with her fellow astronauts.

Commander Francis "Dick" Scobee

Challenger **Pilot Michael J. Smith**

The commander of the mission, forty-six-year-old Francis "Dick" Scobee, had flown in *Challenger* once before. The crew during that 1984 trip repaired a solar satellite in space. Born in Cle Elum, Washington, Scobee rose through the ranks of the Air Force. As a pilot he logged more than 6,500 hours of flight time in forty-five types of aircraft. Before joining the astronaut program in 1978 Scobee piloted the Boeing 747 jet that carried the test shuttle *Enterprise* "piggyback" between landing and launching areas.

Navy Commander Michael J. Smith was a seasoned flier also, but he had never been in space before. The forty-year-old from Beaufort, North Carolina, gladly jumped at the chance to become part of the *Challenger* crew. A United States Naval Academy graduate, Smith flew A-6 Intruder jets from the deck of the aircraft carrier *Kitty Hawk* during the Vietnam War. For his combat services he received a number of high military honors. After five years in the astronaut program, NASA finally chose Smith to pilot the *Challenger*.

Thirty-six-year-old Dr. Judith A. Resnik was a space travel veteran. In 1984 she became the second American woman in space and the first Jewish astronaut. As the shuttle *Discovery* first entered orbit, an enthusiastic Resnik radioed back, "The Earth looks great!" When ice formed on the shuttle's side, Resnik used the craft's long robot arm to break a chunk off. With the rest of the *Discovery* crew, Resnik logged 144 hours and 57 minutes in space. NASA picked the Akron, Ohio, native — trained as an electrical engineer — to be one of the three mission specialists on the *Challenger* flight.

Another mission specialist was thirty-five-year-old Dr. Ronald E. McNair. When this expert laser physicist traveled into orbit in 1984, he became America's second black to travel in space. Growing up in Lake City, South Carolina, during the difficult 1950s and 1960s, McNair learned not to let racial prejudice stand in the way of his goals. It meant "trying a little harder, fighting a little harder to get what you perhaps deserve," he remembered. With an advanced

Mission specialist Judith A. Resnik

Mission specialist Ronald E. McNair

407

Mission specialist Ellison S. Onizuka

Payload specialist Gregory B. Jarvis

degree from the Massachusetts Institute of Technology, McNair joined the astronaut program in 1978. While aboard *Challenger,* orbiting in space, McNair was to launch a small science platform to study Halley's comet.

Air Force Lieutenant Colonel Ellison S. Onizuka first journeyed aloft in January 1985 when the shuttle *Discovery* made a secret military flight. Now NASA chose him to be *Challenger*'s third mission specialist. As a boy in Kealakekua, Kona, Hawaii, the thirty-nine-year-old aerospace engineer dreamed of becoming a space explorer. For the *Challenger* voyage, this Japanese-American explained, "I'll be looking at Halley's comet. . . . They tell me I'll have one of the best views around."

Perhaps the most eager crew member was payload specialist Gregory B. Jarvis. Scheduled for two earlier crews, Jarvis had lost his place first to Utah Senator Jake Garn. The first congressman in space, Garn flew on the *Discovery* in April 1985. Later NASA bumped Jarvis again to allow Florida congressman Bill Nelson to shuttle on the most recent trip of the

Columbia. Finally it seemed the Hughes Aircraft Company engineer would get his chance to fly with the *Challenger* crew. The forty-one-year-old from Mohawk, New York, planned to spend six days in orbit studying weightless liquids and figuring out better ways to build satellites.

NASA assigned Christa McAuliffe additional duties also. While in space the teacher would broadcast two live lessons on television to the nation's schoolchildren. The first would explain the roles of the crew, and the second, the purpose of space exploration. As the launch date neared, a reporter asked if McAuliffe felt fearful. "Not yet," she answered. "Maybe when I'm strapped in and those rockets are going off underneath me I will be, but space flight today really seems safe."

Christa McAuliffe

date. Anxiously they waited for acceptable weather conditions.

On that Saturday NASA postponed the flight because of poor conditions at emergency landing

---

AS THE LAUNCH DATE NEARED, A REPORTER ASKED IF MCAULIFFE FELT FEARFUL. "NOT YET," SHE ANSWERED.

At last the *Challenger* crew flew to Cape Canaveral in preparation for the January 25, 1986, lift-off strips in Africa. On Sunday officials scratched a second attempt because Florida forecasts looked bad.

On Monday high winds made trying to launch unsafe. After waiting five hours while strapped on their backs in shuttle seats, the seven crew members learned of their third delay.

Finally, Tuesday, January 28, 1986, dawned clear and cold in Florida. Although icicles formed on the upended shuttle, NASA officials seemed confident. "Let's go today," a smiling Christa McAuliffe called to reporters as the astronauts left for the launch tower. While they suited up to enter the shuttle, a cheerful NASA technician presented an apple to the teacher for good luck. After two hours of delays, the launch seemed ready for countdown at 11:38 A.M.

On the ground thousands of people with binoculars and cameras prepared to watch *Challenger* roar into space. Close friends and relatives of the crew members stood on bleachers gazing at the

Front row: Michael J. Smith, Francis R. Scobee, Ronald E. McNair Back row: Ellison S. Onizuka, Christa McAuliffe, Gregory B. Jarvis, Judith A. Resnik

NASA tracked *Challenger* from the mission control center of the Johnson Space Center in Houston, Texas.

magnificent shuttle. Eighteen third-grade classmates of Scott McAuliffe waved a banner that read, "Go Christa." From loudspeakers everyone heard the voice of mission control and the public affairs officer.

"T minus 10, 9, 8, 7, 6, we have main engine start, 4, 3, 2, 1. And lift-off. Lift-off of the twenty-fifth space shuttle mission, and it has cleared the tower."

Its engines blazing, *Challenger* thrust quickly up and away. Its rockets trailing clouds of smoke, the shuttle picked up speed.

"Velocity 2,257 feet per second," the loudspeaker announced. Witnesses strained their eyes to watch the spacecraft's progress.

"*Challenger*, go with throttle up," instructed mission control. "Roger, go with throttle up," answered Commander Scobee's voice.

Then, seventy-four seconds after the shuttle left the ground, the sky suddenly lit up with a stunning white-orange fireball. People stared in confusion as the left and right rocket boosters crazily spun away from the explosion.

"Flight controllers here looking very carefully at the situation," informed the public affairs officer. Then after a long pause he solemnly continued, "We have a report . . . that the vehicle has exploded."

413

Spectators at the Kennedy Space Center stare in confusion and disbelief as the space shuttle explodes.

Comrades and loved ones shook with grief on the viewing stand. After fifty million miles of shuttle travel without an accident, the worst possible disaster had just occurred before their eyes. Many still could not believe it. Some kept staring hopefully. Some openly sobbed and hugged one another. Slowly they walked away.

Seven miles west of Cape Canaveral a Coast Guard cutter gently rocked in the water. The *Point Roberts* with its ten-man crew remained stationed below *Challenger*'s flight path. Stunned crewmen watched small fragments of the shuttle rain down into the ocean for an hour. "We were awestruck," explained Lieutenant John Philbin. Soon NASA directed the *Point Roberts* to gather whatever wreckage it could find. Other boats and planes promptly joined the search, but little hope remained that any of the seven crew members survived.

Whatever the reason for the tragedy, the nation mourned its loss as the news spread. Across

Left: The United States flag hangs at half-staff at the Kennedy Space Center on January 28. Above: A young girl cries openly during a memorial mass in Clear Lake City, Texas, on January 29.

the country church bells tolled and citizens lowered flags to half-staff. In Washington, D.C., the chaplain of the House of Representatives

again in other young men and young women who will read about them and learn."

Other American leaders also stepped forward to offer sympathy. Former astronaut Senator John Glenn mourned, "This is a day we've managed to avoid for a quarter of a century. . . . It finally has

"NOW THEIR NAMES BECOME HISTORY."

offered up a prayer. From the floor of the House, Congresswoman Lynn Martin honored the fallen seven.

"Now their names become history. But that drive of the human spirit will not die," she reminded her listeners. "In that flash and fire it will be reborn

arrived. We'd hoped we could push this day back forever."

With tears in his eyes, Senator Garn spoke of confidence in the space program. "I would go again tomorrow. If NASA would let me go, I would go again."

Flying to Cape Canaveral, Vice-President Bush met with the

President and Mrs. Reagan comfort crew members' families at the memorial service at the Johnson Space Center.

crew members' grieving families. Afterwards he remarked, "We must never, as people in our daily lives or as a nation, stop exploring, stop hoping, stop discovering. We must press on."

Word of the shuttle disaster greatly affected President Reagan. Canceling plans to make his annual State of the Union Address that night, he addressed the nation that afternoon instead. In a televised speech from the Oval Office the president declared, "We mourn seven heroes. . . . We mourn their loss as a nation together.

"The families of the seven — we cannot bear, as you do, the full impact of this tragedy, but we feel the loss and we're thinking about you so very much. Your loved ones . . . had that special spirit that says, 'Give me a challenge and I'll meet it with joy.' They had a hunger to explore the universe and discover its truths. They wished to serve and they did — they served us all."

To America's schoolchildren he explained, "I know it's hard to understand that sometimes painful things like this happen. It's all part of the process of exploration and discovery; it's all part of taking a chance and expanding man's horizons. The future doesn't belong to the fainthearted. It belongs to the brave. . . . The crew of the space shuttle *Challenger* honored us by the manner in which they lived their lives. We will never forget them nor the last time we saw them this morning as they prepared for their journey and waved good-bye and 'slipped the surly bonds of earth to touch the face of God.' "

Three days after the tragedy, governors, congressmen, foreign diplomats, and NASA engineers and technicians gathered in Houston. More than fifteen thousand people crowded the lawn of the Johnson Space Center for a national memorial service. An Air Force band quietly played patriotic tunes. Then President Reagan stepped before this audience to speak again.

"What we say today is only an inadequate expression of what we carry in our hearts," he said. "Words pale in the shadow of grief. . . . The best we can do is remember our seven astronauts — our *Challenger* Seven. . . . We remember Dick Scobee . . . Michael Smith . . . Judith Resnik . . . Ellison Onizuka . . . Ronald McNair . . . Gregory Jarvis. . . . We remember

The caskets of the *Challenger* crew arrive at Dover Air Force Base in Delaware.

Christa McAuliffe, who captured the imagination of the entire nation."

Addressing their families he continued, "The sacrifice of your loved ones has stirred the soul of our nation and, through the pain, our hearts have been opened to a profound truth: the future is not free, the story of all human progress is one of a struggle against all odds. . . . Our seven star voyagers . . . answered a call beyond duty."

With words of hope the president promised, "Man will continue his conquest of space, to reach out for new goals and ever greater achievements. That is the way we shall commemorate our seven *Challenger* heroes."

After the president returned to his seat, four roaring T38 jets streaked overhead through the sky. Beneath gray clouds they flew in the "Missing Man" formation, a final tribute to the *Challenger* crew.

In Concord, New Hampshire, during the days that followed, Mrs. Virginia Timmons finally took down from her front window the note Christa McAuliffe had once written to her daughter, Jeanne. "May your future be limited only by your dreams. Love, Christa," it read.

Life slowly returned to normal in Concord and throughout the nation, but never will we forget our teacher, Christa McAuliffe, who encouraged us all to "reach for the stars."

Meet Zachary Kent

At different times in his life, Zachary Kent worked as a taxi driver, a shipping clerk, and a house painter, all to support himself while he wrote. Now he writes full-time. *The Story of the* Challenger *Disaster* is just one of over forty-six books Kent has written for children.

Most of Kent's books are about United States history. He has been fascinated by the subject since he was a young boy. One of his boyhood hobbies that he still enjoys is collecting and studying souvenirs from the lives of United States presidents. His collection includes books, pictures, games, and even some autographed letters.

Another one of Kent's books dealing with United States history is *The Story of Geronimo*.

REMEMBER
Challenger

Create a Tribute

In Their Honor

After the *Challenger* astronauts died, the entire country mourned. In addition to public memorials, thousands of children and adults created personal expressions of their feelings. Make your own tribute to the astronauts. It could be a drawing, a poster, a poem, a song, a speech, or a sculpture. Let your ideas soar!

Teacher in Space

The *Challenger* mission was special in part because Christa McAuliffe was to be the first teacher in space. Make a time line of Christa's life from her selection for the program to the memorials that celebrate her.

Is It Worth It?

Since the 1960s, the United States space program has cost billions of dollars and has resulted in the deaths of at least ten people. Form teams to debate this question: Is the quest for knowledge about space worth the danger and expense?

Catastrophe and Community

Tornado, earthquake, explosion — most disasters devastate a community of people in some way. Think about the catastrophes in the major selections of this theme — *Night of the Twisters, Earthquakes,* and *The Story of the* Challenger *Disaster.* Write about who was affected by each disaster and how they were affected.

KIDS' TRIBUTES TO CHALLENGER

CHILDREN ACROSS AMERICA WERE DEEPLY
AFFECTED BY THE CHALLENGER DISASTER.
THEY WROTE POEMS AND LETTERS AND
CREATED ARTWORK TO EXPRESS THEIR
FEELINGS ABOUT THE LOSS OF THE CREW.
HERE IS A SAMPLE OF THEIR TRIBUTES.

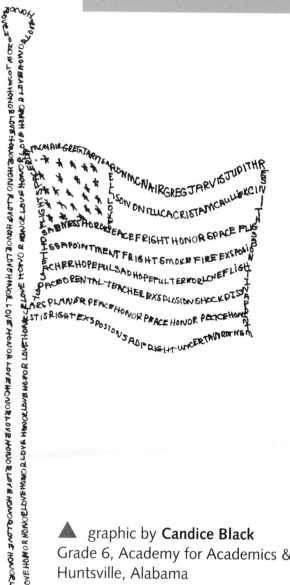

Americans
Striving to explore
Trying to discover
Remaining untold secrets
Onward to the sky
Now we have seven heroes
All very brave
Untold secrets still lie ahead
Till we find a way

▲ poem by **Steven Sharpe**
Grade 5, Christian Central Academy
Buffalo, New York

▲ graphic by **Candice Black**
Grade 6, Academy for Academics & Arts
Huntsville, Alabama

Dear NASA,

My name is Tamara Seraj and I am ten years old. I am so sorry about the shuttle "Challenger." But I believe in the importance of space and the space program. I would like to inquire about sending the first young person into space. If you have been thinking about it and you would like to send one of us in a shuttle, I would like to go. Even after that big tragedy that happened today I would want to go. I have had an interest in flying in a shuttle for a long time.

Sincerely,

Tamara Seraj

▲ letter by **Tamara Seraj**
Grade 5, Jasper Public School
Rancho Cucamonga, California

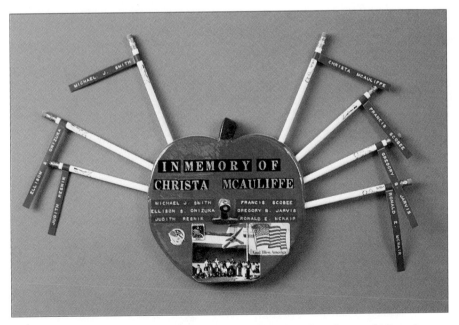

▲ Students from Jesse Keen Elementary School in Lakeland, Florida, designed and built a magnetic "Space Apple" pencil holder as a memorial to the seven *Challenger* astronauts. In September of 1988, the Magnetic Memorial Space Apple traveled with the next space shuttle, *Discovery*.

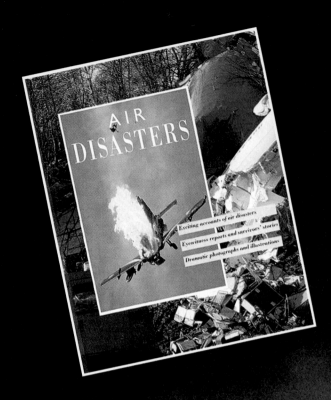

AIR
DISASTERS

Exciting accounts of air disasters

Eyewitness reports and survivors' stories

Dramatic photographs and illustrations

RAMSTEIN
AIR SHOW

On the afternoon of August 28, 1988, the air show at the United States air base in Ramstein, Germany, was nearing its end. The final act was being performed by the Italian Air Force team, the *Frecce Tricolori*. After a series of complex maneuvers, the ten pilots in their MB-339A jet trainer aircraft began the most spectacular part of their performance — a daring maneuver called *Arrow Through the Heart*. At its climax something went horribly wrong. One airplane clipped the tails of two others, causing all three jets to go out of control and crash. The aircraft that hit the other two had been flying straight toward the crowd. It plunged to the ground in front of them and exploded in a ball of flame, showering burning fuel and wreckage over the screaming spectators.

The fireball shot through the crowd, burning many of the people in its path. It also set fire to cars and trucks before burning itself out. A television cameraman from the West German station ARD said, "We saw the fireball racing toward us, so we first threw ourselves down on the ground." When the flames had died down, many people began searching for their friends and relatives, screaming their names. Others just stood still, too shocked to move. In all, 44 spectators and 3 pilots were killed, and more than 340 people were injured.

CRASH

by Roger Coote

This is the horrific sequence of events at the Ramstein Air Show on August 28, 1988.

TOP Nine airplanes split into two groups: five swooped down to the left and four to the right. At about 200 feet from the ground they leveled out and flew through each other. The tenth airplane was supposed to race through the gap. Tragically, the pilot made an error and clipped the tails of two of the airplanes.

MIDDLE One of the airplanes burst into flames in midair and continued toward the crowd of spectators.

BOTTOM The accident happened in seconds, so spectators had no time to avoid the burning wreckage.

OPPOSITE The airplane crashed only feet away from the crowd and rolled over in a ball of flames.

Is it possible to prevent similar disasters from occurring in future? The thing that makes air shows so popular is the very thing that also makes them dangerous — fast jets being flown with immense skill and precision in maneuvers that bring them to within feet of each other. The more thrilling the maneuver, the less room there is for error and the greater the danger. The pilots who fly in air shows realize this, and know that their own lives are at risk. To combat this risk, they train and practice each maneuver until it is perfect. The three Italian pilots who were killed at Ramstein had a total of more than 9,000 hours' flying experience. However, no matter how well trained they are, pilots are human and human beings can make mistakes. What changed the Ramstein crash from an accident involving three pilots into a disaster affecting hundreds of people was that the jets were close to the crowd when they collided, and that one airplane was flying toward the spectators. Since then, aerobatic teams have stepped up safety precautions. They now perform farther away from spectators and parallel to them, just in case another tragedy occurs.

FROM THE PRAIRIE TO THE SEA

FROM THE PRAIRIE TO THE SEA

CONTENTS

READ ON YOUR OWN

The sequel to the Newbery Medal winner *Sarah, Plain and Tall*

Patricia MacLachlan

Skylark

PAPERBACK **PLUS**

Skylark

by Patricia MacLachlan

A drought threatens the life that Sarah, Jacob, Anna, and Caleb have made on the prairie.

In the same book . . .

More about life on the prairie and love of the sea

Old Yeller

by Fred Gipson

When his father leaves for the cattle trail, Travis learns to rely on himself and his big yeller dog.

In the same book . . .

More about the people and animals of the Texas hill country, and a look at life on the cattle trail

BOOKS FOR THE TRAIL

If You Traveled West in a Covered Wagon
by Ellen Levine
The journey west sometimes took six months. Here's an account of daily life on the wagon train.

Bound for Oregon
by Jean Van Leeuwen
Mary Ellen is both excited and sad at the thought of leaving Arkansas for a new home in the West.

Dear Levi: Letters from the Overland Trail
by Elvira Woodruff
When Levi Ives dies in 1913 at age 71, he leaves to his grandchild a packet of letters his older brother wrote while crossing the Overland Trail in 1851.

Off the Map: The Journals of Lewis and Clark
edited by Peter and Connie Roop
In 1803 Lewis and Clark led an expedition through the territory of the Louisiana Purchase. Read about what they saw — in their own words.

The Bite of the Gold Bug: A Story of the Alaskan Gold Rush
by Barthe DeClements
Bucky can't wait to get to Alaska and find gold. But he hasn't counted on such hardships as the Golden Stairs!

America's Prairies
by Frank Staub
What do America's prairies look like today? Learn about the plant and animal life of the tallgrass, shortgrass, and mixed-grass prairies.

THE SANTA FE TRAIL

ARKANSAS

MOUNTAIN BRANCH

CAMP MACKEY

COLORADO

CIMARRON CUT OFF

RIO GRANDE

OKLAHOMA

NEW MEXICO

TEXAS

FORT UNION

CANADIAN

SANTA FE

ALBUQUERQUE

The red line traces the route Marion Russell, her mother, and brother traveled in 1852.

ALONG THE SANTA FE TRAIL
MARION RUSSELL'S OWN STORY

By Marion Russell / Adapted by Ginger Wadsworth   Illustrated by James Watling

435

When she was in her eighties, Marion Sloan Russell began telling her daughter-in-law, Winnie McGuire Russell, the adventures of her life. Winnie Russell wrote down Marion's words, and Marion read and corrected the work. It was published as *Land of Enchantment: Memoirs of Marian Russell along the Santa Fe Trail.*

Marion Russell was born on January 26, 1845, in Peoria, Illinois. Over her lifetime she was to travel back and forth five times on the Santa Fe Trail, which began in Independence, Missouri, and extended almost eight hundred miles to Santa Fe, New Mexico. The trail was primarily an important trade route, and later, a mail and stagecoach route as well. More than five thousand wagons a year used the trail by the late 1860s; by 1880, the railroad had reached Santa Fe, and travel by wagon was no longer necessary.

Marion's memoirs reflect the perspective of white settlers. However, later in her memoirs, she does wonder about the Indians "who watched with bitter eyes that vast migration" across their land. Some Native Americans were understandably hostile as they saw white settlers kill buffalo and claim their homelands.

My story is adapted from Marion Russell's text. I had wanted to write my own version of her first trip on the Santa Fe Trail. Then I realized that my words seemed flat in comparison to Marion's eloquent voice. I returned to her memoirs and used her words as much as possible. In a few places

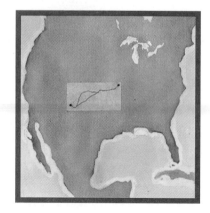

I added transitions or altered phrases so the story would flow smoothly. My version of her first trip is shorter, but the essence of the story is Marion's, in both words and spirit.

For an unknown reason, Marion's name in the original memoirs is spelled *Marian.* But in family papers and on her tombstone, the spelling is *Marion*, which I have used.

Ginger Wadsworth

My stepfather, Mr. Mahoney, was an experienced scout, but he was killed by the Indians while on a scouting expedition on the prairies. I remember mostly my mother and how, when the news came, she leaned against the wall for support, one hand clutching at her throat as if she were choking. I remember the horror in her eyes.

After my stepfather's death, Mother, Will, and I waited two long years in Kansas City for Grandfather to come from California and take us there. He said we might wash out much gold if we cared to. But we waited in vain. That was the year of the cholera epidemic, and Grandfather and both of his sons died in it and were buried in faraway California.

When school closed in the spring of 1852, Mother decided that we would go to California anyway. So we moved to Fort Leavenworth in Kansas, where emigrant trains prepared to travel west. Mother had planned that we were to take passage in Captain Francis Xavier Aubry's train, and she had great confidence in him. Two army officers and a doctor offered Mother, Will, and me transportation as far as Fort Union in New Mexico Territory if Mother would prepare their meals en route for them. Mother agreed. She saved the five-hundred-dollar fare by cooking for the young men.

The dread cholera was raging in Fort Leavenworth the October day our white-hooded wagons set sail on the western prairies. Captain Aubry broke camp first; his great wagon swayed out onto the trail. We heard his powerful voice calling orders to follow. Wagon after wagon rolled onward; the train numbered five hundred wagons. Tar barrels were burning in the streets to ward off the cholera, and clouds of black smoke drifted over us as we pulled out.

After a few days on the trail, we settled into a familiar pattern. Each morning the camp was astir at daybreak. Men began rolling out from under the wagons where they had been sleeping. They stood up in the cold morning air to stretch their arms and to rub their eyes. Through partially closed tent flaps and wagon curtains, women could be seen

slipping their dresses over their heads. I found it hard to button all the buttons that ran up and down the back of my dress. Why couldn't they have been put in front where I could get at them? Will sometimes helped me, for Mother was busy cooking.

Dressed and out in the sunshine, we were all happy. Sunbonnets bobbed merrily over cooking fires, and a smell of coffee was on the air. Packing was done swiftly, and the mules hitched to the wagons. Then the children were counted and loaded. Drivers called, "Get up there! Come along, boys!" Whips cracked, and all about the heavy wagons began groaning. The mules leaned into the collar, and the great wheels began their steady creaking.

The man in charge of our wagon was a Frenchman called Pierre. He almost always walked, but at times he sat swinging his booted feet over the dashboard — perilously close to the brown mules' swinging hips. Sometimes he sang or talked in French to the mules. His limp black hat turned straight up in front. His blue shirt was dotted thickly with little white stars. His dark eyes were like a hawk's eyes, and his nose was like a beak.

Will, who was nine, usually walked with Pierre. He tanned in the sun, and there seemed boundless energy in his slender body.

Mother sat erect on the spring seat, her face rosy in the depth of her bonnet. Frequently she knitted as we bumped along, and often as meal and camp time drew near, she sat there and peeled potatoes.

Our food and cooking things were kept in a great box at the rear of the wagon. Two blackened kettles and a water pail hung from the running gear.

I was seven on this trip, and I could not keep up with Will and Pierre. Often, when I got tired, I would crawl back among the blankets where I would play with my doll or fall asleep.

Each noon we would halt for a brief hour's rest. The lunch was a cold one. The mules fed on the crisp buffalo grass while the drivers rested. I remember the tired men lying under the shade of the wagons, their hats covering their faces as they slept. I can see the tired, sweaty mules rolling over and over in the grass, delighted to be free from the heavy wagons.

After the noon rest, we would go on again, until the sun was low in the West.

The vast open country that is gone from us forever rippled like a silver sea in the sunshine. Running across that sea of grass were the buffalo trails — narrow paths worn deep into the earth. They were seldom more than eight inches across and always ran north and south. A buffalo is a wise animal. It knows instinctively that water flows eastward away from the Rocky Mountains and that the nearest way to running water is always north or south.

Scattered along the buffalo trails were the buffalo wallows, small lagoons of rainwater like turquoise beads strung on a dark-brown string. They were made by buffalo bulls fighting. The bulls would put their heads together and slowly walk round and round, making a depression that caught the rainwater.

Always there were buffalo. Our trail often led among herds of buffalo so numerous that at times we were half-afraid.

Frightening thunderstorms came up suddenly. The drivers would wheel the wagons so that the mules' backs were to the storm. The men who had been walking sought shelter with the women and children inside. The prairies would darken, and a sheet of drenching water would fall from the skies upon us. A fine white mist would come through the tightened canvas, and soon small pearls glistened in Mother's hair. Then, as suddenly as it had come, the storm would pass away.

We would emerge then from the wagons to stretch our cramped limbs. Always we saw our storm, a tattered beggar, limping off across the distant hills.

One evening a great rainbow flashed through the sunlit rain. I called out to Mother, who stood on the wagon tongue. Will, who was busy kindling a cooking fire, said with some eloquence, "There is always a pot of gold at the end of each rainbow."

"Mother, is it really true about the pot of gold?" I asked.

Mother smiled. "The end of the rainbow is always much farther away than it seems, dear. We can only follow the rainbow and hope that it leads to fame and fortune."

For years I thought that the end of the rainbow was in California.

At sunset the prairie sky flared into unbelievable beauty, with long streamers of red and gold flung out across it. Each night there were two great circles of wagons. Inside each great circle the mules were turned after grazing, for ropes were stretched between the wagons and a circular corral made. The cooking fires were inside the corral.

Between the two night circles formed by the wagons was a no-man's land which the children used as a playground. The ball games that went on there, the games of leapfrog and dare base!

And sometimes, far away, we heard the war whoop of the Indians. Men stood on guard each night, rifles in hand. They circled and re-circled the big corrals.

After the evening meal, we would gather around the little fires. The men would tell stories of the strange new land before us, tales of gold and of Indians.

One night when the wind was blowing, Captain Aubry came and held me on his lap. I felt the great, black night closing down upon us and heard the voice of the night wind as it swept across the turbulent prairie. I shivered in the Captain's arms, thinking that only in the circle of the firelight that flickered on Mother's face was there warmth and comfort and home.

While most of the drivers slept under the wagons, the women and children slept inside the wagons or in tents. Each night we pitched our tent close to the wagon, and it spread its dark wings over the three of us. It was easy to hear Pierre snoring outside. Our bed on the matted grass was comfortable, but sometimes in the night I would awaken to hear the coyote's eerie cry in the darkness. Then I would creep close to Mother.

Our long caravan, loaded with heavy, valuable merchandise to be sold in the West, traveled slowly. Sometimes we were alarmed by the Indians, sometimes we were threatened by storms, and always it seemed we suffered for want of water.

I remember so clearly the beauty of the earth, and how, as we bore westward, the deer and the antelope bounded away from us. There were miles and miles of buffalo grass, blue lagoons, and blood-red sunsets, and once in a while, on the lonely prairie, a little sod house — the home of some hunter or trapper.

We paused at Pawnee Rock and Camp Macky; then we moved on.

Babies were born as our wagons lumbered westward.

Death sometimes came.

After about a month, we were on the Cimarron Cutoff. We built our fires with buffalo chips. My chore was to gather the chips. I would stand back and kick them, then reach down and gather them carefully, for underneath lived big spiders and centipedes. Sometimes scorpions ran out. I would fill my long, full skirt with the evening's fuel and take it back to Mother.

It was on this trip that I made my first acquaintance with the big, hairy spider called a tarantula. They lived in holes in the ground. When we found such a hole, we would stamp on the ground and say, "Tarantula, Tarantula! Come out, come out! Tell us what it is all about." And sure enough they would come out, walking on stiltlike legs.

As we continued in a southwesterly direction, there was less and less forage for our mules and horses. We found rattlesnakes and a variety of cactus that resembled trees.

Sometimes little jeweled lizards would dart across our path. Birds with long tails would walk the trail before us. The drivers called them roadrunners.

Once we traveled for two whole days without water, and thirsty child though I was, I felt sorrier for the straining mules than for myself. Captain Aubry told us how the muddy water in the buffalo wallows had often saved human lives. "One dying of thirst," he said, "does not stop for gnats or impurities."

Mother, Will, and I had to wash our faces and hands in the same basin of water. Will washed last, for Mother said he was the dirtiest.

After we had traveled for what seemed like an eternity across the hot, dry land, we awoke one morning to find the air filled with a cool, misty rain, which lasted all day. In the late afternoon we reached a flat mesa. There were a dozen Indian lodges there, and we saw smoke issuing from the tops. We saw Indian children slither through the wet drizzle among the stunted cedar trees and the lodges. Somehow it seemed we had entered a strange land of enchantment. This was different from anything we had seen.

Captain Aubry told us we were now in New Mexico Territory. "This is the land," he said, "where only the brave or criminal come. But it is a land that has brought healing to the hearts of many. There is something in the air of New Mexico that makes the blood red, the heart to beat high, and the eyes to look upward. Folks don't come here to die — they come to live, and they get what they come for."

We were a bit over two months reaching Fort Union in New Mexico. There, our great cavalcade rested.

The tired mules were turned out to graze on the prairies. Freight was unloaded, and two hundred horses turned into the corral. Army officers perched on the fence to look over and choose their horses. The ground was a shambles of buffalo hides, Mexican blankets, and sheep pelts — things to be sent back east.

Our camp was outside the Fort Union gate that stood open, and all day Will and I came and went as we pleased.

When the mules had rested, we struck the westward trail again, starting out on a cold December morning. We were in Santa Fe before we knew it. We passed through a great wooden gateway that arched high above us. We moved along narrow alleylike streets past iron-barred windows. We saw a church with two cupolas. We saw old adobe walls and strings of red peppers drying.

Our caravan wiggled through donkeys, goats, and chickens. We came to a plaza where a tall man with a gun told us where to go. Dogs barked at us. Big-eyed children stared at us; shawled women smiled shyly.

As darkness deepened, there was a great hunting for clean shirts and handkerchiefs. Pierre even drew the comb through his choppy mustache. From the dance hall came the tinkle of guitar and mandolin — a *baile* was forming. We slept in the wagon, or tried to, but the noise and confusion kept us awake. Pierre had gone to the dance, and it was hard to sleep without the sound of his snores near us.

In a few days, we continued our long trek to California. One evening as the wagon train drew near to Albuquerque, New Mexico, Mother discovered that a small workbasket in which she kept her money and jewels was gone.

Some of the jewelry was found, but no part of the money was ever discovered. I was too young to realize what the loss of the money meant to my mother, but I do remember the shadow that settled on her bright face as we journeyed on. Now she did not have enough money to pay for the rest of our passage. When we reached Albuquerque, we had to leave the train that was to have carried us to the gold fields of California.

Will and I went house hunting with her. I remember the tears that rolled down her face as she sold a great yellow brooch and a pair of earrings. She rented an old adobe house on the outskirts of Albuquerque and began taking in boarders.

I remember the morning Pierre carried our luggage into the mud house. He tried to say something, but his mustache only wiggled. Mother tried to speak, too, but as usual when she was stirred deeply, she was silent, pressing her hand to her throat as if choking.

Will and I stood in the bare, windswept yard, watching the long wagon train pull westward. When we turned back, our surroundings seemed desolate.

There was no looking back. We were soon busy cleaning and whitewashing our little adobe, not knowing then how many mud palaces were to be ours in the future, or that in time we would come to love them. When I grew up, I said to myself, I would travel endlessly back and forth over the Santa Fe Trail. I loved the trail and would always live on it. These were the dreams of my childhood.

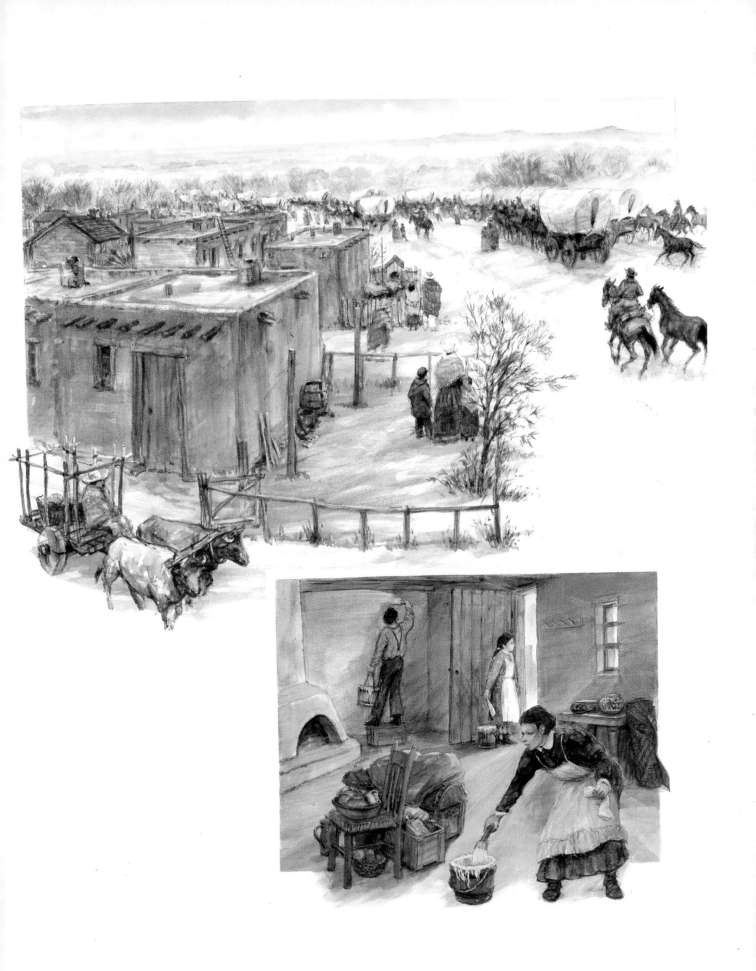

When Marion Russell was nine, Captain Aubry was stabbed to death in Santa Fe during a quarrel.

A few years later, when the Civil War started, Will joined the Union Army. Marion and her mother, Eliza Mahoney, didn't see him again for fifty years. Following the war, he was ordained a Baptist minister. He became a missionary in Calcutta, India, then a minister in Mexico City, and eventually returned to the United States. In 1917, Will was buried near Fort Leavenworth, Kansas, where he, Marion, and their mother had departed with Captain Aubry's wagon train in 1852.

Marion's mother did not remarry. She went back and forth over the Santa Fe Trail many times. As Marion recounts, "She was never quite happy unless she was passing back and forth over it . . . or planning to." She at last traveled to California, and died of old age in Los Angeles.

Marion traveled again and again on the Santa Fe Trail, first with her mother and brother, and then with her husband. She met Lieutenant Richard D. Russell at Fort Union when she was nineteen. They married the following year, in 1865. After the Civil War, they settled in Trinidad, Colorado, to raise their family.

Marion and Richard Russell had nine children, sixteen grandchildren, twenty-two great-grandchildren , and four great-great-grandchildren. Marion died in 1936 at the age of ninety-one, after being struck by an automobile. She was buried beside her soldier husband.

Marion Russell, about 1910.

Meet Ginger Wadsworth

Telling Marion Russell's story brought together many of Ginger Wadsworth's interests. As a "third-generation writer," Wadsworth feels that storytelling is in her blood. She has also been strongly influenced by "western American history and the natural history of plants and animals."

In telling the stories of places, Wadsworth focuses on the stories of people: Her other books for young readers are also biographies. Two of them — *Rachel Carson, Voice for the Earth* and *John Muir, Wilderness Protector* — are biographies of people who loved nature. When she isn't telling stories, Wadsworth explores nature by gardening, hiking, and bird watching.

Meet James Watling

Along the Santa Fe Trail appealed to James Watling's interests in "historical illustration and illustration of nature [and] wildlife." Watling had already illustrated over twenty-four children's books, including *History's Mysteries: The Roanoke Missing Persons Case*, by Anita Larsen, and *Samuel's Choice*, by Richard Berleth. Besides illustrating and teaching, Watling takes care of two cats, three dogs, and six ducks.

BLAZE A TRAIL OF IDEAS!

Write a Journal Entry

Words by Lantern Light

Along the Santa Fe Trail is based on Marion Russell's memoirs. If you had traveled with her wagon train, what would *you* have written about? Take a step back in time to 1852 and write a journal entry from the Santa Fe Trail.

Draw a Diagram

Uncovering the Covered Wagon

Where was the dashboard? What did the tongue look like? Use the words and illustrations in the selection to help you draw a diagram showing the different parts of the covered wagon.

Make a Poster

"There Is Something in the Air of New Mexico . . ."

Captain Aubry has high praise for New Mexico Territory. Let his speech and other words and illustrations from the selection inspire you. Create a poster that invites pioneers to come to New Mexico.

Make a List

A Well-Stocked Wagon Train

Suppose you were about to start out on the Santa Fe Trail in the 1850s. What provisions would you need? Use details mentioned in the selection as well as your own ideas to create a list of food, clothing, and other items for the journey.

VOICES OF THE WEST

They speak to us from diaries written on the trail and in memories recorded years later. They are the people who made their homes west of the Mississippi in the mid-1800s. Here are their words.

What was daily life like for nineteenth-century Native Americans on the Great Plains? Here are two recollections by members of the Hidatsa tribe.

Riding a Dog Travois

Small boys sometimes jumped on a dog travois just for the fun of it. Once I asked my husband to go for wood with me to the timber east of the village. I had three dogs and travois. My son, Goodbird, who was then four or five years old, wanted to go along. My husband and I said, "No, you cannot go." Goodbird wept and wept, so at last we took him with us. As we went along, my little son jumped on and off the travois, walking and riding, and playing with the dogs. The dogs got into a fight and ran off with my little son. He was much frightened and we laugh about it to this day.

Buffalo-Bird Woman

The horse was more efficient at pulling a travois. It could carry four times the weight and travel twice the distance that a dog could. And it didn't fight with other horses!

A Typical Summer Day for a Hidatsa Boy

Breakfast eaten, my father said to me: "It is time for you to take out the horses. Keep careful watch in the hills. If you see any strangers who look like enemies, hasten back to the village. Leave your lariat on the neck of your saddle horse and let it drag, so that if an enemy appears, you can quickly catch your horse."

My mother handed me my midday lunch, a double handful of whole parched corn, mixed with minced pieces of dried kidney fats. It was tied up in a heart skin which I fastened by a string to my belt over my left hip. I also picked out four long ears of white corn from the harvest of the previous year and tied them up, in a piece of cloth. Around this bundle I passed a piece of thong, tied the ends on a loop, passed my left arm through the loop, and so carried the bundle slung on my left elbow.

I caught one of the mares in the corral, and put on her a halter made of a flat rawhide lariat. "That is right," said my father, "drive the horses to the river and let them swim to cool off their bodies, that they may better enjoy their grazing."

As I started off on my mare my father said, "If you meet enemies while you are guarding your horses, try to escape and return home. If you cannot escape, stand against them like a man and make good your arrows!"

A tipi and a buffalo hide showing horses and hunting

461

A Navajo boy sees a
white man for the first
time. Here, he recalls
the astonishing
encounter.

Face to Face

One day I saw a man coming along with big white whiskers all over his face. The skin that showed was around his eyes, just a little bit. I had never seen a white man before. I ran away home and told the people I had seen something out there coming toward the sheep. It looked like a man, I said, but had wool all over its face. I thought the whiskers were wool, and I wasn't sure it was a man.

Roberto, my grandfather, was sitting outside the hogan having coffee and Navajo bread. He said, "That must have been a white man you seen." Pretty soon the man came up, walked up to Roberto, reached under his vest, and pulled out below the left arm a bunch of chili peppers. He peeled off three and gave them to Roberto, then he pointed to the bread and then down his throat. The women didn't want to feed him, but Roberto said, "Give him some." The pile of bread soon went away down.

Then the white man stood up, pointed away to the west, and walked off that way. Next day some of the Indian boys trailed him to see which way he was going. They found where he had spent the night, dug a hole and lit a tiny fire and laid down by it all night. Then his tracks went on toward the west.

Jaime, Navajo

A Navajo herder tends her sheep.

462

Near Independence Rock, on the Oregon Trail

Oregon Trail Diary

Sunday, May 8 — Sunday morning. Still in camp waiting to cross. There are 300 or more wagons in sight and as far as the eye can reach the bottom is covered, on each side of the river, with cattle and horses. There is no ferry here and the men will have to make one out of the tightest wagon bed (every company should have a waterproof wagon bed for this purpose).

Wednesday, June 1 — It has been raining all day long and we have been traveling in it so as to be able to keep ahead of the large droves. The men and boys are all soaking wet and look sad and comfortless. The little ones and myself are shut up in the wagons from the rain. Still it will find its way in and many things are wet. Take us all together we are a poor looking set. And all this for Oregon. I am thinking while I write, Oh, Oregon, you must be a wonderful country. Came 18 miles today.

Tuesday, June 7 — Rained some last night, quite warm today. Just passed Fort Laramie, situated on the opposite side of the river. This afternoon we passed a large village of Sioux Indians. Numbers of them came around our wagons. Some of the

A trail that emigrants might have followed

women had moccasins and beads which they wanted to trade for bread. I gave the women and children all the cakes I had baked.

Monday, July 4 — It has been very warm today. Thermometer up to 110 and yet we can see banks of snow almost within reach. I never saw the mosquitoes as bad as they are here. Chat has been sick all day with fever, partly caused by mosquito bites.

Wednesday, July 20 — Dry traveling today. No grass, water is very scarce. Stopt at noon to water at a very bad place on Snake river 1 1/2 miles or more down a steep bank or precipice. The cattle looked like little dogs down there and after all the trouble getting the poor things down, they were so tired they could not drink and were obliged to travel back and take the dusty road again. We are still traveling on in search of water, water.

Wagon train, 1866

464

Wagon train, 1850

Friday, Aug. 12 — Came 12 miles today. Crossed Burnt river twice. Lost one of our oxen. We were traveling slowly along when he dropped dead in the yoke. We unyoked and turned out the odd ox and drove around the dead one. And so it is all along this road. We are continually driving around the dead cattle.

Saturday, Sept. 10 — This road is cut down so deep that at times the cattle and wagons are almost out of sight, with no room for the drivers except on the bank. A very difficult place to drive, and dangerous, and to make matters worse there was a slow poking train ahead of us which kept stopping every few minutes, and another behind us that kept swearing and hurrying our folks on. There they all were, with the poor cattle all on the strain, holding back the heavy wagons on the slippery road.

Amelia Stewart Knight

An African American prospector who joined the rush for gold in California describes part of his journey west.

Goldminers at a sluice

Reminiscences

I started from St. Louis, Missouri, on the 2nd of April in 1849. There was quite a crowd of neighbors who drove through the mud and rain to St. Joe to see us off. About the first of May we organized the train. There were twenty wagons in number and from three to five men to each wagon.

We crossed the Missouri River at Savanna Landing on or about the 6th, no the 1st week in May. . . . At six in the morning, there were three more went to relieve those on guard. One of the three that came in had cholera so bad that he was in lots of misery. Dr. Bassett, the captain of the train, did all he could for him, but he died at 10 o'clock and we buried him. We got ready and started at 11 the same day and the moon was new just then.

We got news every day that people were dying by the hundreds in St. Joe and St. Louis. It was alarming. When we hitched up and got ready to move, [the] Dr. said, "Boys, we will have to drive day and night." . . . We drove night and day and got out of reach of the cholera. . . .

We got across the plains to Fort Laramie, the 16th of June and the ignorant driver broke down a good many oxen on the trains. There were a good many ahead of us, who had doubled up their trains and

Goldminer panning for gold in northern California, 1890

left tons upon tons of bacon and other provisions. . . .

Starting to cross the desert to Black Rock at 4 o'clock in the evening, we traveled all night. The next day it was hot and sandy. . . .

A great number of cattle perished before we got to Black Rock. . . . I drove our oxen all the time and I knew about how much an ox could stand. Between nine and ten o'clock a breeze came up and the oxen threw up their heads and seemed to have new life. At noon, we drove into Black Rock. . . .

We crossed the South Pass on the Fourth of July. The ice next morning was as thick as a dinner-plate.

Alvin Coffey

Women prospectors on their way to the gold fields

467

Just Another Day?

A Personal Narrative by Michelle Slape

Michelle often helps her dad on his ranch, but one day something unusual happened. This is her true story.

Just Another Day?

Weird things happen in small towns, especially when you live in the country. Tending to cattle is one thing, but delivering a calf is another.

One day I went with my dad to check his cattle. We started our truck and headed for the pasture. It was very quiet unless one of the cows mooed. The sweet smell of freshly baled hay floated around in the cool breeze.

There were about sixty cows in this pasture. When they heard my dad's truck, they all went running to one part of the pasture. Dad had to park our truck and then climb over an old, rusty barbed wire fence to check all the cattle closely. When he was almost finished, he spotted a young cow trying to have a calf.

Dad said, "She can't have the calf by herself, so we'll have to pull it."

My dad roped the cow, but she was so strong that she jumped the fence and ran to the end of a small pasture. We walked down to the cow, and my dad grabbed the rope that was tied to her neck and tied it to a tree. I had to hold the end of the rope so that it wouldn't slip off the tree.

"You'd better hold on to that rope tight!" Dad cautioned me.

"It hurts my hands to hold on tight!" I whined.

"You'd better not let go!" Dad repeated.

I was quite scared. Just imagine a thousand-pound cow that could come charging at you any time!

When we finally got the cow still, my dad started pulling the calf's hooves out. Then he got a smaller rope and tied it to the hooves. My dad had to pull really hard, and every time he pulled the rope, a little more of the calf came out. Finally, the cow lay down, and my dad pulled the calf right out.

When he pulled the calf out, my dad had to clean its mouth so it could breathe. Then the mama cow got up, and we took the rope off her neck. The cow then turned around and started smelling and licking her calf. We still had to get her back in the right pasture, so my dad picked up the calf and carried her and the mama cow followed.

That day I learned that pulling a calf is much harder than people think. If you don't believe me, go try it yourself!

Michelle Slape
Central Elementary School
Tahlequah, Oklahoma

When asked why she chose this experience to write about, fifth-grader Michelle said it was "because I really learned something, and I felt that others might enjoy reading about it."

In addition to taking piano lessons and singing in choir, Michelle enjoys reading, roller skating, and playing basketball and softball. Michelle, who is part Cherokee, would like to be a doctor someday.

BISON

by Tonye Garter

Sioux/Senior, Cheyenne-Eagle Butte High School

Where has he gone?

The great shaggy beast.

The wild one.

The provider,

The warmth from cold.

The food to drive away hunger.

The robe and moccasins for my feet.

The leather for my shirt.

The skin for my tent.

The bones for my tools.

The sinew for my bowstring.

The horn for my spoon and cups.

The stomach for a bag to carry my things in.

The rawhide.

I look for him on the plains and he is not there.

I look for him in the meadows and the valleys

    and the water and

he is not there either.

I cannot live without him.

▲ George Catlin
Oil on cardboard
*Buffaloes Grazing
in the Prairie,*
c. 1855–1870.
18 5/8 x 24 7/8 in.

LINEAGE

by Margaret Walker

My grandmothers were strong.
They followed plows and bent to toil.
They moved through fields sowing seed.
They touched earth and grain grew.
They were full of sturdiness and singing.
My grandmothers were strong.

My grandmothers are full of memories
Smelling of soap and onions and wet clay
With veins rolling roughly over quick hands
They have many clean words to say.
My grandmothers were strong.
Why am I not as they?

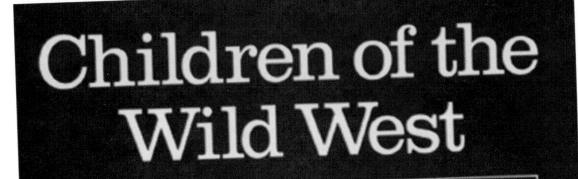

Children of the
Wild West

RUSSELL FREEDMAN

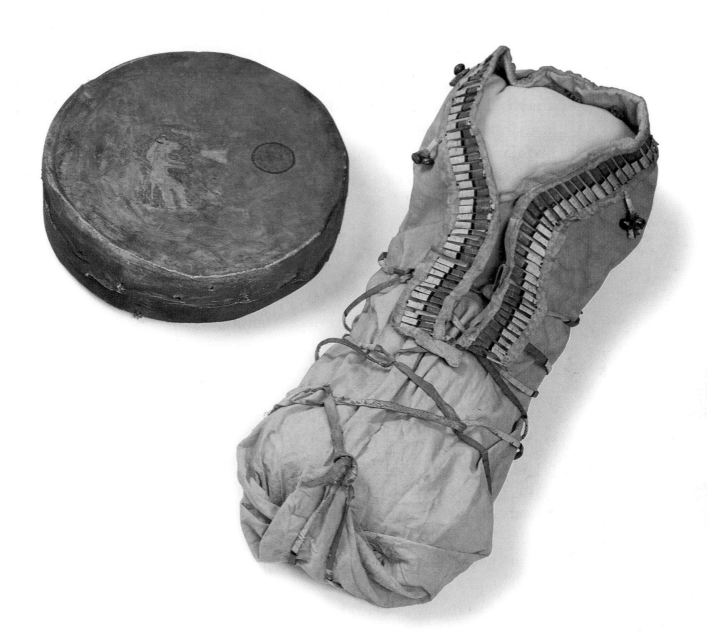

The American Indians

The Oregon Trail cut straight through the heart of the Indian country. When the first wagon trains set out in 1841, most of the land west of the Mississippi River was occupied by Indian tribes.

Hundreds of tribes and bands were scattered through the western territories. Some tribes had lived in the West for thousands of years. Others had arrived only recently from the East. Pushed from their native lands by white settlers, they had been forced to pack up and move across the Mississippi.

These tribes differed greatly among themselves. They spoke different languages, observed different customs, and had different life-styles. The Cheyenne were free-roaming hunters and warriors who followed herds of buffalo across the plains. When they were on the move, they carried their homes with them, living in tipis made of buffalo skin. The Pueblo of the Southwest were settled farmers who lived in large adobe apartment houses and raised corn, cotton, and turkeys. The Chinook of the Northwest were expert fishermen, skilled with canoes. Their houses were built of wood.

At first, most Indian tribes were friendly to the pioneers who began to settle in the West. As wagon trains crossed the continent, Indians often acted as guides. They ferried emigrants across rivers and traded with them along the way. A few tribes were hostile to the newcomers, but to begin with, there was little trouble. All along the trail, meetings between Indians and the emigrants were usually peaceful.

In some regions, Indian children began to attend schools run by Christian missionaries. Some white children had Indian playmates and learned to carry on conversations in tribal dialects.

For the most part, however, the Indians and the whites lived in separate worlds. Indians visited frontier trading posts and towns, but white settlers rarely ventured into an Indian village. Most whites remained ignorant of the Indians' ways. They knew little about these native Americans whose language, dress, and customs were so different from their own.

Anyone who visited an Indian village would see children playing many familiar games. Indian youngsters walked on stilts, rode wooden stick horses, spun tops made of acorns, and tossed leather balls stuffed with animal hair. They enjoyed blindman's buff, cat's cradle, and hunt the button. They competed in one-legged hopping races, breath-holding contests, wrestling matches, and Indian versions of football and field hockey.

An adobe apartment complex in Taos, New Mexico

A Zuni family on the terrace of their adobe apartment

475

Little girls played house with deerskin dolls, putting them to bed in toy tipis or small willow lodges. They dressed up their pet puppies and carried them on their backs, like babies. Small boys set out on make-believe hunts and raids, armed with miniature bows and arrows. Sometimes they caught frogs or killed chipmunks and rabbits. Occasionally they came up against bigger game.

A Sioux tribesman named Ohiyesa recalled his boyhood adventure with a huge moose. He was playing by the shore of a lake with some other boys when they saw the moose swimming toward them.

"We disappeared in an instant, like young prairie chickens, in the long grass. I was not more than eight years old, yet I tested the strength of my bow string and adjusted my sharpest and best arrow for immediate service. My heart leaped violently as the homely but imposing animal neared the shore. . . .

"'Still,' I thought, 'I shall claim to be the smallest boy whose arrow was ever carried away by a moose.' That was enough. I gathered myself into a bunch, all ready to spring. As the long-legged beast pulled himself dripping out of the water and shook off the drops from his long hair, I sprang to my feet. I felt some of the water in my face! I gave him my sharpest arrow with all the force I could master, right among the floating ribs. Then I uttered my war whoop.

"The moose did not seem to mind the miniature weapon, but he was very much frightened by our shrill yelling. He took to his long legs, and in a minute was out of sight."

Youngsters of all ages rode ponies and horses. When children were only two or three years old, they were placed on a gentle horse and tied in the saddle. By the time a boy was five or six, he might have his own pony, a gift from his father or grandfather. He was already a good rider and was able to help herd the horses.

Older boys competed in races and riding contests. They showed off their skill by hanging on the side of a galloping horse, then swinging down to scoop up an object from the ground.

A Kiowa boy on horseback

Sioux boys played a rough-and-tumble game called "throw them off their horses." The boys would choose up sides, mount their steeds, and charge. As their horses reared and neighed, they tried to wrestle each other down to the ground. If a boy lost his grip and fell off his horse, he was counted "dead." He was out of the game.

Children learned the skills and customs of their tribe from their parents, grandparents, aunts, and uncles. Boys were instructed in the arts of hunting, trapping, and fishing, in boat-building and horsemanship. They were taught how to make drums and war bonnets, shields and spears, bows and arrows. When a boy entered his teens, he went along on his first serious hunt. If he made a kill, he was highly praised. His father might celebrate the event by inviting other tribesmen to a great feast.

As a boy grew older, he began to accompany war parties on raids. At first he would help gather wood, hold the horses, and collect the enemy's arrows to be used against them. Gradually he learned to face danger and take his place as a man among the warriors.

Girls began to help their mothers when they were five or six. They learned to cook and sew, to create intricate beadwork and quillwork, to weave blankets, make baskets and pottery, fashion moccasins, decorate clothing, and tan buffalo hides.

Older girls looked after their baby brothers and sisters, carrying them about in softly padded cradleboards. Each tribe had its own style of cradleboard. A tiny dress made of shells or beads might hang near a baby girl's head, a little bow and arrow near a boy's.

"Life was softened by a great equality," a Sioux chief recalled. "All the tasks of women — cooking, caring for children, tanning, and sewing — were considered dignified and worthwhile. No work was looked upon as menial; consequently there were no menial workers."

A Navajo family working at a blanket loom. The five-year-old girl in the foreground is carding wool.

Two Kiowa girls with a baby in a cradleboard

A Bannock family camped near Medicine Lodge Creek, Idaho

Boys and girls alike were taught the traditional myths, rituals, songs, and dances of their tribe. They learned the names of the spirits that dwelt in the trees, rocks, streams, and hills bordering their lands, how to understand those spirits and ask for their help.

Children were scolded for lying, for quarreling, and for disrespect to old people. While most parents were strict, they rarely struck their children. Instead, they disciplined them with stern words and nasty looks. When children really got out of line, they were ridiculed and belittled. The worst punishment a child could receive was to be shamed in the eyes of the tribe.

As more and more settlers arrived in the West and claimed land, troubles arose. The land they claimed was usually Indian land. Indians began to suspect that the white man had come to take permanent control of their hunting grounds.

Most whites believed that it was the destiny of the United States to occupy and develop the entire continent from sea to sea, and to convert the Indians to the white man's own civilized ways. Some settlers regarded the "red man" as a primitive savage, a member of a lesser race who must be expelled from settled regions and packed off to reservations. Settlers were spreading rapidly across the frontier. They felt that the Indians had no right to stand in their way.

During the 1850s, Indian tribes were persuaded or forced to give up more and more of their territory. In return, the United States government signed hundreds of treaties setting aside reservations for the exclusive use of the tribes. The government also promised to pay the Indians for the loss of their lands. But often the treaties were ignored and the promises forgotten. Many Indians found themselves exiled to isolated reservations where they could no longer hunt and live freely as they had in the past. For them, life on the reservation meant poverty and despair.

All along, the Indians were being urged to give up their traditional ways, to exchange their bows and arrows for the white man's plow. On some reservations, the United States government offered to build brick houses if the Indians would agree to settle down and live as the white man said they should. Many Indians used the brick houses for storage and continued to live in their familiar tipis. Some began to wear the clothing of the white man. Others clung to their traditional Indian robes.

On the grassy plains, the hunting tribes had depended on buffalo for their livelihood. Buffalo supplied much of their food and nearly everything else they needed — leather for their tipis and clothing; fur for their rugs and blankets; bones for their cups and spoons, knives, and arrowheads. To the Plains Indians, the buffalo was a sacred animal. It was to be killed only as needed, to be worshiped before every hunt, to be praised and thanked for its many gifts.

Indians were being urged to give up their traditional ways. This photograph was
taken on the Santee Sioux reservation in Minnesota in 1862.

White hunters did not regard the buffalo so highly. During the 1850s and 1860s, millions of the animals were slaughtered for meat and leather and often for sport. At the beginning of the 1800s, perhaps 60 million buffalo had roamed the continent. By 1850, at least 20 million remained. But by 1870, the American buffalo was nearly extinct.

Along with the loss of their buffalo, thousands of Indians lost their lives to new and terrible diseases they had not known before. Pioneers traveling west had carried with them epidemics of cholera, smallpox, and measles. The Indians had no natural immunity to these European diseases, so their death rate was high. Some tribes lost more than half of their members.

Meanwhile, frontier towns and homesteads were springing up everywhere. Pioneers were demanding that more Indian territory be opened to white settlement. Throughout the West, the Indians were being pushed aside by white farmers, miners, and cattlemen. Some tribes gave in peacefully. But others, feeling cheated and betrayed, vowed to resist. They began to fight for the land they regarded as theirs.

Skirmishes and battles erupted between angry tribesmen and United States Army troops. The army made surprise raids on Indian villages. The Indians attacked wagon trains, homesteads, and border settlements. While most settlers never experienced violence by the Indians, they did hear terrifying stories and rumors about Indians on the rampage. In some parts of the West, fearful pioneers slept with loaded rifles by their sides. Wagon trains hurried along the trails, watching for signs of trouble, never knowing if the Indians might attack.

By the 1860s, full-scale warfare had broken out. For years, Indians fought a guerrilla war against the white invaders, while army troops pursued the Indians and fought pitched battles with them. The army battled the Apache in the Southwest, the Nez Percé in the Northwest, the Sioux, Comanche, and Cheyenne on the Great Plains. On both sides, there were raids and reprisals, massacres, and atrocities.

Two Comanche girls

A Kiowa boy

"What do we have to live for?" asked an Indian chief. "The white man has taken our country, killed all our game. Not satisfied with that, he has killed our wives and children. Now no peace. We want to go and meet our families in the spirit land. We have raised the battle ax until death."

The fighting reached its peak between 1869 and 1875, when more than two hundred pitched battles were fought. While the Indians won some important battles, they had no real hope of ever regaining their lands. Outnumbered and poorly armed, wasted by warfare and disease, they were finally subdued. The last major battle of the Indian wars was the massacre at Wounded Knee Creek in South Dakota on December 29, 1890, when more than two hundred Sioux men, women, and children were shot down by army troops.

At one time, the Indians had held all the land in America. By 1890, they held only about 200,000 square miles. The rest of the land — about 3 million square miles — had been taken by the whites. Even then, the Indians did not enjoy the same rights as other Americans. It was 1924 before they were granted citizenship and voting rights.

As the Indian wars ended, the government made new efforts to change the ways of the Indians and bring them into the society of the whites. At schools on reservations, Indian youngsters were taught modern farming methods and practical trades. Many young Indians were sent to special boarding schools in the East, like the Carlisle Indian School in Pennsylvania. Founded in 1879, Carlisle was the first school of its kind to be established off a reservation. Its students came from nearly every tribe in the United States.

The purpose of Carlisle and similar schools was to train young Indians in "the ways of civilization." Richard H. Pratt, the founder of Carlisle, believed that the Indians could flourish in America only if they exchanged their own culture for that of the whites.

Three girls on their arrival at an Indian boarding school in 1878 (above); the same girls fourteen months later (right)

Some graduates of Indian schools went on to take their places in white society. But many others did not want to adopt the white man's version of civilization. They returned to their reservations, where they preferred to live, as much as possible, in the traditional ways of their ancestors.

In 1867, a Comanche chief named Ten Bears had expressed the feelings of his people: "I have heard that you intend to settle us on a reservation near the mountains. I don't want to settle there. I love to roam over the wide prairie, and when I do it, I feel happy and free. When we settle down, we grow pale and die.

"Hearken well to what I say. . . . A long time ago this land belonged to my fathers, but when I go up to the river I see a camp of soldiers, and they are cutting my wood down or killing my buffalo. I don't like that, and when I see it my heart feels like bursting with sorrow. I have spoken."

A group of boys on their arrival at an Indian boarding school in 1878

Some of the same boys fifteen months later

Meet Russell Freedman

When Russell Freedman was a boy, he discovered that nonfiction thrilled him as much as any novel or story. Later, when he saw historical pictures of children at a photographic exhibit, he was fascinated. He wanted to tell the stories behind the photos.

Today, Freedman throws all his energies into uncovering history. He does research and often travels to see places firsthand. He also carefully chooses the photographs he uses, sometimes spending hundreds of hours finding the best images. For Freedman, pictures are essential to the story and "should reveal something that words alone can't express."

Russell Freedman has written over thirty-five nonfiction books for young readers. He provides a different look at the lives of people on the plains in his books *Buffalo Hunt*, *Indian Chiefs*, and *Cowboys of the Wild West*.

RETURN

Make a Chart

Childhood Then and Now

Nineteenth-century Native American children played games and learned important life skills. How similar or different was your childhood? Make a chart comparing and contrasting the childhood of a Native American boy or girl with yours. Use these headings for your chart: *Games, Skills, Values,* and *Discipline.*

Write a Letter

Walk in Another's Moccasins

The United States government sent Native American children to reservation schools and boarding schools "to bring them into the society of the whites." Was this a good idea? Discuss with your classmates the pros and cons of this plan. Then write a letter expressing your views to a newspaper of 1890.

TO THE WEST

Create a Picture

A Day in the Life

In the selection from *Children of the Wild West*, Russell Freedman describes what daily life was like for Native American children. Using the text and the photos as your guide, draw, paint, or construct a scene showing one or more of these everyday activities.

Compare Selections

Culture Clash

Think about how Native Americans are depicted in *Along the Santa Fe Trail* and how they are depicted in *Children of the Wild West*. Write a paragraph explaining how you think Marion Russell's and Russell Freedman's points of view differ, and why.

Where Did They Live?

During the last half of the nineteenth century, people of many cultures called the Great Plains home. Here is what home looked like for some of them.

The tipi was ideal for Native American life on the Great Plains — portable, well lighted and ventilated, dry, snug, sturdy, and efficient.

Hidatsa 4 pole

Cheyenne 3 pole

Native Americans on the Great Plains typically built tipis with three-pole or four-pole foundations.

A miniature Kiowa tipi cover

buffalo-hide cover: tanned and smoked to let in light but not rain or snow

willow lacing pins

door on east side

fuel, food, utensils, etc. stored south of door

anchor stake

Tipi use on the Great Plains

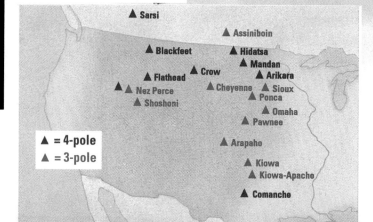

▲ Sarsi
▲ Assiniboin
▲ Blackfeet
▲ Hidatsa
▲ Mandan
▲ Crow
▲ Arikara
▲ Flathead
▲ Cheyenne
▲ Sioux
▲ Nez Perce
▲ Ponca
▲ Shoshoni
▲ Omaha
▲ Pawnee
▲ Arapaho
▲ Kiowa
▲ Kiowa-Apache
▲ Comanche

▲ = 4-pole
▲ = 3-pole

492

lodge poles of pine, cedar, or fir

tipi about 14' high at point

smoke flaps

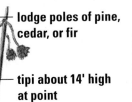

In a Cheyenne camp, the doors of the tipis faced east. This allowed the morning light to flow into the tipis and protected them from the prevailing west winds of the plains.

water bag

willow-rod backrest

This Arapaho tipi used a three-pole foundation and had a buffalo-hide cover. In the later 1800s, covers were made of canvas.

dew cloth (tipi liner): **provides privacy, insulation, and improved air flow**

altar

sleeping pallets of buffalo hides

wooden anchor peg

riding gear, weapons stored north of door

Sarsi (Canadian Plains) women erecting a four-pole tipi. Native American women usually owned, constructed, and erected the tipis.

ADOBES

Hispanic settlers in the Southwest used the materials at hand — clay soil and sparse trees — to build homes well suited to their environment.

canal
(water spout to carry water off roof and away from walls)

bench and cupboard built into wall

An adobe's basic unit was a cube-shaped room about thirteen to fifteen feet wide. The roof beams (*vigas*) could not carry the weight of a wider roof.

wooden bars and shutters

packed-earth floor, made hard with a mixture of animal blood and ashes

plank floor added on

Adobe walls would erode more quickly if not plastered with clay mud. The plaster was applied with the bare hands and later smoothed with a piece of damp sheepskin.

General area in which Hispanic settlers built adobes

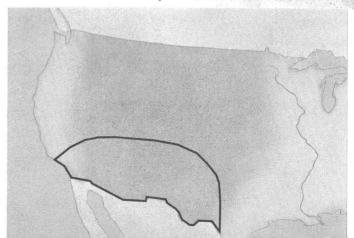

mud-plastered interior wall

roof: wooden rafters, layer of bark (to keep mud from falling into room)**, straw, and 6-12" of adobe**

fireplace

viga (horizontal beam)

mud-plastered exterior wall

Making Adobe

Today some houses are still built with adobe bricks made the traditional way. Adobe earth is screened to remove stones and pebbles. Then it is mixed with straw in a pit.

1) A brick form is wetted so that the mud brick can slide out easily. Some brick forms are much larger than this one.

2) The mold is tightly packed with mud so that no cracks or air pockets remain.

3) The mud bricks are carefully turned out of the mold and left to bake in the sun. The bricks are turned on their narrow sides after a few days so that they bake completely.

Floor Plan

New rooms were often added to an older house, making a long or L-shaped floor plan.

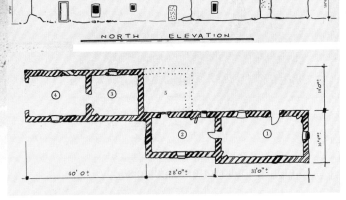

NORTH ELEVATION

1

2

3

SODDIES

The prairie was nearly treeless, so homesteaders were forced to build with the earth beneath their feet.

roof: willow or cedar rafters, then layers of chokecherry brush, prairie grass, and sod (grassy side up)

ceiling cloth of muslin or canvas catch dirt, spider and other drop-i

board to keep weight of settling sod from breaking window glass

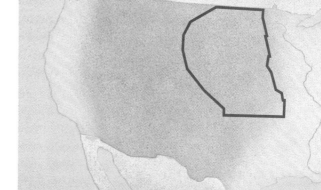

packed-earth floor, sometimes covered with hay and carpet

A family's first "soddy" was often a dugout in the side of a hill.

In time a family might add on to its dugout or build a freestanding soddy.

A soddy lasted about six or seven years. An abandoned or neglected soddy soon returned to the soil.

General area in which most soddies were built

cedar ridge pole

Homesteaders used a grasshopper plow to cut an acre of ground into strips about a foot wide and four inches deep. Then they cut the strips into three-foot-long bricks, jokingly called "Nebraska marble."

An average soddy was fourteen feet by twelve feet and took one week to complete. It was warm in winter and cool in summer, and its heavy roof wouldn't blow away in the strong prairie winds. But in the rain, the roof leaked muddy water onto everything!

sod wall: two bricks thick
(grassy side down)

forked post to help support heavy roof

furniture ordered or brought from the East or made from packing boxes

The sod-house era ended in the 1890s, but some soddies were occupied well into the twentieth century.

497

PECOS BILL

a play by John Tichenor

Characters:
Narrator
Ma
Pa
Pecos Bill
Chuckwagon Chuck
Sourdough Sal
Hardtack Hank
Flap Jack
Sluefoot Sue
(Coyotes and Cattle)

Setting: The dry, brushy plains of west Texas, 1840s.

(*The play opens in* Ma *and* Pa's *homestead in west Texas.* Pa *is busy chopping wood with an ax.* Ma *is standing on a boulder, peering out at the audience, her hand shading her eyes. She's hopping mad.* Narrator *enters, dressed in Western clothes.* Narrator *stands off to one side of the stage and addresses the audience.*)

NARRATOR: Howdy, folks. This here's the story of Pecos Bill, the wiliest, bravest, foolhardiest cowpoke in the West. In fact, you could say Bill was the *first* cowpoke in the West. But let's start at the beginning — out in west Texas, with Bill's ma roarin' like a cornered cougar.

MA: Confound it, Pa! It's happenin' again! Take a look out there.

Pᴀ (*Putting ax down, peering*): Where?

Mᴀ (*Pointing*): Beyond the river, in the next valley. You see that?

Pᴀ (*Squinting*): I don't see a thing, Ma.

Mᴀ: A cabin going up! (*She turns* Pa *around.*) Don't you get it, Pa?
    HOMESTEADERS! Hitch up the wagon! We're movin' on.

(Ma *starts packing up.* Pa *follows her, trying to reason with her.*)

Pᴀ: But, Ma. They must be pert-near twenty miles away!

Mᴀ: Exactly! They got some nerve settlin' so close! Why do you think
    we headed west in the first place?

PA (*Stopping to scratch his head*): To get a better view of the sunset?

MA: No! To get some privacy, that's why. Round up the kids!

PA: Whatever you say, Ma.

(Pa *walks to the edge of the stage and starts hollering.*)

PA: Benjamin, shake a leg! Barnaby, hop to it! Buster, get the lead out! Buford, look alive! Beulah, Blanche, Betty, put some hustle in your bustle! (Pa *looks around.*) Where's Bill? Bill!

(Ma *and* Pa *carry their possessions off-stage.* Bill *enters, fishing.*)

NARRATOR: Little Bill had toddled out of his crib, grabbed a fishin' pole and was over at the pond catchin' himself a mess o' catfish. Not bad for a two-year-old, eh?

PA (*From off-stage*): Come on back, Bill boy! We're headin' west!

(Bill *toddles off. Moments later,* Ma *and* Pa *drive a Conestoga wagon across the stage.*)

NARRATOR: If there's one thing Ma couldn't stand it was the slow, steady drip of civilization. And who could blame her? Stay in one place too long and before you know it you're neck-high in an ocean of cities, states, railroads, and ranches.

MA: Heads up! We're fordin' the Pecos River.

(Bill *sits at the tail end of the wagon. He casts his fishing pole.*)

NARRATOR: Yep. Ma, Pa, and the kids ran smack into the Pecos, a river that sidewinds through Texas like a wild rattlesnake. And just like that, Bill hooked a two-ton Texas trout.

(Bill *is pulled out of the wagon and dragged off-stage.* Ma *and* Pa *drive off in the other direction.*)

BILL: Whoo-weeeeee! Yippee-yi-yay!

NARRATOR: That fish swam Bill halfway to the Rio Grande. If Bill hadn't come up for air, he might still be trailin' that trout. As for Bill's folks, what with bein' so preoccupied with crossin' the river, why, they didn't even know he was gone!

(Bill *re-enters, looking half-drowned. He looks around, scared.*)

BILL: Ma? Pa?!

NARRATOR: Poor little feller. To lose your family and a two-ton trout in the same day. It was more than any two-year-old could take.

BILL (*Sits down, rubbing his eyes*): Waaaaaaaaah!

(Coyotes *howl from off-stage, then enter howling. A few go over to* Bill *and sniff him curiously.*)

NARRATOR: Then, lo and behold, the first person to come along wasn't a person at all. It was a pack of coyotes. Naturally they up and adopted little Bill and raised him as one of their own.

(Coyotes *run around with* Bill. Bill *crawls on his knees, barking.*)

NARRATOR: Ya might say Bill took to a coyote's life like a weed takes to water. What with all the exercise, Bill grew to become the strongest, rip-roarin'est boy in all creation. 'Course, as far as Bill knew, he was a full-blooded coyote. Bill didn't even know what a human was 'til some years later when one came wanderin' by.

(Chuck *enters, singing a cowboy song, and* Coyotes *run off-stage.*)

CHUCK (*Sees* Bill *and stops*): Well, what do we have here? A critter that acts like a coyote but looks like a man! (Bill *fastens on to* Chuck's *ankle with his teeth.*) Hey, amigo! Leggo o' my spur!

BILL: Grrrrrrrr . . .

CHUCK (*Trying to shake* Bill *off*): Have you gone plumb loco? What are you doin' out here in the middle of nowhere in just a diaper?

BILL (*Sitting back on his haunches and howling*): Arrooooooo!

CHUCK: Can't you talk? Talk like me, I mean. Ya know, with words.

BILL (*Trying to sound it out*): Wor . . . ds.

CHUCK: That's right. Let's see if I can learn ya some more.

(Bill *stands up a little shakily.*)

NARRATOR: Bill was as bright as a new silver dollar, so in no time at all he was stringin' words together in complete sentences.

BILL: Ya mean to say I'm not a coyote?

CHUCK (*Slapping* Bill *on back*): Nope, you're practically a full-grown man. 'Course, I never did see one in diapers before.

BILL (*Scratching himself*): But I've got fleas, just like a coyote.

CHUCK: All folks got fleas, fella. Don't mean nothin'.

BILL: What about my tail?

(Bill *looks over his shoulder and turns, trying to find his tail.*)

BILL (*Stops turning*): Huh. That's funny.

CHUCK: Never thought to look, did ya?

BILL: Always just kind of assumed.

CHUCK (*Extending right hand*): The name's Chuckwagon Chuck, on account of my love for grub. What's your name?

BILL (*Shaking* Chuck's *hand*): Ruff. That's what the coyotes call me.

CHUCK: What about your human name?

BILL: Hmmm . . . I've got a few memories from way back before the coyotes found me. Near as I can remember, folks called me Bill.

CHUCK: Just Bill? Here in Texas, everybody's got a nickname. Like Red River Roy or Guadalupe Gwen. And seein' as we're down here by the Pecos, Bill . . . (*Stops short and snaps his fingers*) Pecos Bill! How 'bout that? Here, Pecos — if ya wanna be seen in public, ya better slip into these extra duds o' mine.

(Chuck *reaches into his backpack and removes a shirt, a pair of jeans, and boots.* Bill *tries putting the jeans on over his head.*)

CHUCK (*Laughing*): Looks like I'd better help you before you turn yourself inside out. (Chuck *holds the shirt up.*) First, put your hands through those tubes. We call 'em sleeves.

BILL (*Taking shirt*): You want me to put my paws where?

CHUCK: Not your paws — your hands.

(Chuck *helps* Bill *slip his hands through the sleeves. But he has the shirt on backwards and gets his head caught.*)

BILL: Wait a second, I got my snout caught in here.

CHUCK: Ya mean your nose! Ya got to stop thinkin' like a coyote! Turn it around with the buttons in front!

(Bill *puts the shirt on right, then starts to put on the boots.*)

Hold up there, Pecos. Before ya put your boots on, ya want to slip your hind legs into . . . hoppin' horned toads! Now ya got me doin' it! I mean, ya want to put your pants on next!

(Chuck *helps* Bill *put the pants on.*)

CHUCK: Okay. After ya button up, hunker down and put on your boots. (Bill *sits down and puts the boots on.*) That's fine. And finally, no Texan would feel dressed without his ten-gallon hat.

(Chuck *reaches into his pack and removes a hat.*)

NARRATOR: So just like that, Bill became Pecos Bill. But before he could become a legend, Bill had to do somethin' remarkable. He didn't have long to wait. It so happens the biggest, orneriest rattlesnake to ever slither through sagebrush was takin' a siesta on a nearby boulder — and what with all the commotion, it woke up as mad as . . . well, as mad as a rattled rattlesnake!

(*A huge rattlesnake springs from a boulder and pounces on* Bill.)

CHUCK: Look out, Bill!

(*The snake coils around* Bill. Bill *wrestles it.*)

NARRATOR: But that snake picked the wrong hombre to tangle with. Bill grabbed hold of the rattler and twisted it so tight, he wrung out every last drop of poison. By the time Bill was through, that reptile was just a long thin piece of rattlin' snake-rope!

(Bill *rolls the snake into a coil and hangs it over his belt.*)

BILL: I reckon this'll come in handy someday.

(*The sun sets and* Bill *and* Chuck *set up camp.*)

NARRATOR: Pretty soon, the sun set, as it has a habit of doin' in the West, and Pecos Bill and Chuck built a cracklin' campfire. (Bandana Bandits, *wearing handkerchiefs over their noses and mouths, enter and tiptoe toward* Bill *and* Chuck.) Little did they know, the notorious Bandana Bandits were on the prowl!

(Chuck *sees* Bandits, *jumps up, and raises his hands.*)

BILL (*Turning around, unafraid*): Howdy, friends! Want some grub?

SOURDOUGH SAL (*Speaking through her handkerchief*): Mmmhmmh!

BILL (*Cupping his ear*): How's that?

SOURDOUGH SAL: Mumumhumhum!

BILL (*Pulling her handkerchief down past her chin*): One more time?

SOURDOUGH SAL: I said, "We're bushwhackin' ya!"

BILL (*Confused*): Whackin' bushes? That don't make sense.

SOURDOUGH SAL: No! We're sneakin' up to steal your money!

BILL: Steal? That's a word I haven't heard before. What's it mean?

SOURDOUGH SAL (*Surprised*): Stealin' is . . . well . . . takin' things that don't belong to you.

HARDTACK HANK: Like robbin' trains . . .

FLAP JACK: And stagecoaches . . .

HARDTACK HANK: And banks!

BILL: Why would anyone want to do that?

SOURDOUGH SAL (*Exasperated*): Because it's what we do!

FLAP JACK (*Proudly*): We're the Bandana Bandits!

SOURDOUGH SAL: I'm Sourdough Sal, the leader of this here gang.

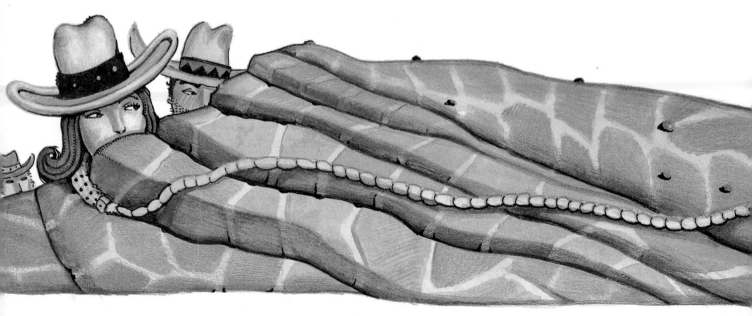

HARDTACK HANK: Hardtack Hank here.

FLAP JACK: They call me Flap Jack. (*He shakes* Bill's *hand.*) Howdy!

SOURDOUGH SAL (*Waving away the politeness*): Enough of this jibber-jabberin'! Let's do what we come to do! Hand over your money!

CHUCK: 'Fraid not, amigos. We're plumb broke.

FLAP JACK (*Throwing hat to the ground*): Rats! Third time this month.

BILL: Maybe you should try another line of work.

HARDTACK HANK: Like what? There's nothin' out here but a bunch of worthless cattle.

BILL: Poor lonesome critters. Wanderin' the prairie, all alone, bawlin' for their mas. There must be someone who wants 'em.

CHUCK (*Snapping his fingers*): There is! Up in Kansas, folks'd pay a ton o' money for Texas beef!

HARDTACK HANK: How in tarnation do we get 'em up there?

SOURDOUGH SAL: We tried rounding 'em up once. We got ourselves some rope, made a loop, and set it on the ground.

FLAP JACK: Then we waited.

BILL: For what?

HARDTACK HANK: For a cow to come by and step into the loop.

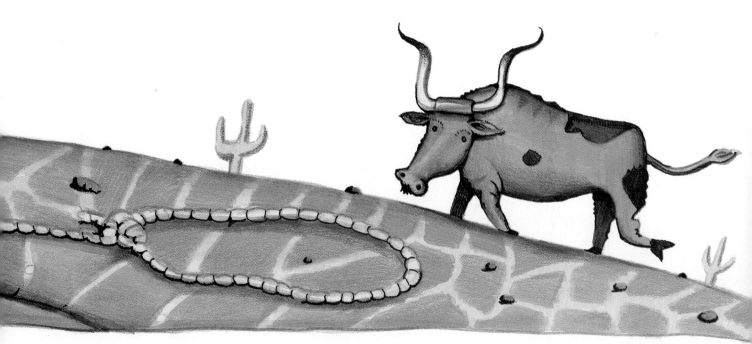

BILL: Supposin' one did?

FLAP JACK: Then we'd jerk real sharp on the rope and snare one.

BILL: And to catch a cow took — what — a couple of hours?

HARDTACK HANK: More like a week.

BILL: Seems to me you bandits got it backwards. Instead of the cow coming to the rope, the rope needs to go to the cow. Watch.

(Bill *uncoils his snake-rope, makes a loop, twirls it over his head, and throws the looped end off-stage.*)

NARRATOR: Bill uncoiled his snake-rope, made a loop, and let the rope fly. And like it had eyes — which it did — that rope landed around the neck of a lonely longhorn. Bill reeled it in just like a Texas trout. And that's how Pecos Bill invented the lasso.

(Bill *pulls a* Texas Longhorn *onto the stage.* Chuck *and* Bandits *practice lassoing and pulling in cows.*)

NARRATOR: It wasn't long before Chuck and the Bandana Bandits got the hang of lassoing. In a week's time, they had rounded up half the longhorns in Texas. But before heading north, Bill said good-bye to the coyote pack that raised him from a pup.

BILL (*Howling*): Arrooooooo . . .

(Coyotes *appear on stage and howl their farewell.*)

NARRATOR: The Bandana Bandits were so touched that they began howlin' along. And thus was born the first cowboy yodel.

BANDITS (Bandits *sing*): Yodelay-hee-oh . . . Yodelay-hee.

(Cows *appear on the stage.* Cowpokes *start to herd them.*)

NARRATOR: The howls and yodels of coyotes and cowboys soon gave way to a thousand cows, mooin' their hearts out. Bill and his cowpokes kept busy roundin' up strays by day and singin' the herd to sleep at night. But by the time they hit the Oklahoma Panhandle, those cows were so parched, their cuds were like concrete. It was the worst drought the West had ever seen.

(Cowpokes *drag their way across the stage.* Chuck *holds an empty canteen over his mouth and shakes it.*)

BILL: Hoo-weee, is it dry!

CHUCK: How dry you reckon it is?

HARDTACK HANK: So dry I'm sweatin' table salt.

FLAP JACK: So dry the windmills are pumpin' dust.

SOURDOUGH SAL: So dry the cactuses packed up and walked to Arizona.

NARRATOR: When they reached the Kansas border, the herd was so skinny it looked more like beef jerky than cattle.

509

(Sluefoot Sue, *wearing a prairie dress with a "Miss Kansas 1860" sash, sashays in carrying a sunflower.*)

SLUEFOOT SUE: Welcome to Kansas! The name's Sluefoot Sue! (*She points to* Cows.) What in tarnation are *those* mangy things?

(Bill *removes his hat and gazes adoringly at* Sluefoot Sue.)

BILL: We call 'em Longhow Corns . . . I mean, Longhorn Cows, ma'am.

SLUEFOOT SUE: Ya could've fooled me. Why'd ya bring 'em up here?

BILL: We aim to bell 'em to the slyest hitter . . . I mean, sell 'em to the highest bidder!

NARRATOR: The plain fact is, Bill's brain didn't know what his tongue was sayin'! One look at Sluefoot Sue and he'd fallen hat over boots in love.

510

SLUEFOOT SUE: Sell *those* scrawny things? I'd sooner buy a plate of sand. It seems like you came a long way for nothin.'

SOURDOUGH SAL: Blast! I told ya this cattle drive was a tom-fool idea! Quick! Where's the nearest bank?

BILL: Sluefoot Sue, will you marry me?

(Cowpokes *gasp.*)

SLUEFOOT SUE: What?! Why should I marry you?

(Bill *jumps up on a boulder.*)

BILL: 'Cause I'm Pecos Bill, the greatest cowboy in the world! I'm strong as an ox, quick as a jackrabbit, and I sing like a coyote! I'm a fair sight to look at, and I'm good with children, too!

SLUEFOOT SUE: And that makes you good enough for me?

BILL: I kind of figured it would, yeah.

SLUEFOOT SUE: Well, listen up, buster. (Sluefoot Sue *pushes* Bill *off the boulder and takes his place.*) I'm Sluefoot Sue, premiere interpreter of the waltz-clog, hootenanny, two-step, and polka. I can rope and ride as good as any man, bust a bronc, and fix a shoe. And I'm a fair sight better-lookin' than you are!

BILL: You surely are special, Sue. I reckon you deserve me.

SLUEFOOT SUE: The question is, do *you* deserve *me?* If you're so terrific, do something really special. Make it rain!

NARRATOR: Well, Bill liked nothing better than a challenge. He looked around and saw opportunity on the horizon in the form of an ugly black cloud. Was it rain? No such luck.

(*The sky darkens and a sound like the roar of a train can be heard.*)

CHUCK (*Pointing off-stage*): Tornado!

SLUEFOOT SUE (*Shading her eyes*): Never seen one that big!

FLAP JACK: Head for the . . . Where should we head, Bill?

SOURDOUGH SAL: We got nowhere to turn!

CHUCK: It's gettin' closer!

HARDTACK HANK: The cows'll be blown sky-high!

BILL: Hold on. I got me an idea.

> (Bill *uncoils the snake-rope and throws the loop end off-stage.*)

NARRATOR: Sure as shootin', Bill lassoed that twister, jumped on its back, and went for a spin that took him from Eldorado to Wichita Falls.

> (Bill *is pulled off-stage.* Cowpokes *look up into the sky, following the tornado back and forth across the stage.*)

BILL (*From off-stage*): Yee-haw! This is more fun than a buckin' bronco!

NARRATOR: Bill cinched up the lasso and pulled it tight, choking the rain right out of that twister. (*Lightning flashes, thunder roars, and it begins to rain.*) And down below, cows and cowpokes and Kansans alike lapped up the sweetest water they ever tasted.

> (Sluefoot Sue, Cowpokes, *and* Cows *dance around the stage.*)

FLAP JACK: Whooooeee, is it wet!

HARDTACK HANK: How wet do you reckon it is?

> (Bill *enters, wet but happy.*)

BILL: Wet enough! And whaddya say we just leave it at that!

NARRATOR: After three days of rain, the grass turned green, the cows got fat, and the Bandana Bandits gave up bushwhackin' for good.

> (Cowpokes *toss their hats in the air and cheer.*)

SOURDOUGH SAL: I told ya this cattle drive was a brilliant idea.

> (*All* Cowpokes *except* Bill *pick up their hats and exit.*)

NARRATOR: And that's the story of how Pecos Bill invented the cattle drive. As for him and Sluefoot Sue, well, that's another story.

> (Bill *and* Sluefoot Sue *exit together, holding hands, leaving* Narrator *and* Bill's *hat on-stage.* Narrator *slowly walks over to the hat.*)

NARRATOR: Whatever happened to Pecos Bill? Well, some folks say what with the big cities and highways, Bill died of a broken heart. (*He picks up the hat, dusts it off, and puts it on his head.*) But I say Pecos Bill's still with us, wanderin' the land, wearin' his favorite hat, tellin' stories, and singin' with the coyotes. Arrrooooooooo!

(Coyotes *howl from off-stage.* Narrator *exits. Lights go dark.*)

Meet the Author JOHN TICHENOR

John Tichenor wrote his adaptation of "Pecos Bill" for a children's theater group in New Hampshire. In writing the play, he tried to capture the fun side of history. "I've been hooked on stories that blend history and fiction . . . ever since I was a kid. Most of my favorite books were historical fiction. 'Pecos Bill' clicked into that interest — with a fanciful touch."

Tichenor believes that stories like "Pecos Bill" offer a lot to young readers. "Kids see characters who think for themselves and who use their imagination. They also get to enjoy themselves." Tichenor has written or developed at least twenty plays for children and is currently writing a novel for kids aged nine to twelve. He says, "I try to use humor and the world of fantasy and make-believe to reach kids at an important turning point in their lives."

Meet the Illustrator ETHAN LONG

Ethan Long comes from a long line of Long artists: His father is an architect and his grandfather worked in watercolors. As a boy, Long liked riding his unicycle and juggling. However, his real love was art. When Long attended one of the Ringling Schools in Sarasota, Florida, he didn't study at the Circus School but at the School of Art and Design. He now lives in Pennsylvania with his wife, their child, and their dog.

Lasso Some

Write a Tall Tale

The Adventures of . . .

Mom to the rescue! Neighbor saves the day! Life is full of people who perform heroic deeds. Write a tall tale about someone you know who is a real hero or heroine. Use the exaggerated style of *Pecos Bill* to tell about that person's heroic acts.

Write a Diary Entry

When Bill Met Sue

It was a red-letter day in the lives of Pecos Bill and Sluefoot Sue when the two characters met. Write the entry for that day in the diary of Bill or Sue. Or write about a red-letter day when you met a new friend.

Wild Ideas

Have a Discussion

The Wild (and Crazy) West

Lassoing with a snake?? Riding a tornado?? The West shown in *Pecos Bill* is different from the West in *Along the Santa Fe Trail* and *Children of the Wild West*. In a discussion with classmates, compare and contrast Western life in the three selections.

Make a List

Don't Bark With Your Mouth Full!

It wasn't easy for Pecos Bill to change his coyote ways! Put yourself in his place. Make a list of some activities that fill your day. In another column, make a list of problems that those activities might create for someone raised by coyotes.

517

HOME ON THE RANGE

Sung around many a campfire, the song "Home on the Range" was first published as a poem. "Oh, Give Me a Home Where the Buffalo Roam" appeared in December 1873 in *The Smith County Pioneer* newspaper in Kansas.

Words by Dr. Brewster M. Higley

Music by Daniel E. Kelley

Oh, give me a home, where the buf - fa-lo roam,

Where the deer and the an - te-lope play; . . .

Where sel - dom is heard a dis - cour - ag-ing word

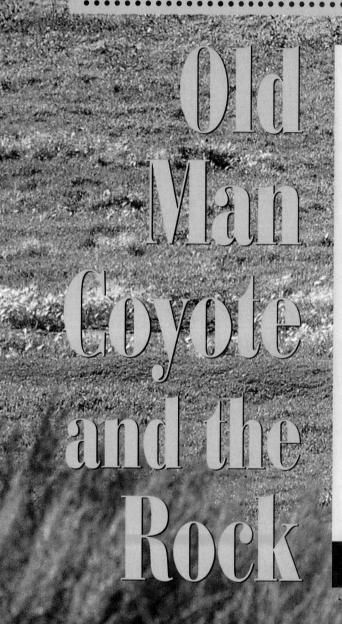

Old Man Coyote and the Rock

KEEPERS OF THE EARTH

Native American Stories and Environmental Activities for Children

Michael J. Caduto and Joseph Bruchac

Foreword by N. Scott Momaday

Illustrations by John Kahionhes Fadden and Carol Wood

told by Joseph Bruchac

Old Man Coyote was going along.

It was quite a while since he had eaten and he was feeling cut in half by hunger. He came to the top of a hill and there he saw a big rock. Old Man Coyote took out his flint knife.

"Grandfather," Old Man Coyote said to the rock, "I give you this fine knife. Now help me in some way, because I am hungry."

Then Old Man Coyote went along further. He went over the top of the hill and there at the bottom was a buffalo that had just been killed.

"How lucky I am," Old Man Coyote said. "But how can I butcher this buffalo without a knife? Now where did I leave my knife?"

Then Old Man Coyote walked back up the hill until he came to the big rock where his knife still lay on the ground.

"You don't need this knife," he said to the big rock.

Then he picked his flint knife up and ran back to where he had left the buffalo. Now, though, where there had been a freshly killed buffalo, there were only buffalo bones and the bones were very old and gray. Then, from behind him, Old Man Coyote heard a rumbling noise. He

turned around and looked up. The big rock was rolling down the hill after him. **GA-DA-RUM, GA-DA-RUM.**

Old Man Coyote began to run. He ran and ran, but the stone still rumbled after him. **GA-DA-RUM, GA-DA-RUM.** Old Man Coyote ran until he came to a bear den.

"Help me," he called in to the bears.

The bears looked out and saw what was chasing Old Man Coyote. "We can't help you against Grandfather Rock," they said.

GA-DA-RUM, GA-DA-RUM. The big rock kept coming and Old Man Coyote kept running. Now he came to a cave where the mountain lions lived and he called out again.

"Help me," Old Man Coyote said. "I am about to be killed!"

The mountain lions looked out and saw what was after Old Man Coyote. "No," they said, "we can't help you if you have angered Grandfather Rock."

GA-DA-RUM, GA-DA-RUM. The big rock kept rumbling after Old Man Coyote and he kept running. Now he came to the place where a bull buffalo was grazing.

"Help me," Old Man Coyote yelled. "That big rock said it was going to kill all the buffalo. When I tried to stop it, it began to chase me."

The bull buffalo braced his legs and thrust his head out to stop the big rock. But the rock just brushed the bull buffalo aside and left him standing there dazed, with his horns bent and his head pushed back into his shoulders. To this day all buffalo are still like that.

GA-DA-RUM, GA-DA-RUM. The big rock kept rolling and Old Man Coyote kept running. But Old Man Coyote was getting tired now and the rock was getting closer. Then Old Man Coyote looked up and saw a nighthawk flying overhead.

"My friend," Old Man Coyote yelled up to the nighthawk, "this big rock that is chasing me said you are ugly. It said you have a wide mouth and your eyes are too big and your beak is all pinched up. I told it not to say that and it began to chase me."

The nighthawk heard what Old Man Coyote said and grew very angry. He called the other nighthawks. They began to swoop down and strike at the big rock with their beaks. Each time they struck the big rock a piece broke off and stopped rolling. **GA-DA-RUM, GA-DA-RUM.**

The rock kept rolling and Old Man Coyote kept running, but now the rock was much smaller. The nighthawks continued to swoop down and break off pieces. Finally the big rock was nothing but small pebbles.

Old Man Coyote came up and looked at the little stones. "My, my," he said to the nighthawks, "Why did you wide-mouthed, big-eyed, pinch-beaked birds do that to my old friend?" Then Old Man Coyote laughed and started on his way again.

Now the nighthawks were very angry at Old Man Coyote. They gathered all of the pieces of the big rock and fanned them together with their wings. The next thing Old Man Coyote knew, he heard a familiar sound behind him again. **GA-DA-RUM, GA-DA-RUM.** He tried to run, but he was so tired now he could not get away. The big rock rolled right over him and flattened him out.

Meet the Author

Joseph Bruchac

In "Old Man Coyote and the Rock," as in much of his writing, Joseph Bruchac drew on two major sources of inspiration. Those sources are nature and the Native

American experience. Throughout his career, Bruchac — whose Abenaki tribal name is Sozap — has worked to spread awareness of modern Native American literature both for adults and for children. For Joseph Bruchac and his readers, "The heritage of American Indian oral literature (which is still very much alive today . . .) is a truly great one."

Do You Believe

Grand View Ship Hotel, a steamboat in the mountains near Pittsburgh, PA.

Cranberry Cocktail, on Cape Cod, MA.

The Elephant Hotel at Margate City, one of the oldest landmarks, near Atlantic City, N. J.

The Elephant Hotel, near Atlantic City, NJ.

This??

HAINES The Shoe Wizard SHOE HOUSE YORK, PA.

Shoe House, near York, PA.

FAMOUS ONE-LOG HOUSE
Free ADMISSION

One Log House, in San Francisco, CA.

WE'RE AT... *norman johnson's* UpSiDe-DoWN House
SUNRISE GOLF VILLAGE, FLA
UPSIDE DOWN ENTRANCE

Upside-Down House, in Sunrise Village, FL.

Ice Cream
TOASTED FRANKFURTS
Ice Cream
TOASTED HAMBURGS
TOASTED SANDWICHES
Ice Cream
MILK DRINKS

Roadside Ice Cream Stand, in Berlin, CT.

Do You Believe This??

Contents

Just an Ordinary Day?

POST CARD

UNITED STATES POSTAGE

GEORGE WASHINGTON 1789–1797

1 CENT 1

What a Character!

You Won't Believe Your Eyes

The Kid in the Red Jacket

by Barbara Park

What do you do when you're new in town and your only friend is a pesky six-year-old who won't take a hint?

In the same book . . .

More about moving and being the new kid on the block

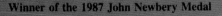

Winner of the 1987 John Newbery Medal

SID FLEISCHMAN
The Whipping Boy

PAPERBACK PLUS

The Whipping Boy

by Sid Fleischman

The adventures of a spoiled prince named Brat, a brave lad named Jemmy, and a pair of kidnappers

In the same book . . .

More about Sid Fleischman and castles of the world

Reading Is Believing!

The Case of the Mummified Pigs and Other Mysteries in Nature
by Susan E. Quinlan
Who made mummies of dead pigs? Why did a herd of reindeer disappear? The author searches for the answers to these and other mysteries.

All the Money in the World
by Bill Brittain
A leprechaun grants Quentin three wishes. He wishes for all the money in the world — and gets more than he bargained for!

Surtsey: The Newest Place on Earth
by Kathryn Lasky
On a November morning in 1963, a volcano erupted under the ocean off the coast of Iceland. When the lava settled, Earth had a new island.

Grand Canyon
by Patrick Cone
The author-photographer presents outstanding photographs and a geo-logical history of this incredible natural wonder.

Wanted . . . Mud Blossom
by Betsy Byars
Only the Blossom family would put a dog on trial! The Blossoms think Mud is responsible for the mysterious disappearance of a pet hamster.

The Boggart
by Susan Cooper
Emily receives a desk that belonged to a Scottish relative. She opens it and lets loose the Boggart, a centuries-old sprite who causes all kinds of mischief.

Meet Gary Soto

When Gary Soto was growing up in Fresno, California, he attended Jefferson Elementary School. One year the school held a talent show, and a classmate of Gary's decided to pantomime to the song "Sugar Shack." On stage in the middle of his performance, Soto's friend forgot the words. That event later became the inspiration for the story "La Bamba."

Like many of Soto's stories, "La Bamba" builds on Soto's memories of his childhood and of the neighborhood where he grew up. Living in California, Soto played a lot of baseball, soccer, and four-square. "I was a playground kid," he says.

Today Soto is a writer and a college professor. He has published short stories, such as "The Skirt" and "The Pool Party," and longer fiction for both adults and younger readers. A new collection of his short stories is *Local News*.

Meet David Diaz

Born in New York City, David Diaz grew up in southern Florida. In the second grade, Diaz set his sights on being an artist. His art explorations have since led him to sculpture, pottery, and ceramics as well as illustration. Diaz has worked with Gary Soto's material before, illustrating *Neighborhood Odes*, a book of poetry. Diaz currently lives with his wife and three children in San Diego, California.

LaBamba

BY GARY SOTO

Baseball
in April

AND OTHER STORIES
GARY SOTO

Manuel was the fourth of seven children and looked like a lot of kids in his neighborhood: black hair, brown face, and skinny legs scuffed from summer play. But summer was giving way to fall: the trees were turning red, the lawns brown, and the pomegranate trees were heavy with fruit. Manuel walked to school in the frosty morning, kicking leaves and thinking of tomorrow's talent show. He was still amazed that he had volunteered. He was going to pretend to sing Ritchie Valens's "La Bamba" before the entire school.

Why did I raise my hand? he asked himself, but in his heart he knew the answer. He yearned for the limelight. He wanted applause as loud as a thunderstorm, and to hear his friends say, "Man, that was bad!" And he wanted to impress the girls, especially Petra Lopez, the second-prettiest girl in his class. The prettiest was already taken by his friend Ernie. Manuel knew he should be reasonable, since he himself was not great-looking, just average.

Manuel kicked through the fresh-fallen leaves. When he got to school he realized he had forgotten his math workbook. If his teacher found out, he would have to stay after school and miss practice for the talent show. But fortunately for him, they did drills that morning.

During lunch Manuel hung around with Benny, who was also in the talent show. Benny was going to play the trumpet in spite of the fat lip he had gotten playing football.

"How do I look?" Manuel asked. He cleared his throat and started moving his lips in pantomime. No words came out, just a hiss that sounded like a snake. Manuel tried to look emotional, flailing his arms on the high notes and opening his eyes and mouth as wide as he could when he came to *Para bailar la baaaaammmba.*

After Manuel finished, Benny said it looked all right, but suggested Manuel dance while he sang. Manuel thought for a moment and decided it was a good idea.

"Yeah, just think you're like some rock star," Benny suggested. "But don't get carried away."

During rehearsal, Mr. Roybal, nervous about his debut as the school's talent coordinator, cursed under his breath when the lever that controlled the speed of the record player jammed.

"Darn," he growled, trying to force the lever. "What's wrong with you?"

"Is it broken?" Manuel asked, bending over for a closer look. It looked all right to him.

Mr. Roybal assured Manuel that he would have a good record player at the talent show, even if it meant bringing his own stereo from home.

Manuel sat in a folding chair, twirling his record on his thumb. He watched a skit about personal hygiene, a mother-and-daughter violin duo, five first-grade girls jumping rope, a karate kid breaking boards, and a skit about the pilgrims. If the record player hadn't been broken, he would have gone after the karate kid, an easy act to follow, he told himself.

As he twirled his forty-five record, Manuel thought they had a great talent show. The entire school would be amazed. His mother and father would be proud, and his brothers and sisters would be jealous and pout. It would be a night to remember.

Benny walked onto the stage, raised his trumpet to his mouth, and waited for his cue. Mr. Roybal raised his hand like a symphony conductor and let it fall dramatically. Benny inhaled and blew so loud that Manuel dropped his record, which rolled across the cafeteria floor until it hit a wall. Manuel raced after it, picked it up, and wiped it clean.

"Boy, I'm glad it didn't break," he said with a sigh.

That night Manuel had to do the dishes and a lot of homework, so he could only practice in the shower. In bed he prayed that he wouldn't mess up. He prayed that it wouldn't be like when he was a first-grader. For Science Week he had wired together a C battery and a bulb, and told everyone he had discovered how a flashlight worked. He was so pleased with himself that he practiced for hours pressing the wire to the battery, making the bulb wink a dim, orangish light. He showed it to so many kids in his neighborhood that when it was time to show his class how a flashlight worked, the battery was dead. He pressed the wire to the battery, but the bulb didn't respond. He pressed until his thumb hurt and some kids in the back started snickering.

But Manuel fell asleep confident that nothing would go wrong this time.

The next morning his father and mother beamed at him. They were proud that he was going to be in the talent show.

"I wish you would tell us what you're doing," his mother said. His father, a pharmacist who wore a blue smock with his name on a plastic rectangle, looked up from the news-paper and sided with his wife. "Yes, what are you doing in the talent show?"

"You'll see," Manuel said with his mouth full of Cheerios.

The day whizzed by, and so did his afternoon chores and dinner. Suddenly he was dressed in his best clothes and standing next to Benny backstage, listening to the commotion as the cafeteria filled with school kids and parents. The lights dimmed, and Mr. Roybal, sweaty in a tight suit and a necktie with a large knot, wet his lips and parted the stage curtains.

"Good evening, everyone," the kids behind the curtain heard him say. "Good evening to you," some of the smart-alecky kids said back to him.

"Tonight we bring you the best John Burroughs Elementary has to offer, and I'm sure that you'll be both pleased and amazed that our little school houses so much talent. And now, without further ado, let's get on with the show." He turned and, with a swish of his hand, commanded, "Part the curtain." The curtains parted in jerks. A girl dressed as a toothbrush and a boy dressed as a dirty gray tooth walked onto the stage and sang:

> *Brush, brush, brush*
> *Floss, floss, floss*
> *Gargle the germs away — hey! hey! hey!*

After they finished singing, they turned to Mr. Roybal, who dropped his hand. The toothbrush dashed around the stage after the dirty tooth, which was laughing and having a great time until it slipped and nearly rolled off the stage.

Mr. Roybal jumped out and caught it just in time. "Are you OK?"

The dirty tooth answered, "Ask my dentist," which drew laughter and applause from the audience.

The violin duo played next, and except for one time when the girl got lost, they sounded fine. People applauded, and some even stood up. Then the first-grade girls maneuvered onto the stage while jumping rope. They were all smiles and bouncing ponytails as a hundred cameras flashed at once. Mothers "aahed" and fathers sat up proudly.

The karate kid was next. He did a few kicks, yells, and chops, and finally, when his father held up a board, punched it in two. The audience clapped and looked at each other, wide-eyed with respect. The boy bowed to the audience, and father and son ran off the stage.

Manuel remained behind the stage shivering with fear. He mouthed the words to "La Bamba" and swayed from left to right. Why did he raise his hand and volunteer? Why couldn't he have just sat there like the rest of the kids and not said anything? While the karate kid was on stage, Mr. Roybal, more sweaty than before, took Manuel's forty-five record and placed it on the new record player.

"You ready?" Mr. Roybal asked.

"Yeah . . ."

Mr. Roybal walked back on stage and announced that Manuel Gomez, a fifth-grader in Mrs. Knight's class, was going to pantomime Ritchie Valens's classic hit "La Bamba."

The cafeteria roared with applause. Manuel was nervous but loved the noisy crowd. He pictured his mother and father applauding loudly and his brothers and sisters also clapping, though not as energetically.

Manuel walked on stage and the song started immediately. Glassy-eyed from the shock of being in front of so many people, Manuel moved his lips and swayed in a made-up dance step. He couldn't see his parents, but he could see his brother Mario, who was a year younger, thumb-wrestling with a friend. Mario was wearing Manuel's favorite shirt; he would deal with Mario later. He saw some other kids get up and head for the drinking fountain, and a baby sitting in the middle of an aisle sucking her thumb and watching him intently.

What am I doing here? thought Manuel. This is no fun at all. Everyone was just sitting there. Some people were moving to the beat, but most were just watching him, like they would a monkey at the zoo.

But when Manuel did a fancy dance step, there was a burst of applause and some girls screamed. Manuel tried another dance step. He heard more applause and screams and started getting into the groove as he shivered and snaked around the stage. But the record got stuck, and he had to sing

Para bailar la bamba
Para bailar la bamba
Para bailar la bamba
Para bailar la bamba

again and again.

Manuel couldn't believe his bad luck. The audience began to laugh and stand up in their chairs. Manuel remembered how the forty-five record had dropped from his hand and rolled across the cafeteria floor. It probably got scratched, he thought, and now it was stuck, and he was stuck dancing and moving his lips to the same words over and over. He had never been so embarrassed. He would have to ask his parents to move the family out of town.

After Mr. Roybal ripped the needle across the record, Manuel slowed his dance steps to a halt. He didn't know what to do except bow to the audience, which applauded wildly, and scoot off the stage, on the verge of tears. This was worse than the homemade flashlight. At least no one laughed then, they just snickered.

Manuel stood alone, trying hard to hold back the tears as Benny, center stage, played his trumpet. Manuel was jealous because he sounded great, then mad as he recalled that it was Benny's loud trumpet playing that made the forty-five record fly out of his hands. But when the entire cast lined up for a

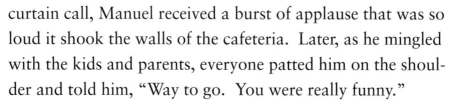

curtain call, Manuel received a burst of applause that was so loud it shook the walls of the cafeteria. Later, as he mingled with the kids and parents, everyone patted him on the shoulder and told him, "Way to go. You were really funny."

Funny? Manuel thought. Did he do something funny?

Funny. Crazy. Hilarious. These were the words people said to him. He was confused, but beyond caring. All he knew was that people were paying attention to him, and his brothers and sisters looked at him with a mixture of jealousy and awe. He was going to pull Mario aside and punch him in the arm for wearing his shirt, but he cooled it. He was enjoying the limelight. A teacher brought him cookies and punch, and the popular kids who had never before given him the time of day now clustered around him. Ricardo, the editor of the school bulletin, asked him how he made the needle stick.

"It just happened," Manuel said, crunching on a star-shaped cookie.

At home that night his father, eager to undo the buttons on his shirt and ease into his La-Z-Boy recliner, asked Manuel the same thing, how he managed to make the song stick on the words

Para bailar la bamba.

Manuel thought quickly and reached for scientific jargon he had read in magazines. "Easy, Dad. I used laser tracking with high optics and low functional decibels per channel." His proud but confused father told him to be quiet and go to bed.

"Ah, *que niños tan truchas*," he said as he walked to the kitchen for a glass of milk. "I don't know how you kids nowadays get so smart."

Manuel, feeling happy, went to his bedroom, undressed, and slipped into his pajamas. He looked in the mirror and began to pantomime "La Bamba," but stopped because he was tired of the song. He crawled into bed. The sheets were as cold as the moon that stood over the peach tree in their backyard.

He was relieved that the day was over. Next year, when they asked for volunteers for the talent show, he wouldn't raise his hand. Probably.

YOUR IDEAS — UP IN LIGHTS!

Make a Poster

Draw a Crowd!

Mr. Roybal has asked you to make a poster advertising the school talent show. How will your poster make people come to see it? Use various art materials, magazine pictures, or even photographs to create your poster.

Make a Program

Get Your Program!

With so many performers, the audience needs a guide to the talent show. Put together a written program that lists and briefly describes each act. Make up a name for the show and decorate the front of your program.

Write a Review

Thumbs Up, Thumbs Down

The talent show is over; the school auditorium is dark. But Ricardo, the editor of the school bulletin, still has work to do — he has to write a review of the show. Write the review for him! Describe and give your opinion of each act in the show. Which act stole the show?

Write a Story

From Where I Sit . . .

"La Bamba" is told from Manuel's point of view. But what if someone else — Petra Lopez, Benny, Mario, Mr. Roybal, Ricardo, or Manuel's father — had told the story? Which parts of the story would that person tell? Write the story from the point of view of one of these characters.

MISTAKES THAT WORKED

BY CHARLOTTE FOLTZ JONES

VELCRO

For thousands of years, man has walked through fields of weeds and arrived home with burrs stuck to his clothing. It's amazing no one took advantage of the problem until 1948.

George de Mestral, a Swiss engineer, returned from a walk one day in 1948 and found some cockleburs clinging to his cloth jacket. When de Mestral loosened them, he examined one under his microscope. The principle was simple. The cocklebur is a maze of thin strands with burrs (or hooks) on the ends that cling to fabrics or animal fur.

By the accident of the cockleburs sticking to his jacket, George de Mestral recognized the potential for a practical new fastener. It took eight years to experiment, develop, and perfect the invention, which consists of two strips of nylon fabric. One strip contains thousands of small hooks. The other strip contains small loops. When the two strips are pressed together, they form a strong bond.

"Hook-and-loop fastener" is what we call it today. VELCRO, the name de Mestral gave his product, is the brand most people in the United States know. It is strong, easily separated, lightweight, durable, and washable, comes in a variety of colors, and won't jam.

There are thousands of uses for hook-and-loop fasteners — on clothing, shoes, watch bands, or backpacks; around the house or garage; in automobiles, aircraft, parachutes, space suits, or space shuttles; to secure blood pressure cuffs and artificial heart chambers. The list is never-ending.

The only bad thing about hook-and-loop fasteners is the competition they give the snap, zipper, button, and shoelace industries!

DOG GUIDES FOR PEOPLE WHO ARE BLIND •••••••••••••••••••••

World War I lasted more than four years — from 1914 to 1918. During that time, approximately 8.5 million people were killed and 21 million were wounded.

Near the end of World War I, a doctor was walking outside a German military hospital with a soldier who had been blinded in battle. The doctor's dog joined the walk and when the doctor was called into one of the buildings, the blind soldier was left alone with the dog.

Soon the doctor returned, but the blind man and the dog were missing. When he found them, he discovered the dog had led the blind patient across the hospital grounds.

The doctor was amazed at what his untrained pet dog had done and decided to see how well a trained working breed of dog could lead a blind person. The results were great and the German government soon expanded the dog guide program.

POTATO CHIPS •

Americans spend almost $4 billion every year on a treat we know as potato chips.

A popular story says they were invented in 1853 in Saratoga Springs, New York. Many wealthy people vacationed at the Carey Moon Lake House in Saratoga Springs and a Native American chef named George Crum worked in the kitchen there.

One day a customer kept sending his plate of fried potatoes back to the kitchen asking that they be sliced thinner and fried longer. George Crum had a bad temper, and he decided to get even with the complaining diner. He sliced the potatoes very thin, fried them till they were curly crisps, and salted them. Certain the guest would hate them, he had the potatoes delivered to the table. To everyone's surprise, the patron was delighted and asked for more.

Word spread quickly of these crispy potatoes and until the early 1900s they were known as Saratoga chips after the town where they were introduced.

Today over 816 million pounds of potato chips are consumed in the United States each year. A total of 3,468 billion pounds of potatoes end up as America's number one snack food: potato chips.

Extraordinary Art

When is a French fry not just a French fry? When it's an eight-foot sculpture, of course! Here are some examples of how artists can show us the "extraordinariness" of ordinary things.

▼ **Salvador Dalí**
Oil on canvas
*The Persistence
of Memory,* 1931.
13 x 9$\frac{1}{2}$ in.

René Magritte
Oil on canvas
Time Transfixed, 1938.
$57\frac{7}{8}$ x $37\frac{7}{8}$ in.

Claes Oldenburg ▶
Sculpture
*Shoestring Potatoes
Spilling from a Bag,* 1966.
108 x 46 x 42 in.

◀ **George Segal**
Sculpture
The Diner, 1964–1966.
$98\frac{3}{4}$ x $144\frac{1}{4}$ x 96 in.

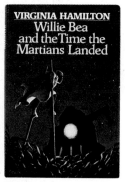

Willie Bea and the Time the Martians Landed

by Virginia Hamilton

It is October 30, 1938. Millions of Americans are in a state of panic. They have heard on their radios what sound like news reports of Martians invading Earth! Willie Bea, a young girl with a vivid imagination, has another idea. Because she has a pattern of lines in her palm that her aunt Leah calls a "Star of Venus," Willie Bea is sure the invaders are from the planet Venus. She thinks she might be able to communicate with them and stop the attack.

Willie Bea's friend Toughy Clay claims to have seen one of the aliens on the nearby Kelly farm, where the corn harvest is in high gear. Wearing their Halloween costumes, she and Toughy go off on their stilts toward the farm. They pay no attention to the panicked warnings of a neighbor.

Willie Bea and Toughy went, striding as fast as their legs and arms propelling the stilts would take them, their capes bouncing.

"No!" hollered the farmer after them. His children and wife commenced shouting. "That's the wrong way! You're headin' the direction of that Kelly farm. That's where the Martians is. . . ."

But Willie Bea and Toughy were gone. They were in the dark, invisible in the night.

Her hands and face were cold now.

So cold! she thought. Glad for the capes of sheets!

Out here where there were only cornfields, the cold seemed to sift down from the sky into the ground and come up again. Willie Bea longed to stop and just take stock of things. Her muscles were mighty sore, holding on so tightly to the stilts. Her fingers cramped her, and her legs were stiff and chilled. They were starting to ache.

"Maybe we oughtn't to come out here," she said softly. All was so still around them. "Toughy, maybe we ought to just go on back."

Toughy strode ahead of her. They had slowed somewhat, for thick trees along the road blocked out the bonfire light behind them. They crossed onto a narrower gravel strip with fields on either side. Gravel was tricky beneath their stilts. Willie Bea saw that there was no fence on either side of the gravel road.

"This is a private road," Toughy told her.

"Whose private?" she asked him.

"It's the Kelly private," Toughy said. "Cuts right through the corn, and they own it. Can say who walk and stride on it, too." Toughy had never been on the Kelly road before. But he recognized it from the years of stories he had heard about the farm.

"Are we that close? Keep your voice *down*," she whispered.

"Look there," Toughy said. He stood, shifting back and forth to keep his balance.

Willie Bea shifted, too. But she was better at balancing than Toughy was. Just arm pressure and flexing leg muscles was all that was necessary. And once in a while moving the stilts an inch or two. "Look at what?" she said.

"There. Come over here," Toughy said.

She came up beside him. And what she saw made her feel like someone had shut down all her tiredness. Had turned off the cold of her hands and face. She didn't realize she was shivering, but the cold had got way under the hobo costume she had made.

They were on the private Kelly road and it had risen over a hillock. At first Willie Bea looked down at the reach of land.

"Is it the ice-skating lake?" she asked in the softest voice. Who could tell anything in this deep night?

"Uh-uh," Toughy said. "I hear the lake is on the other side of the house. Here is only the fields on each side of the private road."

"Well, I'm glad of that," Willie Bea said.

She thought to look up, gazing across and beyond the black land-reach to where there had to be some sort of hill. Over there, situated high and handsome, was the biggest house Willie Bea had ever seen. It was enormous. And it was lit up like a carnival, like a birthday cake.

"Havin' a Halloween ball?" she asked in awe.

She thought she heard strains of music coming from the mansion.

"Think they just own a lot of light," Toughy said. "Think they must be listenin' to their Victrola phonograph."

They don't even know the Venus ones are here! Willie Bea thought.

"Did you hear that?" she said. "Did you hear them laughing over there, them Kellys?" she asked Toughy. Her voice was dreamy and faraway.

"No," he said. "They don't act like they care about Martians, though."

"Not Martians," Willie Bea said. "They are from Venus."

"That's what you said before. But how you know that?" he asked her.

"Aunt Leah read my palm and she found in it the Star of Venus. Aunt Leah says it is a sign of great good luck."

"You sure?" Toughy asked. But he knew anything Leah Wing told was true. Everyone knew that Leah Wing was the best fortune lady ever did live among the people. And rich, like the Kellys.

"So you lookin' for the Venus ones. So, see what they have to say to you?" Toughy asked.

Willie Bea nodded in the dark. "I don't know what-all will happen," she said in a misty voice. She never took her eyes from that Kelly mansion of enchantment. "But maybe it will stop the attack from them. Maybe if they see there's somebody here that has the Star of Venus . . ." Her voice seemed to drift off on the air.

"I don't know," Toughy murmured. He imagined it could be true. In the deep dark of Halloween night, the Kelly farm was a magic kingdom. Invading men from Venus were *boldacious* monsters, close about. Watch out! Anything could be true.

"Where'd you see the monster?" Willie Bea asked. "Was it over there? You can see some big, dark trees by the light from those windows."

Toughy shifted uneasily on his stilts. He cleared his throat, about to tell his lie again, when Willie Bea said, "Come on! We'll follow the road closer."

It was deep, dark going, and their stilts made grating sounds on the gravel. When they were down there, it didn't feel or look much different than on the rise. It was cold. The cornfields looked full of tall rows of dark.

"There's no lake that I can tell," Willie Bea said.

"I told you. Say the lake is on the other side of the house," Toughy said.

"Well, you don't have to yell," Willie Bea told him.

"I'm not yelling!" he yelled back.

They were both yelling. Noise, a deep rumbling, was coming out of the ground. Willie Bea couldn't hear herself breathe, or think.

"What's that?" she hollered at Toughy.

"Don't know. Can't tell where it is or what it is!" he hollered.

It was getting closer. Willie Bea thought she saw something. Like the blackest night moving.

"You see that?" she thought she yelled. Her mouth moved, but she couldn't hear what came out. "Toughy!" she screamed.

"Willie Bea!" he was screaming back. "Willie Bea!"

Now they could guess what the noise was. The great black dark that moved was one of the monsters. It was a rolling, ear-splitting, outlandish alien. And huge.

The thing must have turned a corner in front of them from behind the house, somehow. It had turned toward them and they saw its evil eye.

An awful, white, wicked, round eye. It could have been its heat ray, but it didn't hurt them. It was just blinding.

"Wait! I got the Star!" cried Willie Bea.

The great black dark came straight for them. And another huge blackness came on behind it. Giants as tall as houses, tall as trees, on the move.

Another one came after the second. Two of them marching, rolling behind the first. They spread out to the left of the first one. Their blinding eyes outlined the first one. Illuminated it for Willie Bea to see plainly that it was a deadly, monstrous alien.

"It's true! It's an invasion!" Toughy was yelling. "Run. Run, Willie Bea!"

Willie Bea couldn't hear him. She couldn't move. She was transfixed by the monsters. The first one's neck wasn't in the center of its body, where it should have been. It was on the right *side* of it! The long neck was like a wide stovepipe jutting out of its side. Its head that fitted on its neck was *all* V-shaped.

Suddenly, it seemed that the first monster spoke to her. She was staring into its awful eye, into its noise. The darkness moving one by one was overpowering.

All went quiet inside Willie Bea. She no longer heard the monster's roaring noise. Its sound of voice was right with her, like it was all around in her head. It seemed to be right by her, right in her ear.

"Huh?" Willie Bea said, staring wildly into the evil eye.

"Willie Bea, I come here, too. I got here late. I was looking for you. Heard you shouting." Spoken loud and as clear as a bell in her ear.

The white eyes of the monsters coming on held her hypnotized. She thought she told them, "Look. I hold the Star of Venus in my palm. Turn off your rays. Don't fight. We only want to be friends!" She held up her palm for them to see.

"Willie Bea, we'd better get back. You coming back with me?"

The first monster was now to the left side of the road. Its head on the side, on its long neck, was coming right at her.

"Oh, no, I can't go back to Venus with *you!*" she told it.

"You're just scared and tired. Follow me close behind."

The second monster was passing along beside the gravel road. Willie Bea looked up at its head.

"No! Get away!" she hollered.

Then she was backing away from the third monster. She thought its light was bearing down. "You leave me be!" She flailed her arms backward and one stilt leg slipped in the gravel. She twisted, trying to untangle herself from the foot wedges. She was falling. Something grabbed at her. She saw the last monster's head turn in her direction. Its light was full on her. It was coming for her.

Willie Bea, falling. And something, someone had hold of her, was falling with her. She hit the ground, falling hard on part of someone. Something struck her a glancing blow on the forehead.

All went dark for Willie Bea. The dark filled with glowing comets and stars. Great planets of Venus and Mars. All such colors of worlds, pumpkin yellow and orange in a Halloween universe.

Willie Bea opened her eyes on an alien standing over her. She thought she saw its V-shaped mouth: "Willie Bea! Are you hurt?"

"No. I won't go back with you, either," she told it. "I like my own world."

"You hit your head. It knocked you silly," the alien said.

Willie Bea's head started hurting. Suddenly, she felt cold all over. Her legs were aching. Her hand with its Star felt numb as she came to.

She saw a great light. It was upon her and the someone who stood over her.

"Where . . . ?" was all she could think to say.

She heard fast footfalls on the gravel. She lifted her head and was blinded by the white monster-light. The monster made its roaring sound, but it wasn't moving now.

"What happened?" it hollered, sounding frightened. "What are you kids doing where we are harvesting? Did we hit someone? . . . Oh, little child!"

Willie Bea saw a man in the light. He knelt beside her. "Did the combines scare you, child? We might've run you over!"

Willie Bea was damp and clammy from the gathering cold and mist. Tired and confused, she closed her eyes. Her insides flopped and the inky night of a dizzying universe returned.

Where a giant black cat sat on a pumpkin world. Where aliens were Kelly kings. They took away the Star in her palm. Willie Bea was so small, so unimportant. They made her polish their V-shaped crowns of gold.

Meet Virginia Hamilton

Like many of her stories, *Willie Bea and the Time the Martians Landed* is filled with Virginia Hamilton's childhood memories. Hamilton grew up in the same southern Ohio farm country that Willie Bea and Toughy Clay stilt across in the story. Hamilton and her cousin Marleen made stilts just like Willie Bea's. Even Willie Bea's personality is based on Hamilton's memories of herself when she was young and "given to wild imaginings."

Hamilton also builds on old family stories in her fiction. Telling stories was one way her family passed its history on to the children and grandchildren. Hamilton has absorbed all this family lore into her imagination. She says she can see her hometown "through my eyes, my mother's eyes, and my grandmother's eyes." As a writer, Hamilton says she likes to take those views and "weave . . . a tale out of the mystery of my past and present."

One of Hamilton's other novels, *M. C. Higgins, the Great*, won the Newbery Medal. Hamilton was the first African American writer to win that award.

Meet Charles Lilly

When Charles Lilly was in high school, he wanted to become a nuclear engineer. Then one day Mr. Burns, the head of the school's art department, saw something Lilly was drawing. "Mr. Burns told me I was going to be an artist," Lilly remembers. "He didn't ask me; he just told me."

Mr. Burns was right. Lilly graduated from the School of Visual Arts in New York City in 1970, and has been painting and teaching illustration ever since. He also gives lectures about his work at local schools.

Lilly now lives in Jamaica, New York. His son, Eliott, is also a talented artist.

Stride Through a

Portrait of a Mistake

Willie Bea mistook a corn harvester in the
dark for something very scary. Think about a
time when you mistook an ordinary object for
something strange or scary. Then draw a picture of what you thought the object was —
and what it turned out to be.

Night Harvest Nightmare

Was it a Martian or was it a girl on stilts?
Think about what the combine driver saw
and felt on the night of Willie Bea's field walk.
Then write that part of the story from his
point of view.

Field of Ideas!

Write a Newspaper Article

What Really Happened?

Suppose you were a reporter covering the strange incident on the Kelly farm the night of October 30, 1938. What were the facts? What were the rumors? Write an article for the local newspaper about what happened.

Have a Discussion

Surprise!

Both Manuel in "La Bamba" and Willie Bea in *Willie Bea and the Time the Martians Landed* had to face something completely unexpected. Think about the way each character reacted to his or her situation. Then discuss how their reactions were different and how they were alike.

Invasion from Mars

by Howard Koch

THE PANIC BROADCAST

portrait of an event
by Howard Koch

... "LADIES AND GENTLEMEN:
WE INTERRUPT THIS PROGRAM
FOR THE FOLLOWING
ANNOUNCEMENT...STRANGE
BEINGS HAVE LANDED IN
THE JERSEY FARMLANDS
TONIGHT AND ARE THE
VANGUARD OF AN INVADING
ARMY FROM MARS...THEY
ARE NOW IN CONTROL OF
THE MIDDLE SECTION OF..."

"Run for your life! The Martians have landed!"

On the night of October 30, 1938, Orson Welles and the Mercury Theater Company broadcast the radio play *Invasion from Mars*, adapted from the novel *The War of the Worlds* by H. G. Wells. Before the play was over, thousands of listeners all over the country were convinced that a Martian army had landed and was attacking Earth. In this scene from the play, newsman Carl Phillips is broadcasting live from the New Jersey farm where a strange metal cylinder has crash-landed. How would *you* have reacted to hearing these words on your radio?

PHILLIPS: I wish I could convey the atmosphere . . . the background of this . . . fantastic scene. Hundreds of cars are parked in a field in back of us. Police are trying to rope off the roadway leading into the farm. But it's no use. They're breaking right through. Their headlights throw an enormous spot on the pit where the object's half buried. Some of the more daring souls are venturing near the edge. Their silhouettes stand out against the metal sheen.

(Faint humming sound)

One man wants to touch the thing . . . he's having an argument with a policeman. The policeman wins. . . . Now, ladies and gentlemen, there's something I haven't mentioned in all this excitement, but it's becoming more distinct. Perhaps you've caught it already on your radio. Listen: *(Long pause)* . . . Do you hear it? It's a curious humming sound that seems to come from inside the object. I'll move the microphone nearer. Here. *(Pause)* Now we're not more than twenty-five feet away. Can you hear it now? Oh, Professor Pierson!

PIERSON: Yes, Mr. Phillips?

Orson Welles

PHILLIPS: Can you tell us the meaning of that scraping noise inside the thing?

PIERSON: Possibly the unequal cooling of its surface.

PHILLIPS: Do you still think it's a meteor, Professor?

PIERSON: I don't know what to think. The metal casing is definitely extraterrestrial . . . not found on this earth. Friction with the earth's atmosphere usually tears holes in a meteorite. This thing is smooth and, as you can see, of cylindrical shape.

PHILLIPS: Just a minute! Something's happening! Ladies and gentlemen, this is terrific! This end of the thing is beginning to flake off! The top is beginning to rotate like a screw! The thing must be hollow!

VOICES: She's a movin'!
Look, the darn thing's unscrewing!
Keep back, there! Keep back, I tell you!
Maybe there's men in it trying to escape!
It's red hot, they'll burn to a cinder!
Keep back there. Keep those idiots back!

(Suddenly the clanking sound of a huge piece of falling metal)

VOICES: She's off! The top's loose!
Look out there! Stand back!

PHILLIPS: Ladies and gentlemen, this is the most terrifying thing I have ever witnessed . . . Wait a minute! *Someone's crawling out of the hollow top.* Someone or . . . something. I can see peering out of that black hole two luminous disks . . . are they eyes? It might be a face. It might be . . .

(Shout of awe from the crowd)

PHILLIPS: Good heavens, something's wriggling out of the shadow like a gray snake. Now it's another one, and another. They look like tentacles to me. There, I can see the thing's body. It's large as a bear and it glistens like wet leather. But that face. It . . . it's indescribable. I can hardly force myself to keep looking at it. The eyes are black and gleam like a serpent's. The mouth is V-shaped with saliva dripping from its rimless lips that seem to quiver and pulsate. The monster or whatever it is can hardly move. It seems weighed down by . . . possibly gravity or something. The thing's raising up. The crowd falls back. They've seen enough. This is the most extraordinary experience. I can't find words . . . I'm pulling this microphone with me as I talk. I'll have to stop the description until I've taken a new position. Hold on, will you please, I'll be back in a minute.

(Fade into piano)

Many people tuned in late to the radio program. Many didn't listen long enough to realize that what they were hearing was simply a play.

Citizens of Grover's Mill discuss the radio play that put their town on the map.

ANNOUNCER TWO: We are bringing you an eyewitness account of what's happening on the Wilmuth farm, Grover's Mill, New Jersey. *(More piano)* We now return you to Carl Phillips at Grover's Mill.

PHILLIPS: Ladies and gentlemen (Am I on?). Ladies and gentlemen, here I am, back of a stone wall that adjoins Mr. Wilmuth's garden. From here I get a sweep of the whole scene. I'll give you every detail as long as I can talk. As long as I can see. More state police have arrived. They're drawing up a cordon in front of the pit, about thirty of them. No need to push the crowd back now. They're willing to keep their distance. The captain is conferring with someone. We can't quite see who. Oh yes, I believe it's Professor Pierson. Yes, it is. Now they've parted. The professor moves around one side, studying the object, while the captain and two policemen advance with something in their hands. I can see it now. It's a white handkerchief tied to a pole . . . a flag of truce. If those creatures know what that means . . . what anything means! . . . *Wait!* Something's happening!

(Hissing sound followed by a humming that increases in intensity)

A humped shape is rising out of the pit. I can make out a small beam of light against a mirror. What's that? There's a jet of flame springing from that mirror, and it leaps right at the advancing men. It strikes them head on! Good Lord, they're turning into flame!

(*Screams and unearthly shrieks*)

Now the whole field's caught fire. (*Explosion*) The woods . . . the barns . . . the gas tanks of automobiles . . . it's spreading everywhere. It's coming this way. About twenty yards to my right . . .

(*Crash of microphone . . . then dead silence*)

ANNOUNCER TWO: Ladies and gentlemen, due to circumstances beyond our control, we are unable to continue the broadcast from Grover's Mill. Evidently there's some difficulty with our field transmission.

The radio play continues: the creatures in the cylinder are the front line of an army of Martian invaders. Thousands of people frantically try to flee as cylinders land all over the United States. Tall as skyscrapers, the machines advance on long metal legs toward major cities. They knock out communications and use their "heat ray" and poisonous black smoke to defeat all in their way. It seems like the end for humans — but the Martians are eventually killed themselves. How? By Earth's bacteria, against which they have no defenses — in other words, by the common cold.

EXTRA! EXTRA!

Invasion from Mars *had an unexpected and powerful effect on thousands of listeners. Here's some of what happened, as reported in* **The New York Times** *the next morning, October 31, 1938.*

A wave of mass hysteria seized thousands of radio listeners throughout the nation between 8:15 and 9:30 o'clock last night when a broadcast of a dramatization of H. G. Wells's fantasy, "The War of the Worlds," led thousands to believe that an interplanetary conflict had started with invading Martians spreading wide death and destruction in New Jersey and New York.

The broadcast, which disrupted households, interrupted religious services, created traffic jams and clogged communications systems, was made by Orson Welles, who as the radio character, "The Shadow," used to give "the creeps" to countless child listeners. This time at least a score of adults required medical treatment for shock and hysteria.

In Newark, in a single block at Heddon Terrace and Hawthorne Avenue, more than twenty families rushed out of their houses with wet handkerchiefs and towels over their faces to flee from what they believed was to be a gas raid. Some began moving household furniture.

Throughout New York families left their homes, some to flee to nearby parks. Thousands of persons called the police, newspapers and radio stations here and in other cities of the United States and Canada seeking advice on protective measures against the raids.

The program was produced by Mr. Welles and the Mercury Theatre on the Air over station WABC and the Columbia Broadcasting System's coast to coast network, from 8 to 9 o'clock.

The radio play, as presented, was to simulate a regular radio program with a "break-in" for the material of the play. The radio listeners, apparently, missed or did not listen to the introduction, which was: "The Columbia Broadcasting System and its affiliated stations present Orson Welles and the Mercury Theatre on the Air in 'The War of the Worlds' by H. G. Wells". . . .

The switchboard of THE NEW YORK TIMES was overwhelmed by the calls. A total of 875 were received. One man who called from Dayton, Ohio, asked, "What time will it be the end of the world?" A caller from the suburbs said he had had a houseful of guests and all had rushed out to the yard for safety. . . .

Jersey City police headquarters received similar calls. One woman asked Detective Timothy Grooty, on duty there, "Shall I close my windows?" A man asked, "Have the police any extra gas masks?" Many of the callers, on being assured the reports were fiction, queried again and again, uncertain in whom to believe.

Scores of persons in lower Newark Avenue, Jersey City, left their homes and stood fearfully in the street, looking with apprehension toward the sky. A radio car was dispatched there to reassure them.

The incident at Hedden Terrace and Hawthorne Avenue, in Newark, one of the most dramatic in the area, caused a tie-up in traffic for blocks around. The more than twenty families there apparently believed the "gas attack" had started, and so reported to the police. An ambulance, three radio cars and a police emergency squad of eight men were sent to the scene with full inhalator apparatus.

They found the families with wet cloths on faces contorted with hysteria. The police calmed them, halted those who were attempting to move their furniture on their cars and after a time were able to clear the traffic snarl. . . .

Expressing profound regret that his dramatic efforts should cause such consternation, Mr. Welles said: "I don't think we will choose anything like this again." He hesitated about presenting it, he disclosed, because "it was our thought that perhaps people might be bored or annoyed at hearing a tale so improbable." ■

WHOPPERS

TALL TALES AND OTHER LIES

collected by Alvin Schwartz

Hey, did you hear the one about the man who was so tall that he had to duck his head to let the moon go by? For as long as human beings have existed, they have exaggerated some of their stories. Call these stories what you will — tall tales, lying tales, windies, gallyfloppers, whoppers — they're great fun to tell and to read.

Painting

This artist was so talented that when he painted a dog it bit him.

But he should have known better. Earlier he had painted a snowstorm and caught cold.

Farming

There are places where the soil is so miserable nobody can raise anything, not even a fuss.

On this one farm, the people are so poor all they eat is pancakes. And the pancakes are so thin they only have one side.

On another, they are so poor they feed their chickens sawdust instead of chicken feed. But that doesn't work too well. For some of the chickens lay eggs with splinters. And others lay knotholes.

The Canyon

This trapper lived in a cabin deep in the mountains at one end of a long box gulch, which is a kind of canyon that after a while runs into a cliff.

Although he lived far from civilization, he had everything he needed. Each night, for example, he would look down the canyon, take a deep breath, and shout:

"Good morning! Good morning!"

Then he would climb into his blanket roll and fall asleep. Seven hours later, to the very minute, the echo of his voice would come booming back.

"Good morning! Good morning!" he would hear himself shout.

Then he would stretch and yawn and crawl out of bed, ready to start another day.

The Fog

One foggy morning a farmer hired a man to shingle the roof of a small barn. It didn't seem like much of a job, but the man didn't come back until dinner time.

When he finally returned, he said, "That's an almighty long barn of your'n."

And the farmer replied, "Not very long."

And the man replied, "Well, I've been at work the whole day, but with the fog and all I am nowhere near finished yet."

And the farmer replied, "Well, you're a lazy fellow. That's all I've got to say."

Then they went down to the meadow to see what he had done. By the time they got there, the fog had lifted a little, so they got a good look. And they both just stood there and stared.

The man had worked hard, all right. He had shingled a hundred feet of fog along with the barn.

Halfway

Have you heard about the man who swam halfway across the ocean, then decided he couldn't make it and swam back?

Meet the Author

Sid Fleischman

As a child, Sid Fleischman had a passion for performing magic tricks. During his spare time he often "disappeared" into the local public library. There, he read so much about magic tricks that during his teenage years he became a professional magician. His writing career began at age nineteen, when he decided to write down some of his tricks. That book was the first of many that Sid Fleischman has written.

Fleischman is a magician when it comes to writing fiction too. He loves to write about tricky characters like McBroom. Fleischman says, "I cannot resist . . . heroes capable of a kind of sleight-of-mind in outwitting the villains." When asked about tall tales like *McBroom Tells the Truth*, Fleischman says he writes them "for the sheer fun of it." Readers who enjoy reading this story as much as Fleischman enjoyed writing it may want to read some of Fleischman's other books, *Here Comes McBroom*, *The Midnight Horse*, and *Jim Ugly*.

Meet the Illustrator

Jennifer Beck Harris

Jennifer Beck Harris has had a zest for drawing zany characters since she was a child. At the age of six, she drew comic strips featuring crazy piano-playing chickens. One of her later comic strips starred a surfer named Cold Wave. Today, Harris takes her inspiration from the stories she illustrates instead of from the funny pages. Her favorites are tall tales like *McBroom Tells the Truth*. Why? Because, she says, "I like stories that are really off the wall."

McBroom Tells the Truth

by Sid Fleischman

There has been so much tomfool nonsense told about McBroom's wonderful one-acre farm that I had better set matters straight. I'm McBroom. Josh McBroom. I'll explain about the watermelons in a minute.

I aim to put down the facts, one after the other, the way things happened — exactly.

It began, you might say, the day we left the farm in Connecticut. We piled our youngsters and everything we owned in our old air-cooled Franklin automobile. We headed West.

To count noses, in addition to my own, there was my dear wife Melissa and our eleven red-headed youngsters. Their names were Will*jill*hester*chester*peter*polly*tim*tom*mary*larry*andlittle*clarinda*.

It was summer, and the trees along the way were full of birdsong. We had got as far as Iowa when my dear wife Melissa made a startling discovery. We had *twelve* children along — one too many! She had just counted them again.

I slammed on the brakes and raised a cloud of dust.

"Willjillhesterchesterpeterpollytimtommarylarryandlittleclarinda!" I shouted. "Line up!"

The youngsters tumbled out of the car. I counted noses and there were twelve. I counted again. Twelve. It was a baffler as all the faces were familiar. Once more I made the count — but this time I caught Larry slipping around behind. He was having his nose counted twice, and the mystery was solved. The scamp! Didn't we laugh, though, and stretch our legs in the bargain.

Just then a thin, long-legged man came ambling down the road. He was so scrawny I do believe he could have hidden behind

a flagpole, ears and all. He wore a tall stiff collar, a diamond stickpin in his tie, and a straw hat.

"Lost, neighbor?" he asked, spitting out the pips of a green apple he was eating.

"Not a bit," said I. "We're heading West, sir. We gave up our farm — it was half rocks and the other half tree stumps. Folks tell us there's land out West and the sun shines in the winter."

The stranger pursed his lips. "You can't beat Iowa for farmland," he said.

"Maybe so," I nodded. "But I'm short of funds. Unless they're giving farms away in Iowa we'll keep a-going."

The man scratched his chin. "See here, I've got more land than I can plow. You look like nice folks. I'd like to have you for neighbors. I'll let you have eighty acres cheap. Not a stone or a tree stump anywhere on the place. Make an offer."

"Thank you kindly, sir," I smiled. "But I'm afraid you would laugh at me if I offered you everything in my leather purse."

"How much is that?"

"Ten dollars exactly."

"Sold!" he said.

Well, I almost choked with surprise. I thought he must be joking, but quick as a flea he was scratching out a deed on the back of an old envelope.

"Hector Jones is my name, neighbor," he said. "You can call me Heck — everyone does."

Was there ever a more kindly and generous man? He signed the deed with a flourish, and I gladly opened the clasp of my purse.

Three milky white moths flew out. They had been gnawing on the ten dollar bill all the way from Connecticut, but enough remained to buy the farm. And not a stone or tree stump on it!

Mr. Heck Jones jumped on the running board and guided us a mile up the road. My youngsters tried to amuse him along the way. Will wiggled his ears, and Jill crossed her eyes, and Chester twitched his nose like a rabbit, but I reckoned Mr. Jones wasn't used to youngsters. Hester flapped her arms like a bird, Peter whistled through his front teeth, which were missing, and Tom tried to stand on his head in the back of the car. Mr. Heck Jones ignored them all.

Finally he raised his long arm and pointed.

"There's your property, neighbor," he said.

Didn't we tumble out of the car in a hurry? We gazed with delight at our new farm. It was broad and sunny, with an oak tree on a gentle hill. There was one defect, to be sure. A boggy looking pond spread across an acre beside the road. You could lose a cow in a place like that, but we had got a bargain — no doubt about it.

"Mama," I said to my dear Melissa. "See that fine old oak on the hill? That's where we'll build our farmhouse."

"No you won't," said Mr. Heck Jones. "That oak ain't on your property."

"But, sir — "

"All that's yours is what you see under water. Not a rock or a tree stump in it, like I said."

I thought he must be having his little joke, except that there wasn't a smile to be found on his face. "But, *sir!*" I said. "You clearly stated that the farm was eighty acres."

"That's right."

"That marshy pond hardly covers an acre."

"That's wrong," he said. "There are a full eighty acres — one piled on the other, like griddle cakes. I didn't say your farm was all on the surface. It's eighty acres deep, McBroom. Read the deed."

I read the deed. It was true.

"*Hee-haw! Hee-haw!*" he snorted. "I got the best of you, McBroom! Good day, neighbor."

He scurried away, laughing up his sleeve all the way home. I soon learned that Mr. Heck was always laughing up his sleeve. Folks told me that when he'd hang up his coat and go to bed, all that stored-up laughter would pour out his sleeve and keep him awake nights. But there's no truth to that.

I'll tell you about the watermelons in a minute.

Well, there we stood gazing at our one-acre farm that wasn't good for anything but jumping into on a hot day. And that day was the hottest I could remember. The hottest on record, as it

594

turned out. That was the day, three minutes before noon, when the cornfields all over Iowa exploded into popcorn. That's history. You must have read about that. There are pictures to prove it.

I turned to our children. "Will*jill*hester*chester*peter*polly*tim-*tom*mary*larry*andlittle*clarinda*," I said. "There's always a bright side to things. That pond we bought is a mite muddy, but it's wet. Let's jump in and cool off."

That idea met with favor and we were soon in our swimming togs. I gave the signal, and we took a running jump. At that moment such a dry spell struck that we landed in an acre of dry earth. The pond had evaporated. It was very surprising.

My boys had jumped in head first and there was nothing to be seen of them but their legs kicking in the air. I had to pluck them out of the earth like carrots. Some of my girls were still holding their noses.

Of course, they were sorely disappointed to have that swimming hole pulled out from under them.

But the moment I ran the topsoil through my fingers, my farmer's heart skipped a beat. That pond bottom felt as soft and rich as black silk. "My dear Melissa!" I called. "Come look! This topsoil is so rich it ought to be kept in a bank."

I was in a sudden fever of excitement. That glorious topsoil seemed to cry out for seed. My dear Melissa had a sack of dried beans along, and I sent Will and Chester to fetch it. I saw no need to bother plowing the field. I directed Polly to draw a straight furrow with a stick and Tim to follow her, poking holes in the ground. Then I came along. I dropped a bean in each hole and stamped on it with my heel.

Well, I had hardly gone a couple of yards when something green and leafy tangled my foot. I looked behind me. There was a beanstalk traveling along in a hurry and looking for a pole to climb on.

"Glory be!" I exclaimed. That soil was *rich!* The stalks were spreading out all over. I had to rush along to keep ahead of them.

By the time I got to the end of the furrow the first stalks had blossomed, and the pods had formed, and they were ready for picking.

You can imagine our excitement. Will's ears wiggled. Jill's eyes crossed. Chester's nose twitched. Hester's arms flapped. Peter's missing front teeth whistled. And Tom stood on his head.

"Willjillhesterchesterpeterpollytimtommarylarryandlittle-clarinda," I shouted. "Harvest them beans!"

Within an hour we had planted and harvested that entire crop of beans. But was it hot working in the sun! I sent Larry to find a good acorn along the road. We planted it, but it didn't grow near as fast as I had expected. We had to wait an entire three hours for a shade tree.

We made camp under our oak tree, and the next day we drove to Barnsville with our crop of beans. I traded it for various seeds — carrot and beet and cabbage and other items. The storekeeper found a few kernels of corn that hadn't popped, at the very bottom of the bin.

But we found out that corn was positively dangerous to plant. The stalk shot up so fast it would skin your nose.

Of course, there was a secret to that topsoil. A government man came out and made a study of the matter. He said there had once been a huge lake in that part of Iowa. It had taken thousands of years to shrink up to our pond, as you can imagine. The lake fish must have got packed in worse than sardines. There's nothing like fish to put nitrogen in the soil. That's a scientific fact. Nitrogen makes things grow to beat all. And we did occasionally turn up a fish bone.

It wasn't long before Mr. Heck Jones came around to pay us a neighborly call. He was eating a raw turnip. When he saw the way we were planting and harvesting cabbage his eyes popped out of his head. It almost cost him his eyesight.

He scurried away, muttering to himself.

"My dear Melissa," I said. "That man is up to mischief."

Folks in town had told me that Mr. Heck Jones had the worst farmland in Iowa. He couldn't give it away. Tornado winds had carried off his topsoil and left the hardpan right on top. He had to plow it with wedges and a sledge hammer. One day we heard a lot of booming on the other side of the hill, and my youngsters went up to see what was happening. It turned out he was planting seeds with a shotgun.

Meanwhile, we went about our business on the farm. I don't mind saying that before long we were showing a handsome profit. Back in Connecticut we had been lucky to harvest one crop a year. Now we were planting and harvesting three, four crops a *day*.

But there were things we had to be careful about. Weeds, for one thing. My youngsters took turns standing weed guard. The instant a weed popped out of the ground, they'd race to it and hoe it to death. You can imagine what would happen if weeds ever got going in rich soil like ours.

We also had to be careful about planting time. Once we planted lettuce just before my dear Melissa rang the noon bell for dinner. While we ate, the lettuce headed up and went to seed. We lost the whole crop.

One day back came Mr. Heck Jones with a grin on his face. He had figured out a loophole in the deed that made the farm ours.

"*Hee-haw!*" he laughed. He was munching a radish. "I got the best of you now, Neighbor McBroom. The deed says you were to pay me *everything* in your purse, and you *didn't*."

"On the contrary, sir," I answered. "Ten dollars. There wasn't another cent in my purse."

"There were *moths* in the purse. I seen 'em flutter out. Three milky white moths, McBroom. I want three moths by three o'clock this afternoon, or I aim to take back the farm. *Hee-haw!*"

And off he went, laughing up his sleeve.

Mama was just ringing the noon bell so we didn't have much time. Confound that man! But he did have his legal point.

"Willjillhesterchesterpeterpollytimtommarylarryandlittleclarinda!" I said. "We've got to catch three milky white moths! Hurry!"

We hurried in all directions. But moths are next to impossible to locate in the daytime. Try it yourself. Each of us came back empty handed.

My dear Melissa began to cry, for we were sure to lose our farm. I don't mind telling you that things looked dark. Dark! That was it! I sent the youngsters running down the road to a lonely old pine tree and told them to rush back with a bushel of pine cones.

Didn't we get busy though! We planted a pine cone every three feet. They began to grow. We stood around anxiously, and I kept looking at my pocket watch. I'll tell you about the watermelons in a moment.

Sure enough, by ten minutes to three, those cones had grown into a thick pine forest.

It was dark inside, too! Not a ray of sunlight slipped through the green pine boughs. Deep in the forest I lit a lantern. Hardly a minute passed before I was surrounded by milky white moths — they thought it was night. I caught three on the wing and rushed out of the forest.

There stood Mr. Heck Jones waiting with the sheriff to foreclose.

"*Hee-haw! Hee-haw!*" old Heck laughed. He was eating a quince apple. "It's nigh onto three o'clock, and you can't catch moths in the daytime. The farm is mine!"

"Not so fast, Neighbor Jones," said I, with my hands cupped together. "Here are the three moths. Now, skedaddle, sir, before your feet take root and poison ivy grows out of your ears!"

He scurried away, muttering to himself.

"My dear Melissa," I said. "That man is up to mischief. He'll be back."

It took a good bit of work to clear the timber, I'll tell you. We had some of the pine milled and built ourselves a house on the corner

of the farm. What was left we gave away to our neighbors. We were weeks blasting the roots out of the ground.

But I don't want you to think there was nothing but work on our farm. Some crops we grew just for the fun of it. Take pumpkins. The vines grew so fast we could hardly catch the pumpkins. It was something to see. The youngsters used to wear themselves out running after those pumpkins. Sometimes they'd have pumpkin races.

Sunday afternoons, just for the sport of it, the older boys would plant a pumpkin seed and try to catch a ride. It wasn't easy. You had to grab hold the instant the blossom dropped off and the pumpkin began to swell. Whoosh! It would yank you off your feet and take you whizzing over the farm until it wore itself out. Sometimes they'd use banana squash, which was faster.

And the girls learned to ride corn stalks like pogo sticks. It was just a matter of standing over the kernel as the stalk came busting up through the ground. It was good for quite a bounce.

We'd see Mr. Heck Jones standing on the hill in the distance, watching. He wasn't going to rest until he had pried us off our land.

Then, late one night, I was awakened by a hee-hawing outside the house. I went to the window and saw old Heck in the moonlight. He was cackling and chuckling and heeing and hawing and sprinkling seed every which way.

I pulled off my sleeping cap and rushed outside.

"What mischief are you up to, Neighbor Jones!" I shouted.

"*Hee-haw!*" he answered, and scurried away, laughing up his sleeve.

I had a sleepless night, as you can imagine. The next morning, as soon as the sun came up, that farm of ours broke out in weeds. You never saw such weeds! They heaved out of the ground and tumbled madly over each other — chickweed and milkweed, thistles and wild morning glory. In no time at all the weeds were in a tangle several feet thick and still rising.

We had a fight on our hands, I tell you! "Willjillhesterchesterpeterpollytimtommarylarryandlittleclarinda!" I shouted. "There's work to do!"

We started hoeing and hacking away. For every weed we up-rooted, another reseeded itself. We were a solid month battling those weeds. If our neighbors hadn't pitched in to help, we'd still be there burning weeds.

The day finally came when the farm was cleared and up popped old Heck Jones. He was eating a big slice of watermelon. That's what I was going to tell you about.

"Howdy, Neighbor McBroom," he said. "I came to say goodbye."

"Are you leaving, sir?" I asked.

"No, but *you* are."

I looked him squarely in the eye. "And if I don't, sir?"

"Why, *hee-haw*, McBroom! There's heaps more of weed seed where that came from!"

My dander was up. I rolled back my sleeves, meaning to give him a whipping he wouldn't forget. But what happened next saved me the bother.

As my youngsters gathered around, Mr. Heck Jones made the mistake of spitting out a mouthful of watermelon seeds.

Things did happen fast!

Before I had quite realized what he had done, a watermelon vine whipped up around old Heck's scrawny legs and jerked him off his feet.

He went whizzing every which way over the farm. Watermelon seeds were flying. Soon he came zipping back and collided with a pumpkin left over from Sunday. In no time watermelons and pumpkins went galloping all over the place, and they were knocking him about something wild. He streaked here and there. Melons crashed and exploded. Old Heck was so covered with melon pulp he looked like he had been shot out of a ketchup bottle.

It was something to see. Will stood there wiggling his ears. Jill crossed her eyes. Chester twitched his nose. Hester flapped her arms like a bird. Peter whistled through his front teeth, which had grown in. Tom stood on his head. And little Clarinda took her first step.

By then the watermelons and pumpkins began to play themselves out. I figured Mr. Heck Jones would like to get home as fast as possible. So I asked Larry to fetch me the seed of a large banana squash.

"*Hee-haw!* Neighbor Jones," I said, and pitched the seed at his feet. I hardly had time to say goodbye before the vine had him. A long banana squash gave him a fast ride all the way home. I wish you could have been there to see it. He never came back.

That's the entire truth of the matter. Anything else you hear about McBroom's wonderful one-acre farm is an outright fib.

Harvest Your Ideas!

Write a Story

No Lie!

Josh McBroom aims to "put down the facts" about how he came to own his fabulous farm. But what if Heck Jones decided to "set matters straight"? Write a story, a play, or a poem that tells the tale from Heck's point of view.

Draw a Cartoon

Worth a Thousand Words

Rambunctious youngsters. A scheming neighbor. Crops that explode out of the ground. Sid Fleischman uses words to tell his tall tale. Now you tell part of the story in a different form. Make a cartoon drawing or strip, with or without speech balloons, of your favorite scene in *McBroom Tells the Truth*.

Role-Play a Scene

Our First Guest Is — Josh McBroom!

What if McBroom were interviewed on a television talk show for farmers about how to increase crop production? Role-play what might happen. How might the host and the studio audience react?

Compare Selections

Trading Places

Both "La Bamba" and *McBroom Tells the Truth* include unexpected events, but the first selection is realistic fiction and the second a tall tale. Turn the tables. Discuss with your classmates how you would turn "La Bamba" into a tall tale and *McBroom Tells the Truth* into realistic fiction.

607

Lost Words

A Story by Katrina Powell

What happened to all the words in the easy library books? In Katrina's story, someone plays a very mysterious prank at school.

Lost Words

Each week Mrs. Porter's fifth-grade class chose books to read to their kindergarten reading buddies. On this day Deborah picked <u>Little Critter</u> and <u>Two Bad Ants</u>. She went to her seat to read her books, but when she opened the first book, her mouth gaped when she saw the pages had no words. She told the librarian, "Mrs. Scribner, this book doesn't have any words in it."

When other students found the same thing, Mrs. Scribner walked briskly to a bookshelf, pulled out her favorite book, <u>Amelia Bedelia</u>, and was astonished to find blank pages! Mrs. Porter and Mrs. Scribner nervously checked all the books in the easy section. None of them had any words! Then Mrs. Scribner summoned Detective Arbelo. He had to solve this case quickly!

After checking the books, Detective Arbelo walked as fast as his feet could carry him to the school office. He asked

Mrs. Mullen, the school's secretary, "May I see some letters you have typed? I've got a hunch it's going to help us put the words back in the books. When you've been solving cases as long as I have, you get hunches! Now I must find out what has happened!"

"Detective, do you mind if I tag along?"

"I don't mind, if you bring the typed pages."

The first classroom they came to was Mrs. Jackson's fourth grade. No one was in the room, but all the students' spelling books were opened to Chapter Seven. Mrs. Mullen and Detective Arbelo walked around the room. "Come here quickly," said Mrs. Mullen. One spelling book was open like all the others, but it had no words. "What is this circular area?" asked Mrs. Mullen.

"There is an imprint the size of a soda can here," answered the detective, "but the reason you noticed it is this blue dust on the desktop. Whose desk is this?"

Mrs. Mullen looked inside the book and saw Crystal Brown's name. "Crystal is one of the sweetest and most well-behaved children in this school. She would never do anything to get in trouble," she said defensively.

"I'm sure she wouldn't," said Detective Arbelo.

Detective Arbelo and Mrs. Mullen then walked into the three other fourth-grade rooms but found nothing out of the ordinary. On the way to the third-grade wing, Detective Arbelo noticed several blue handprints on students' writings stapled onto the walls. The words were missing wherever the handprints appeared. He knew Mrs. Mullen was irritated with him for suspecting a sweet fourth grader could ever pull a prank, so he didn't mention the handprints.

In the third-grade wing outside Mr. Smith's door, Detective Arbelo noticed more of the blue dust. "Let's have a look in this class." When they entered the room, Detective Arbelo noticed an energetic youngster grab his book bag, run across the room, and stuff it in his cubbyhole. As they approached the boy, he began squirming.

"Vernon, what is your problem?" asked Mrs. Mullen. Then she saw blue all over his hands. "All right, Vernon, you'd better start talking."

After more squirming, Vernon explained, "I didn't do anything. It's all Mrs. Porter's fault. She gave the stuff to my brother."

Detective Arbelo went to Vernon's cubby, pulled out his book bag, reached inside, and pulled out a can labeled Disappearing Dust.

"How did it get on the books in the easy section and on Crystal Brown's spelling book?" demanded Mrs. Mullen.

"Vernon likes Crystal," another third grader, Jason, teased.

"And Vernon got in trouble in the library last week," said Mr. Smith, "so Mrs. Scribner made him put all the easy books in alphabetical order. Now I know why you were gone to the bathroom so long this morning, Vernon."

"We need to go see Mrs. Porter," said Detective Arbelo.

When they told Mrs. Porter what they had discovered, she explained that one of her students, Brandon, had invented Disappearing Dust for the Science Fair. "I never dreamed the concoction would work! The other day when I was cleaning out my closet, I gave Tyrone the can. Tyrone is Vernon's brother."

"How are we going to get the words back in these books?" asked Mrs. Mullen.

"Well, if Disappearing Dust worked, I have something else Brandon invented that may help, but I'm going to need you to type plenty of letters for me, Mrs. Mullen," answered Mrs. Porter.

"I told you I had a hunch," said Detective Arbelo. "We already have the typed pages!"

Mrs. Porter went to her closet and took out an unusual-looking spray can with an elephant and a frog on it.

Mrs. Mullen, Mrs. Porter, and Detective Arbelo went to the easy section in the library, picked out a book, and sprayed Special Sand on the pages. They got the typed pages and started tearing them up on every single page. The words started reappearing. Mrs. Mullen, Detective Arbelo, and Mrs. Porter got book after book and replaced the words. When all of the words were back, everyone, especially Mrs. Scribner, was happy.

Katrina Powell
James J. Davis Elementary School
Dale, South Carolina

After writing this story in the fifth grade, Katrina said that while writing "is enjoyable, it can be hard." She wrote more than one draft of "Lost Words" before she was satisfied with it. "I read a lot," Katrina said, "and I think reading is helping me to improve my writing skills." Katrina's hobbies are reading and singing, and she hopes to pursue singing as a career in the future.

TRAPPED IN TAR

Fossils from the Ice Age

by Caroline Arnold

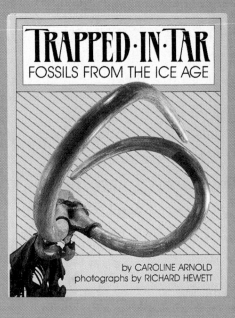

TRAPPED·IN·TAR
FOSSILS FROM THE ICE AGE

by CAROLINE ARNOLD
photographs by RICHARD HEWETT

In the shadow of skyscrapers, a model of an imperial mammoth appears to bellow with rage as it struggles to free itself from the sticky tar below the surface of the water. Like sabertooth cats, giant ground sloths, and many other ancient animals, real mammoths are extinct. Long ago, these animals roamed the grassy plain that is now the busy city of Los Angeles. Then, as now, pools of tar sometimes seeped to the surface of the earth. Water often hid the dangerous tar from view, and thirsty animals came to drink. Little did they know that what looked like a refreshing pool could become their deathtrap.

Large deposits of oil lie under much of southern California. In some places, the oil seeps upward through cracks in the earth's crust. When the oil evaporates, it leaves pools of asphalt, or tar. In cool weather, the tar hardens and the pools become hidden by a layer of leaves and dust. In summer, the hot sun softens the tar into sticky puddles.

A small animal such as a squirrel or a bird could become stuck when the tar coated its fur or feathers. When a larger animal such as a mammoth waded into the water, its weight made it sink. Its feet became stuck in the tar below and, unable to get out, it eventually died. Then meat-eating animals such as wolves, sabertooth cats, and giant vultures would attack the animal. They too often slipped into the tar and died.

The bones of this American mastodon *(Mammut americanus)* were found at Rancho La Brea.

As the flesh of the dead animals rotted away, the bodies floated on the surface of the tar. Later, when the bones became soaked with tar, they sank to the bottom.

The deposits of asphalt that trapped these ancient animals are the Rancho La Brea (*Bray-a*) tar pits. *Brea* is a Spanish word meaning "tar." Once California was part of Mexico and the land around the tar pits was called Rancho La Brea, or ranch of tar. Later, California became a part of the United States and the land belonged to Captain G. Allen Hancock, who operated oil wells there. Today the oil wells are gone, and the land is a county park named after Captain Hancock. In the park are both the tar pits and the George C. Page Museum of La Brea Discoveries.

"Asphalt Is Sticky," an exhibit inside the museum, helps people feel what it might be like to get stuck in tar. Visitors try to lift long steel rods that are immersed in the tar. The tar seems to grab the rods and hold them tight. In the same way, an animal such as a mammoth that stepped into a tar pool found it nearly impossible to escape.

The bones and plant remains in the Rancho La Brea tar pits are a record of life that existed between 10,000 and 40,000 years ago. Then mammoths, mastodons, sabertooth cats, lions, wolves, sloths, camels, horses, and many other animals lived in North America. The oldest fossil found so far at Rancho La Brea is 38,000 years old. However, most of the fossils are between 14,000 and 16,000 years old.

The fossils in the Rancho La Brea tar pits are from a period of the earth's history known as the Ice Age. Then great sheets of ice, called glaciers, covered much of the Northern Hemisphere. An ice and land bridge connected Asia and North America. Both people and animals migrated across this bridge.

Southern California near Rancho La Brea may have looked like this during the Ice Age. Shown, left to right, are giant ground sloths (background), a saber-tooth cat, an ancient North American camel, and teratorn vultures.

Many different kinds of animals lived near Rancho La Brea. The climate was mild, and food and water were plentiful. When the Ice Age ended about 10,000 years ago, the climate changed. Most of the lakes and streams dried up, and food became scarce. Many of the animals that had once been numerous became extinct.

Today we know about the Ice Age animals because the tar that caused their death also preserved their bones. As the oily tar soaked into the bones, it prevented their decay. Over many years the tar hardened into a solid block composed of tar, dirt, and fossils. Encased in this protective covering, the buried bones were safe for centuries.

Usually we think of fossils as living things that have been turned to stone. However, a fossil is any part of a plant or animal or even the impression of a plant or animal that has been preserved in some way.

For hundreds of years, the native Americans and early European settlers living in California used the tar at Rancho La Brea as a glue for baskets and tools. They also used it to waterproof boats and the roofs of houses. Tar was dug out of the ground at Rancho La Brea and hauled by wagon to wherever it was needed. Although some people noticed bones embedded in the tar, no one paid much attention to them.

Then, in 1906, fossils from Rancho La Brea, which included those of a giant ground sloth, were shown to Dr. John C. Merriam at the University of California. He realized their importance and arranged with Captain Hancock, who owned the land around the tar pits, to remove the bones.

Early excavations were simply holes dug in the ground. The scientists removed the largest bones in the pits and threw away everything else. They took the bones they saved to the Los Angeles County Natural History Museum. There they cleaned them and assembled them into whole skeletons. The skeletons were then displayed in the museum.

Over one hundred pits have been dug in Hancock Park since the early 1900s. Most of them were covered over when the park was landscaped in the 1950s. From the beginning, as each new pit was dug, it was given a number. Currently, you can see six pits. These include the lake pit, which used to be an asphalt quarry, as well as Pit 91, where visitors can watch people dig for fossils.

Today the excavations are much more careful than the early digs. Each section of the pit is marked, the location of each fossil is precisely noted and recorded, and everything is saved.

To prevent the sides of the pit from collapsing, heavy boards are held against the walls with metal bars. When needed, new boards are added at the bottom. Each year the pit becomes approximately $\frac{1}{2}$-foot deeper. Like most fossil deposits, those at Pit 91 form a large cone shape that becomes narrower as the pit gets deeper. The oldest fossils are found in the lowest layers.

Scientists want to know what is found in the pit as well as where it is found. The bottom of the pit is divided into sections of 3 by 3 feet.

**Above: Fossil bone fragments must be pieced together.
Below: The paintbrush and the teaspoon become specialized tools.**

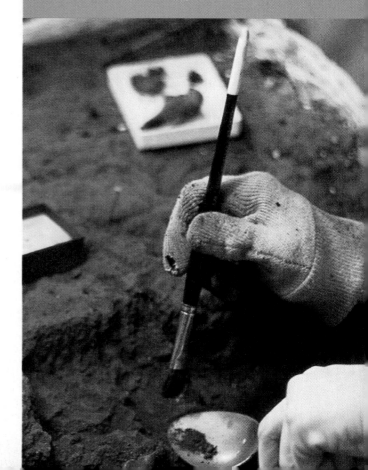

When any bone over $\frac{1}{2}$-inch long is revealed, it is measured and photographed in place before it is removed.

Everything that is taken from the pit is placed in large cans. Each can is filled and hauled to the top of the pit. Then it is stored inside the museum until the material can be cleaned and sorted. So many fossils have been excavated recently that scientists will need many years to study all of them.

Outdoor excavation at Rancho La Brea is done for only a few months each year. Recently, however, an indoor excavation project was begun that allows people to work year-round.

Between 1906 and 1977, all the material found at the Rancho La Brea tar pits was kept in the Los Angeles County Natural History Museum in Exposition Park. As more and more material was found, it began to overflow the storage rooms at the museum. George C. Page, a Los Angeles businessman, was fascinated with the Rancho La Brea fossils. In 1973, he donated money to build a new museum just for the La Brea discoveries. The museum would also be a center for scientific research.

In 1975, as bulldozers began to dig the foundation for the new museum, they unearthed a huge deposit of bones. Everyone knew that to excavate these bones at the site would take a long time. This might delay the construction of the museum for years. Instead, they decided to move the asphalt in large chunks and excavate the bones later. Each portion was cut out, wrapped in a sturdy plaster coating, and stored until the new museum and laboratory were finished. Today visitors can watch through windows as these bone deposits are excavated inside the museum laboratory.

People who study the remains of ancient plants and animals are called paleontologists. Much of the work at Rancho La Brea is done by specially trained volunteers. Some of them are students of paleontology; others are people who just want to know more about our ancient heritage. By identifying and studying the bones and plants, paleontologists find they can guess what events might have taken place thousands of years ago.

For example, one block of tar and bones contained the skull of a sabertooth cat and parts of the skeletons of two baby horses. Probably the horses became stuck in the tar and then were attacked by the cat. These ancient horses, although similar to present-day horses, became extinct at the end of the Ice Age.

After a bone is removed from the tar and dirt in which it was embedded, it must be cleaned. First, loose dirt is brushed or scrubbed off. Then the bone is soaked and washed in a solvent, a liquid that dissolves the tar. The tar stains the bones brown, so even after cleaning, the bones remain dark. The clean bones are then labeled and set aside for identification and cataloguing.

MEET CAROLINE ARNOLD

Caroline Arnold always intended to be a children's book illustrator. But a funny thing happened on the way to the drawing board: She started writing books instead. Arnold liked writing so much that she decided to keep at it. More than eighty books later, Arnold has written on subjects ranging from Australia to zebras. "I particularly like to write about animals and health science topics," she explains. However, that hasn't stopped her from writing about birthdays, gardens, jugglers, and whatever else sparks her curiosity. "One of the beauties of writing for children," she says, ". . . is that each project is something new."

Other books by Caroline Arnold that you might enjoy are *The Ancient Cliff Dwellers of Mesa Verde* and *Dinosaurs All Around: An Artist's View of the Prehistoric World*.

627

SINK YOUR TEETH INTO THESE IDEAS!

The Way It Might Have Been

Write a description of what might have happened to a prehistoric animal who became trapped in one of the La Brea tar pits. Use the selection to help you see and hear the details.

15,000 Years Ago

Fossil bones and tar pits! Sabertooth cats and mastodons! Using information from the selection and your own ideas, plan a museum display about the La Brea discoveries. Write and draw a description of what your display would include.